PARENTING THE CHILD
You have

Re-Imagining the Parent-Child Relationship
Through the Lens of Human Design

AYPRIL PORTER

Edited by Laurie Knight
Cover art by Imogen Porter

HUMAN
DESIGN
P R E S S

An Imprint for GracePoint Publishing (www.GracePointPublishing.com)

GracePoint Matrix, LLC
624 S. Cascade Ave
Suite 201
Colorado Springs, CO 80903
www.GracePointMatrix.com
Email: Admin@GracePointMatrix.com

SAN # 991-6032

A Library of Congress Control Number has been requested and is pending.

ISBN: (Paperback) 978-1-951694-84-5
eISBN: 978-1-951694-83-8

Books may be purchased for educational, business, or sales promotional use.
For bulk order requests and price schedule contact:
Orders@GracePointPublishing.com

DISCLAIMER

The author of this book does not dispense medical advice. The information contained in this book is for informational purposes only and may not be the best fit for your personal situation. It shall not be construed as medical advice. The information shared here is not intended or implied to supplement or replace professional emotional, physical, or medical treatment or advice, and/or diagnoses. Always check with your physician or medical professional before trying or implementing any information read here. The information found within this book is not intended to be a textbook, but a compilation and reflection of the author's learning and experience, both in her own life as well as through the hundreds of clients she's worked with. In the event you use any of the information contained within this book, which is your constitutional right, the author and publisher assume no responsibility for your actions.

Don't believe me. Go experiment for yourself.
~RA URU HU

For all the children of the world present and future.
May you always know the way back home to your Authentic Self
and have the courage to let your light shine brightly.

ENDORSEMENTS

In her book, *Parenting The Child You Have*, Aypril Porter artfully weaves her in-depth knowledge of the Human Design System and Quantum Human Design with her experience as a mother of two. You'll want to share this book with every parent (and parent-to-be) you know! Like no other book in the world, this book teaches parents how to understand their children at the deepest level possible from the moment they are born. I was inspired by the new insights this treasure of a book brought to my awareness. It's a must-have for everyone!

   - **Morganne Tayler Zabek**, Subtle Energy Practitioner

Aypril has written an incredibly digestible map for any parent wanting to improve their connection with their child. I am fascinated with how accurate this is to each of my six children.

   - **Amanda Hooghkirk-Newman**

Knowing about human design has helped me in a lot of ways. It has helped me to learn more about myself and understand more of me. It helps me connect to my inner self and it helps me find out more of what I'm about. I am a projector and I understand that I have bigger and more sensitively triggered emotions. It's always been hard for me to know how I'm feeling when I'm feeling it, and human design helps me figure out why. I love my mom, and I love human design.

   - **Athalia,** age 12

Learning about Human Design has helped me learn about myself. It has impacted how I react to certain situations, and how I interact in relationships. It has helped me a lot in figuring out who I am as a person.

   - **Imogen,** age 14

TABLE OF CONTENTS

FOREWORD

Parenting is hard.

There is no formula for raising a child correctly. Most of the time you're flying by the seat of your pants, deeply invested with all of your heart and soul, trying to do the best that you know how with a small human who has the potential to trigger all of your deepest fears, wounds, and inadequacies. At the same time, you're probably chronically sleep deprived and wondering why the heck you thought this was a good idea in the first place.

It's a job that doesn't come with an instruction manual or any training—other than on-the-job training and your own experiences from your family of origin. Your child does *not* come with instructions; in addition, if you have more than one child, you'll quickly learn that every child you try to raise is totally different from all the others.

As the mother of five biological children and three stepdaughters, I have felt the overwhelm, fear, and despair of being a parent. For most of my parenting career, I was a full-time, single mother trying not only to raise a family but also get the bills paid and—hopefully—be able to give my children the gift of a college education.

I have had many maternal moments of feeling like an utter failure, wracked with guilt and completely terrified that I was going to screw my children up in every way possible. With one of my children, in particular, I was deeply worried that they would either choose suicide or end up in jail if I didn't figure out how to be the parent they needed.

Fortunately for me (and for my children), I encountered Human Design when my children were still pretty young. While knowing Human Design didn't excuse me from doing my own inner healing so that I could be more present and emotionally available to my children, it certainly gave me important information that helped me be the parent that each of my children needed. (And in the case of one of my children, I'm pretty sure that without knowing their Human Design, they might not have made it to adulthood.)

Human Design, in essence, is the instruction manual that we long for when our children are born. When the founder of Human Design, Ra Uru Hu, had his revelatory encounter with "The Voice" he was told that Human Design is for the children, but that the adults had to learn it first in order to better serve the future generations. Understanding your own energy dynamics, in addition to your child's, will help you understand the way you experience the world and what you need to be a better parent.

Years ago, I taught a parenting class called Redirecting Children's Behavior. Although the class focused on powerful parenting techniques and how to use them with your children, the "secret sauce" to the class was really about redirecting the behavior of parents. It was magical to witness how, when parents started feeling better about themselves and more deeply connected with their own emotional awareness, their children's behavior changed in response.

The bulk of what I taught parents at that time was rooted in the teachings of Dr. Rudolf Dreikurs. Dreikurs, in his book *Children: The Challenge,* gave parents a very accessible way to address why children misbehave, how to interpret their misbehavior, and how to support children in learning to get their needs met appropriately. Dreikurs argued that children can't communicate their needs effectively so they misbehave as a way of getting parents to respond to their unmet needs. Dreikurs outlined out a vital process that helps parents interpret their children's needs so that they can better help their children learn how to get the support and love they require to grow into being healthy, resilient adults with high self-esteem.

Human Design adds even more depth to understanding the needs of your child and helps you tailor your parenting in order to best support your child in growing into the person they were born to be. Aypril Porter has, in a very personal and compassionate way, skillfully built upon the knowledge of Dreikurs and shows you exactly how to "see" your children for who they are.

In *Parenting the Child You Have*, Aypril outlines the basics of Human Design and blends it with good parenting concepts so that you can tailor your parenting to be the parent you dreamed of being before you even had children. If you follow Aypril's teachings, you'll be able to break free from your own reactive parenting patterns and cultivate showing up for each of your children the way they need you to. The skillset that Aypril teaches helps you raise a child, not only with a strong sense of who they are but also with a deep sense of their lovability and value.

Research shows that when we don't feel lovable, valued, and safe expressing our authentic selves, it literally takes a toll on the body, creating the experience of micro-traumas. When we internalize the message that it's not okay for us to be who we are or how we are, we learn to build a life rooted in other people's expectations and we end up exhausted, stressed, and at risk for depression. This experience of feeling like you must hide who you are begins in childhood. Aypril's book gives you sound and strong strategies to help your children feel safe and loved while fully expressing who they were born to be—even when their expression doesn't fit your parental expectations or fantasies.

I like to think of parenting as being a sacred stewardship. We are still combatting our collective conditioning that teaches us that children need to somehow be formed or trained to become healthy, successful adults. Trying to figure out strategies to reward, bribe, and punish children is exhausting and leaves you, as the parent, responsible for your child's success or lack of success in life. A "good" child is somehow the result of "good" parenting. If you can just do it "right" everything will be ok.

Yet, in my years of being a parent educator and a child development specialist, I saw a lot of good parents who had challenging children who defied everything the parenting "experts" told them would work. I also saw a lot of strong adults who grew up to do amazing things in spite of dysfunctional family patterns.

The goal of good parenting is not to raise a "good" child, meaning one who follows the rules and is blindly obedient. Good parents are stewards, nurturing their children in becoming who they were born to be, helping their children learn how to bend and flow with the changes and challenges life brings, and guiding their children to cultivate a high sense of self-worth. Good parents help their children know how to connect to the north star of their own inner compass so that they know what to do and how to make the right choices in a rapidly changing world.

Parenting the Child You Have lays out a systematic process for you to be a good steward for the child you have. Aypril also reminds you that children will pattern themselves based on what they see modeled for them. Take this book to heart and remember that good parenting takes time and compassion for both you and your child. The more you heal your own self-worth and lovability, the more you'll be able to help your child do the same. The more you model alignment with your authentic self, the more you show your child what living authentically and being resilient looks like.

When you encourage your children to stay connected to who they were born to be, they will remain clear-minded, optimistic, and enthusiastic. They will remain balanced and flexible. They will remain in a state of grace. They will remain in a state of well-being. And they will make wonderful choices.

Your children will become the architects who build the future we all dream of.

Karen Curry Parker
Author of *Understanding Human Design*
Creator of Quantum Revolution Podcast, Quantum Human Design™ methodology, and Quantum Alignment System™ training program.

INTRODUCTION

Hi Friend,

I hope that this book helps you to better understand your child, yourself, and even your relationship with your parents. Parents often have the idea that their child will arrive and be just like them in some ways. Yet other parents hope that their child is nothing like them. We want our children to be better than us. We want to see them succeed, and it's so hard to watch them struggle. When the child you're gifted is not quite like you thought they'd be, it can be difficult.

When I became a parent, I had to learn to adjust from what I thought I would do before actually having kids, to what my kids needed. By the time the second kid came around, I figured things would go similarly to the first child. I had no idea that two kids from the same parents just a couple of years apart could be so different from such a young age. What worked with the first child didn't work the same with the second. Having been an only child, I had no idea what to expect; I thought it was a simple repeating process. Parenting one kid was a wild ride but parenting two has been even more intense having no personal experience to draw from. Or perhaps it's been freeing because I have nothing to compare it to. When Human Design came into my life, it explained so much about my children that I wondered why this information wasn't given out at birthing centers and hospitals! I could only imagine how much more I would have understood my children's needs early on if I'd been armed with this level of information about my children, and myself, when they were born.

Being a child once myself, I know what it's like to feel like the child you are is not what your parent thought you'd be. A lot of the things I felt I was not living up to were, I'm sure, perceived, but it always left me wondering why I didn't fit in. Why did my father seem to want me to be someone else, and why couldn't he accept me for who I was? I believe he just didn't understand, and I still don't think he understands me, even as an adult. Would he have read this book when I was a kid? Nope. Probably never. But that's okay. This book is not for him. It's for the parent who knows that their child is not just like them and wants to support who they truly are so that they can grow up feeling seen, heard, loved, and valued by being the unique magical being that they are.

My greatest wish is that our children grow up confident in who they are and resilient enough to share their hearts with the world.

We are currently on the edge of a new space in time, where the old is meeting the new. We are ushering out the old paradigms of our parents and ancestors and making room for a new way of being.

Our history as humans has evolved from an existence of a primal need for survival to one of more emotional intelligence and relating to one another. In Human Design we are continuing to rapidly undergo transformation as we approach 2027, when our Emotional Solar Plexus will evolve from an emotional awareness center to a spirit awareness center. Connection to others through this emotional awareness will allow us to become one as we navigate this new world and create systems that support humanity and each other. Rather than being an "every human for themself" society, I see us becoming an "every human together" society where we care for and support one another while remaining individuals, contributing to the Collective in a way that no one else can. Now is our time to step forward into this new consciousness and see what is possible.

If we think about this survival-based time we continue to evolve from, deception, the need for power, and the growing desire to have *all the things* has not allowed us to focus so much on each other but has centered around our own needs primarily. As we continue to awaken to this deeper level of emotional awareness, we move into an era where we've had enough of the stuff, and we want to connect on a deeper level. It's no coincidence that after a year of being stuck at home people are still buying like never before, but it's not more *things* we are craving.

We are trying to fill an emptiness inside, a hurt, a trauma, a way to hide until we know how to make real change. What we long for is a deeper connection. We want something deeper than a network of "friends" showing fabricated social media photos that display the life *we want* to be living. We want to live the life we've created in our minds that allows for us to take the time with our kids, to check out of work at the end of the day so we make it to the kids' events, to follow our passions, and to gather with friends and family celebrating with one another, as well as supporting each other as we grieve. We want the time and space to connect on a heart level.

We are desperate for this connection to one another, and we're not quite there yet. We're still rushing through our days and wearing ourselves out to pay for *all the things* thinking they'll make us happy or at least provide a temporary dopamine hit. Even with all the fancy apps and internet tools, Zoom meetings, and platforms, we still aren't connecting on the level we all desire. If 2020 has taught us anything, it is that more technology is not what we crave.

We see previously-accepted systems breaking down around us, and that breakdown feels like a threat to our safety, but these systems must break down for us to build something better—something new and an advanced way of being that allows us to connect again. We are leveling up. Now is the time for change. It is time to change how we work, how we live, what we value, how we treat each other, how we see each other, and how we come together. We are breaking generational patterns that are no longer serving us and creating a new future for our children. Just because something has always been a certain way, doesn't mean it must not change. Just because something has always been certain, doesn't mean it must always be that way. We get to create the life we want to live and choose what we pass on to our children.

This requires that we look at how we parent, who we are as parents today, how we were parented, how our parents still are, and how they may have a harder time shifting into this new consciousness. I believe Human Design allows us to accept each other where we are and allows us to set healthy boundaries when we realize there are things about people that they, or we, just cannot change. It gives us the freedom to stop trying to be something we're not and finally embrace who we truly are.

How To Use This Book

This book is designed to be read front to back and then used as a reference as your child grows and changes, as new people come into your family or life, and as you learn more about yourself. My hope is that you will read it, look up your and your child's, or children's, charts, and start to see the special little humans that came to this earth to teach you, and how that child was meant just for you. Whether you are brand new to Human Design or you've experimented with it already, I hope that this book gives you a new lens through which to see your child in order to help them remain true to themselves as they grow. You will notice that the most common themes related to children and parenting are discussed in a few different places in this book. I have done this intentionally for your ease of reference. You will also find the Glossary in the back of the book for common Human Design terms.

While this book is centered around parenting and Human Design, I want to remind you that this is not a typical parenting book. I want to empower you with the knowledge you need to get curious about yourself, your child, your partner, and your parents. We are all just walking around, bouncing into each other's auras, looking for the ones that make us feel the best while trying to navigate with grace the ones that don't.

Please take what you read here and lean deeply into your curiosity. Take baby steps with the information until you find your trust in this system of understanding yourself and each other. Experiment, play, and, for goodness' sake, do not become dogmatic about this system. Human Design is simply a tool to help you on your journey. Though it could not possibly explain everything about you or anyone else, in my six years of experimenting with this system, I have found profound personal freedom, understanding, and growth, and I hope you do too.

CHAPTER ONE

WHAT IS HUMAN DESIGN?

The human mind, once stretched by a new idea,
never regains its original dimensions.
~RALPH WALDO EMERSON

Human Design is a relatively new concept that was brought forth by a Canadian man. Ra Uru Hu, born Robert Allan Krakower, had an encounter with what he called *the Voice* on the island of Ibiza that began on January 3, 1987. The information he was given through the Voice was assembled, tested, shared, and eventually became taught throughout the world and has gained a lot of attention in the last five or so years. Human Design is a synthesis of several ancient and modern sciences and systems already familiar, and yet it is none of them in their entirety. It is something all its own providing a template to see what the soul came here to earth to experience in this lifetime. It won't predict what choices you will make in life or what job you're here to have, but it will help you understand your behavior, your preferences, and why you do things the way you do while allowing you to embrace the truth of who you are. If you learn about Human Design as an adult, it can help lead you back to the identity and person you know yourself to be before family and societal conditioning altered your life's course. It can be described as coming home, being seen, and being given permission to be you. It can help you interact with others from a place of understanding and compassion, rather than judgment and criticism.

The Human Design System is a synthesis of the I Ching, the Kabbalah Tree of Life, astrology, quantum mechanics, and the Hindu Brahmin Chakra System.

Human Design is here to help children and future generations live as their authentic selves, but it also must be embodied and lived by the parents first, who can then help their children navigate life through their own unique way of being. The time has come for us to share this system beyond the confines of those who are "woo-woo" or on the fringes and bring it more into the mainstream where it can reach more people in an accessible and practical way. This system is vast and deep, yet it offers insights to those who only scratch the surface. Many people never venture deep and they can still greatly benefit from its use. In fact, I think sometimes the deeper you go, the more limited your view can become, and you can lose sight of the key aspects of Human Design, which are to trust your own inner guidance and navigate your life in an authentic way through your Type, Strategy, and Authority. If you understand these three elements of your design and how your energy works, you can make aligned decisions for yourself allowing the deeper aspects to fall into place and live out the full expression of your chart. Of course, the more details you learn within your unique chart the more it allows for easier navigation through life.

Many who have come before me have shared their interpretation of the system, just as I bring my interpretation through the lens of parenting in this book. While Ra Uru Hu had a way of communicating the system that was shocking, Karen Curry Parker has brought a new language to elements of the chart through her Quantum Human Design™ language, and I value both perspectives. This new language encourages us to operate at a higher vibrational frequency and not to get so lost in the defined/undefined, have/have not. When we first see our chart, we can easily get stuck in a limiting belief of have/have not because our minds want to categorize what is and what isn't. We want to sort and label everything and everyone, so we understand where we all fit, but this system is not about fitting you into a neat and tidy box. It is about helping you understand, as Karen says, that you are a once in a lifetime cosmic event and that each part of the chart is an archetype with a range of expressions that can be experienced. What you see in your chart does not mean that you will be a positive or negative force. There are no *bad* charts. None. But you still must show up, do the work to decondition from living in the not-self, and recognize within yourself the areas you need to understand most. Only then can you interact with others in a way that feels good to yourself and other people. We are still accountable for being the best version of ourselves as we know how, and "because it's in the chart" is a poor excuse for reckless, low-expression behavior with self or others.

I have learned so much from Ra's and Karen's teachings as well as many others who have taken the original work and shared their interpretation and experience. All of these interpretations have broadened my understanding of the system and in how many different ways it can be expressed. These include Richard Rudd's Gene Keys, Rosy Aronson's Wisdom Keepers, Kim Gould's Holographic Human Design, and more. We learn different things from different people and their interpretations of this system, so I cannot say with absolute certainty that one is right and the other wrong. I can only say that the Human Design System can be liberating to those who choose to experiment with it in their lives. Try it and see if it helps you to feel more yourself, more confident as the parent you know you can be, and curious about how you show up in the world and interact with others.

When looking at charts, the defined (colored in) parts show what is consistent for that person. The undefined (white) elements of the chart are not missing, they are simply energies that we get to experience through relationships. I assure you that we all have all parts of the chart. The undefined area in a chart is where we can become very wise to the world around us. We learn lessons about ourselves and others through these dynamics. To be alive on this earth and live this human experience is a gift and even in our struggles, we learn lessons to shape us into who we will become.

I love to use Human Design in my work with clients in all areas of their lives, including parenting, business, health, and relationships to help them approach their lives with curiosity. Everything is all just one big experiment, and if we are open to changing the variables and looking at life or situations as an experiment, we are open to learning more. This understanding allows us to relate to one another better and can free ourselves from the boxes we have either been put into or we have put ourselves into.

CHAPTER TWO

GETTING TO KNOW YOUR WAY AROUND YOUR CHART

There can be as much value in the blink of an eye
as in months of rational analysis.
~Malcolm Gladwell,
Blink: The Power of Thinking Without Thinking

The entirety of the Human Design Chart is complex and layered. This book is not to teach you how to read charts. It is to teach you, the parent, how to take the most essential and implementable elements and benefit now while you're in the thick of it.

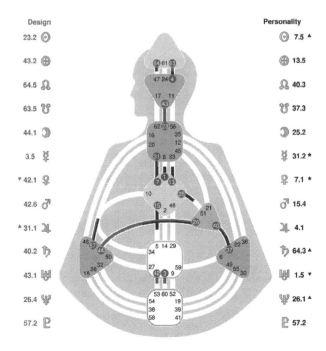

The way I break down the chart in the following pages shows you aspects of your child's design. Your child is not just one of these parts. Each element tells a portion of your child's story, and when looked at together, tells the overarching story of who your child is. Before you can see how all the elements work together, you need to break down the parts to understand the fundamental aspects of the chart. I have included the fundamentals in this book: Type, Strategy, Authority, Centers, and Profile. I have added some advanced elements of the chart that I find particularly helpful to my clients who are in the trenches of parenting, trying to understand themselves, their children, their own parents, and the struggles they have experienced over their lifetime. Because this system takes time to understand, and you must live it to experience it, I recommend having a reading for your child and yourself, if possible. A chart reading can provide insight you may not be able to synthesize from your own understanding of your chart – sometimes we're too close to it to see it. Like with coaching, an outside perspective is always helpful. Whether you have found this book before or after having a Human Design reading, it will help you reinforce the concepts and gain more insight into your child and yourself. If you can't get a reading right now, that's okay too; there is more than enough information here to make a significant impact in your parenting life. The most important aspects are to know and live by your Type, Strategy, and Authority, and as you master those, everything else will begin to fall into place as it's designed to.

The Human Design BodyGraph is made up of several parts and can be both mesmerizing and overwhelming at the same time if you've never seen it before. Some people look at their chart and feel a deep sense of recognition even if they don't understand it on an intellectual level yet, while others need time to warm up to it and peel back the layers of conditioning to remember who they are.

Head over to www.geneticmatrix.com and download a copy of your chart and anyone else's chart you'll want to reference as you read along. The following are some common terms you will see throughout the book that relate to different elements of the chart, which are important to understand as you read.

BODYGRAPH CHART

Undefined Channel
No Color

Defined Gate
Can be red, black or red and black

Defined Channel
Can be red, black or red and black

Undefined Gate
No color

Defined Center
Center is colored in

Undefined Center
No color. It has one or more gate activations

Open Center
No color in Center and no gate activations

Defined

The definition in the chart is determined at birth and remains consistent throughout our lives. We can think of this as the nature aspect of who we are. Definition tells us what consistent energy we carry with us wherever we go and what we broadcast out to the people around us. This defined energy is not fixed in the sense that it can only be expressed one way and is limiting, but rather that there is a consistency in it we can rely on throughout our lives.

Undefined/Open

The areas that are open or undefined in our chart are the areas where we are receiving information and learning about the world, other people, and that energy in our lives. These are areas where we receive the most conditioning and they correlate with the nurture aspect of who we become.

Conditioned/Not-Self

The conditioned or not-self in Human Design refers to how we live out the expression of our chart that goes *against* our design. We are conditioned most by the people in our lives. For example, a Projector's Strategy is to wait for the invitation; however, if they live in a conditioned or not-self way, they are impulsive and take action without waiting for recognition and an invitation. Another example would be someone who has an open Sacral Center who is continually pushing and working, not knowing when enough is enough, and is living through conditioning to do more physical work than they are designed for.

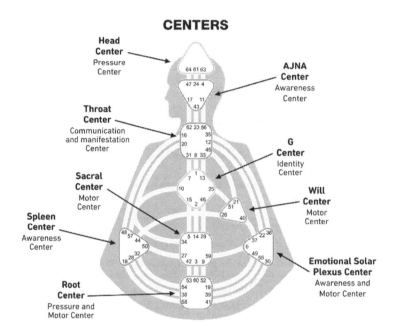

Centers

The chart contains nine energy centers. The chart originally had just seven centers, like the chakra system, but in 1781 it underwent a change. Two of the centers split into two each, resulting in the nine-centered beings currently reflected in the charts. The energy centers carry a specific theme and tell us more about the nine main themes of energy in the chart. What is defined and consistent within your centers or is open and fluctuates depends on who you're around and the environment. These centers are what you will hear most often talked about in Human Design in terms of definition. Clients who have studied their charts before, often come to me for a session and tell me that they or their family members "only have two centers" or "one channel" defined. This is not a game of who has the most defined centers or channels, **we all have all of the components in the chart**, definition shows what is more consistent for us.

CONSCIOUS/UNCONSCIOUS

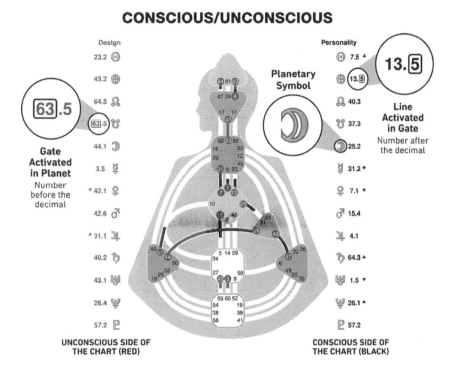

Conscious (Black)

The right side of the chart has a list of planetary symbols with the gates and lines listed in black. These represent what planets were activating the gates of the chart at the moment of birth. The gates listed here are what we can most easily see in ourselves. This side of the chart represents the mind and is labeled as Mind, Soul, Personality, or Conscious depending on the software used to calculate the chart.

Unconscious (Red)

On the left side of the chart is a duplicate of the list of planetary symbols with the gates and lines listed in red. These represent what planets were activating the gates of the chart approximately three months before birth. This side of the chart can feel a little more elusive, especially at first when just learning the energies of the centers, gates, and channels, and is commonly referred to as the *unconscious side*. This part of the chart represents the physical form (body) and can also be labeled Body, Design, Life, or Unconscious depending on the software used to calculate the chart. The energy represented on this side of the chart is generally more easily seen by the people in your life than by you.

Magnetic Monopole

The Conscious and Unconscious sides of the chart are energetically held together through something called the Magnetic Monopole that resides in your G (Identity) Center. You also have a Design Crystal in the Ajna Center and a Personality Crystal in the Head Center. These are not actual crystals you could locate, but energetic.

The Magnetic Monopole is like a one-way magnet holding both aspects of your design together, keeping you feeling like one person with different aspects of yourself rather than two completely different people living within the same body. It also aligns us with our life path as it pulls us along our trajectory through space and time.

Planets

There are twenty-six total planet activations, located in both the Conscious and Unconscious sides of the birth chart, representing what gate activation was present in each planet at the moment of birth (conscious) and approximately three months before birth (unconscious).

The planets each have a specific theme in the big picture of our life, which we won't go into in this book, as you need to have a good understanding of the foundational elements before diving into the next layer of information.

Gates

The 64 gates correlate with the Chinese I Ching hexagrams. While the gates in Human Design represent a separate archetype on their own, we cannot look at them in isolation as we are not merely one of our parts, but a synthesis of our entire chart. The gates are located in the centers in the BodyGraph, and their themes correlate to the overarching theme of that energy center. For example, a gate in the

G Center will have the theme of love, identity, or direction, while a gate in the Spleen Center will have to do with the immune system, instincts, intuition, or fears. The gates numbered 1- 64 are located in the centers and are also connected to the theme of the planet that was highlighting the gate at the moment of birth.

Lines

Each of the sixty-four gates have six possible line activations, creating 384 possible gate activations within a chart. Each of the six lines has a unique theme that correlates with the Profile lines. For example, if you have Gate 25.1 activated in your chart, it represents Gate 25, with line 1 as the specific gate expression. The first line is The Investigator in the Profile lines, so this line energy brings those investigative qualities to the expression of this gate. This gate has the energy of someone drawn to investigate their spirituality and feel secure in it before sharing with others. Depending on the software you use, you will see the line written as the number after the decimal (25.1) or as what looks like an exponent (25^1).

Channels

The channels, when defined, create a consistent archetypal theme of that particular channel's energy, throughout your whole life. Channel definition in a chart creates definition in the energy centers on either end of the channel. The gates located at each side of a channel have a related theme.

If you look at the BodyGraph now, you'll see, for example, that Gate 12, coming out of the right lower side of the Throat Center connects on the other end of that channel through Gate 22 in the Emotional Solar Plexus (ESP). By having both Gate 12 and Gate 22 defined, we now have the defined Channel 12-22 *and* a defined Throat Center and ESP.

This channel definition in your birth chart originates from what gates were activated by the planets in the Personality or Design side of your chart. Channels can also be temporarily experienced through connections with other people, or as the planets transit through the gates, throughout your life. While these connections through people or planets give us a different understanding of what it is like to embody that energy, they are not as consistent and reliable for us as the channels in our birth chart. The definition in our birth chart is always the same. It is an energy that is consistently there and transmits to the world who we are. The expression of that energy is on a spectrum and is experienced in a variety of ways. When you are around people with a different definition in their charts, you will create a temporary experience of what it is like to feel the energy of that gate, channel, or center, which can create an unconscious attraction to people who have the gates defined in their chart that you do not, especially if they complete a channel for you.

Where to Learn About the Gates

I have learned about the gates through multiple sources, and I encourage you to do the same. We all learn differently and take in information in a variety of ways, so I recommend finding what resonates for you. Look in the Resources Section for recommendations.

I suggest that you not only print out your own chart, but that of everyone in your home, and hang them up where you all can see them and as you learn. Talk about it with your children and show them how new discoveries relate to their charts. Seeing the chart gives your children a way to anchor in the information you're telling them, which can sound like a foreign language at first. Put your charts next to each other and notice the differences as well as the likenesses. Human Design is a universal language that is not affected by your religious background, gender, or skin color. I've never even seen the majority of my clients, as we work over the phone. The parts of their lives that they tell me about give me clues as to how they grew up, where they are now, and their heritage. Those are all parts of the story of who you are. And, as much as those aspects of you matter, in Human Design, we are taken back to the same basic elements to see the truth of who we are at our core before conditioning came in and told us who to be and how to be. We are all represented by the same BodyGraph, the same 64 gates, 9 centers, 36 channels, 4 energy types, and 26 planetary activations, but in all different combinations. We are one, yet we are all different, and still, we are more alike than not.

You Don't Have to Go Deep!

Please remember that you do not need to go deep into the chart to benefit from its gifts. You can only take in the information you are ready for, one layer at a time. If you begin reading this and struggle, take in the parts you can and go out into the world and work with the information. When you're ready, you'll be drawn back to it to learn more and integrate the next pieces. You may find yourself absorbing all this information easily and wanting more. We all have our unique paths, and I encourage you to find the teacher or mentor with whom you resonate and with whom your own inner Authority resonates. There is no perfect way, only the way that allows you to remember the truth of who you are and allows you to see your child as the unique individual they are.

To begin, keep it simple and start with the basics: Type, Strategy, and Authority, and then dive into your Profile and Centers, which will give you more insight into yourself and your child. It sounds simple, especially when looking at a Human Design Chart and seeing the depth available to you, but everything in Human Design comes back to the first three things – Type, Strategy and Authority. Learn and embody these three foundational elements, and you will be able to navigate your life and any further Human Design studies in the correct way for you. As you read through this book, if something does not resonate with you, listen to that voice or *knowing*. Is it calling you to lean in and look more closely, or is it not for you right now? Only you will know the answer to that, and I fully support and encourage you to make decisions that feel right for you and not to take my word for it. Lean into your Authority as you learn more and more how to identify what is correct for you.

Deconditioning

The process of coming home to yourself is referred to as *deconditioning* in Human Design. It is peeling back the layers of what you've been taught and told about how and who to be in order to remember the truth of who you are. Children receive most of their conditioning in the first seven years of life, which is why the younger we can support them in living as their authentic and true selves, the better. As adults, we go through deconditioning in seven-year cycles. Children who are aware of how their energy works and who have parents who support them from a young age to be who they truly are, do not have to go through the heavy deconditioning cycles that we as adults do, however they are still conditioned by their parents and the world around them. We are never free from the conditioning of the world and the goal is *not to be free* from it, but rather to be *aware* of it and what is self, versus not-self. The goal is to come home to ourselves and recognize what other people and planetary shifts bring to our life (lessons, experiences, and their unique story) as well as our connection to the Collective.

CHAPTER THREE

WHY DOES UNDERSTANDING YOUR CHILD THROUGH HUMAN DESIGN MATTER?

We are cups, constantly and quietly being filled.
The trick is knowing how to tip ourselves over and
let the beautiful stuff out.
~Ray Bradbury

In a world where we are being homogenized every time we turn around to be like everyone else, to look like everyone else, have the same things, same experiences, same lifestyle, etc., it can be hard to both be the kid who doesn't "fit in," and to be the parent of a kid who doesn't "fit in."

We're given the message that we're not enough. Not good enough, not ambitious enough, not quiet enough, not loud enough, not smart enough, not same enough. I don't know about you, but I don't want to live in a world of sameness. I assume, since you're reading this, you also want to embrace and understand what is different about your child as well as yourself.

Bullying is at an all-time high. Kids are dying by suicide at younger and younger ages. Now is the time. Now is the time for us to stop comparing ourselves to one another, stop singling each other out for being different, and begin celebrating our differences. We need to build bridges rather than create divides. When we look at each other through the lens of Human Design, we are all the same but uniquely different. We all have all of the chart, but there are definitions in our chart that create more consistency in certain areas, making us unique. We are drawn to what is different from us, and rather than picking on those differences as a bully would, we can look at them and celebrate them. We can learn from the differences, share our experiences and wisdom, and realize how much we depend on one another, as well as where each of us fits because *we all belong.*

Sometimes we feel like we've been dropped into the wrong family and don't fit in, but I assure you that your people are out there. Even when we don't understand the family we're born into—*especially* when we don't understand the family that we're born into—it is a perfect time to look at your family through the lens of Human Design. That parent who never seems to see you? Look into their chart and see how different their energies are from yours. Your child whose energy is off the wall all the time and exhausts you? Maybe they're a Sacral energy being, and you're not; they just need more exercise, and you need more rest.

What matters is that when you can see the differences in people and the inherent energies consistently present in a person, you can understand that it's not personal. And if it's not personal, it's not something you did or didn't do to create this pattern. It is simply the resulting mechanics of both of your energies coming together, and you can find ways to navigate that. For example, sometimes just knowing that a child who always makes you feel pressured to do what they want has a defined Root Center and you don't, can allow you to see them and yourself in a new light.

Having a child that you don't understand is nothing new. Somehow, we forget along the way from childhood to parenthood what it's like to be a kid. How many times did you hear your parents or a friend's parents say, "I just don't understand you or the decisions you make?" We're given the child that we're supposed to raise, and in turn, they raise us as well, if we let them.

Overbearing parental authority is tired. So, let's put that shit to bed. When the child is young, a parent does need to set boundaries to keep them safe and healthy. But at what point does keeping the child safe become making the child conform, killing their spirit, and dimming their light? How does one person think that they know what is best for another for eighteen or more years? And why do we assume that children couldn't do anything without us? How much do we let our ego control our parenting decisions?

Generations came before us who repeated what their ancestors did. Unfortunately, not all of what they did was for the highest good of everyone involved. You now have an opportunity to change what patterns you will repeat and whether your child will carry those habits, conditioning, and traumas forward. Shifting generational patterns may feel like a huge responsibility, but if not you, who? And if not now, when? We can all alter the patterns when we change our behavior, which changes our children's conditioning. We are all conditioning each other all throughout our lives, and the objective is not to stop ourselves from conditioning our child but to have more positive influences rather than negative ones.

When our children have a strong sense of self, they grow up to be adults who enter healthier relationships, have healthier boundaries, and know their worth.

Human Design gives you the grace to know it's not all on you to figure it out and that differences are not yours to "correct" out of your child. You can become a witness to your child's growth and who they are here to be without breaking their spirit. Are you ready?

CHAPTER FOUR

PARENTS

The journey of a thousand miles begins with a single step.
~LAO TZU

Accepting our Parents for the People They Are - It's Not Personal, It's Mechanics and Energy

When you thought about the family you had growing up and the one you would create one day, I would imagine you had a picture of what that would look like, what roles you and your family members would play, and what kinds of things you'd do together.

We build our families upon our ideals that are based on how we were raised and what we have experienced in life. We express these ideals as a desire to duplicate our experience or to veer far from that and create the total opposite of what we experienced growing up.

When you picked your partner to parent with (or perhaps you just picked someone to spend time with and accidentally created a family) and you grew your tiny human or awaited their arrival in whatever means they took to become part of your family—adoption, surrogacy, unexpectedly raising a friend's or family's children—I'm sure you had an idea of how things would work in your home. But sometimes, the family we get is not the family we thought we'd have or even understand. Sometimes the children from your DNA feel the most foreign. So even if they look like you, talk like you, and have some of the same quirks you do, you can have moments where you stand back and watch them and wonder *Why is this child this way? Did I teach them this? Did I create these habits, patterns, or mood swings?*

This type of questioning can leave us asking the same things about the people who raised us. We know that there are similarities, yet sometimes we despise the fact that we can be so similar to someone we feel has never understood us. Human Design both allows new insights into the lives of those we love, and new understandings of the relationships with whom we struggle most.

I grew up craving my father's pride, but rarely ever feeling like I received it unless I was doing something he approved of. After my parents divorced when I was eight, the times he was involved in my life were hard. I always wondered why he couldn't just be there for me like other dads, why he couldn't quit drinking, or why he couldn't listen and just hear me and my needs. I always felt railroaded by him. Everything he said to me was so authoritarian that I wanted to rebel, and at the same time, I wanted to do what he said to receive that moment of praise which seemed so ever elusive. It pissed me off that I cared what he thought when I wanted nothing more than to *not* care. I wanted to hurt him as he'd hurt me, and in another breath, I just wanted him to hug me and say, "I love you no matter what," and mean it. My relationship with my dad taught me lots of lessons around boundaries throughout my life that helped make me who I am today, by choosing to do the work to decondition from what my child-self thought she understood about herself. I'm a work in progress. I don't see an end goal. Life just keeps revealing new lessons, and I learn more about myself through each new deconditioning cycle.

I struggled for decades with the way that he was so selfish, stubborn, and bull-headed, and I always wondered why I never came first for him, though he always said I did. His comments made me feel guilty for not being the daughter I thought he wanted, but it wasn't until I looked at him through the lens of Human Design that I had the insight I needed to understand him more and what it must be like to be him through exploring his chart. I learned that he is designed to have to do things the hard way to see what is most important in his life. He's designed to be nurturing and also have big ups and downs emotionally, yet from what I saw, he was raised in a family where men didn't show emotion to other men other than frustration and anger when provoked. Softness and comfort were not supported emotions for men in the time he grew up, so he was likely conditioned to suppress those feelings. The only time I ever felt the softer emotions from my father was when he'd been drinking, and his guard was down, and then probably because he'd bottled them up for so long, they came out in a rush at the wrong time, in front of the wrong people, and I felt embarrassed both for him and myself. Knowing that the emotions I wanted to feel and the words I needed to hear from him were only available to me when he'd been drinking, covered in blame and guilt as to why I wasn't the daughter he wanted me to be, were just too much. One time when I was about twelve, I recall his telling me that he loved his girlfriend's kids more than he could ever love me; it was after he'd been drinking, and he was lashing out at me for not behaving the way he wanted me to. I had to keep learning lessons in boundary setting. I'd set a boundary, and he'd blow through it. I'd say, "I don't want to talk to you if you're drinking," and then he'd shut me out until he'd call me, drunk, telling me how much he loved me.

Being a 5/2 Profile, I now understand that a lot of what he was dealing with was being projected onto me, but as a child, I got the message that who I was, was not acceptable to him. I was not good enough.

While I've done a lot of healing work around these hurts and traumas in my life, Human Design gave me a new lens to see him through that I didn't even know was possible with someone who doesn't talk about his feelings. We still don't get to have those Hallmark heart to hearts, but we have moments, however brief, where we can touch on the past, and it no longer fills me with pain and shrinks me to the hurt child I once was. I see it differently now. He's grown older and calmer and no longer drinks as he did. Through Human Design I get to see him as a person, not just as my dad, and forgive him.

So, as you read through this book and you see places where you recognize not just your child but yourself in the text, I invite you to look up the charts of your parents and siblings. Consider who they are as individuals outside of the family dynamic in which you were raised and open your mind to what life may have been like for them in your family and the roles they played, as well as in your relationship with one another.

When we can see the other as just a person working through their own experiences and have compassion for the struggles and things that make them unique, we free ourselves from the binds that family hurts have caused us throughout our lives. It frees us from the past repeating itself and from you bringing those experiences into your current and future relationships with partners, children, friends, co-workers, and anyone you meet along your life's path.

The Parent's Work

As a parent, you've probably spent a good chunk of time considering what is right for your child, what opportunities you'd like them to have, and how you'd like them to grow up and be. You've probably noticed what they are naturally gifted at doing, and maybe you even have a family tradition of being a tradesperson, a professional, or an expectation of them going to college. You probably remember the pressures you felt to be a certain way, whether it was about what you'd be when you grew up or who you should be (or perhaps who you *shouldn't* be). You may even hear the voice of a parent in your head right now as you read this and consider your own life experiences.

We are shaped largely by the people who raised us–who they were, how they were raised, how they were treated, and what their parents before them were like and were taught. But I know that you're looking to break those patterns because you're reading this book and looking for a new way forward–a way to shift the patterns that have felt heavy to carry on your life's journey. You want something different for your child(ren), and this book will help you navigate your relationships with curiosity for who they are, who *you* are, and who you want to be both as a parent and as a person. The work you choose to do will help you, your children, their children, and the children after that. According to Mark Wolynn in his book *It Didn't Start with You* multi-generational healing in all directions is possible through the work you do now.

Your work as the parent is to see where your limiting beliefs or stories are being repeated with your children, for good or bad. Consider the judgment you place on the stories you carry; do you label them as either *good* or *bad* when you reflect upon them? You are seeing your children through your personal lens, which was likely created by events in your own childhood experience. Seeing that we're stuck in an old story is the first step, and then we must work to change the story we tell about what is good and bad regarding children's behavior, through our adult lens. For example, if you grew up with a family that valued having dinner together at 5:00 every day, and considered this as what a "good" family does, are you expecting that for your family now? And if your family can't make that happen regularly, do you consider that "bad" parenting/family behavior? What would it be like to toss that old story out and create a new narrative for the family you have? Could telling a new story allow everyone to feel more peaceful during mealtime, whether it's at 5:00 or 8:00, together or separate? Disengaging from what you think should be and opening to the possibilities of what could work best for your family can allow you to create a way of being for your family that works for everyone and honors each individual.

Because people tend to get stuck in the emotional charge of the memory when the event took place, journaling, life coaching, counseling, Reiki, meditation, hypnotherapy, and the Emotional Freedom Technique (EFT) are all examples of ways to support your process as you journey into your and your child's charts (and any other family members you run charts for). Make sure you're taking care of yourself through this process so that you can be good support for your child(ren). Take breaks when needed and talk to someone so you're not carrying the things that come up all on your own.

Of course, you don't have to dig into your own work at all and can just read through this book for insight into your child's behavior, and that is your choice. But for the pattern to change, you must look at the places in your life where you are not living authentically. Not all at once, of course, but as issues come up, if you can meet them and get the support to work through them, you give that gift to your child as well as yourself.

CHAPTER FIVE

ENERGY TYPE AND STRATEGY

To dream of the person you would like to be is
to waste the person you are.
~SHOLEM ASCH

Each energy type has a Strategy for navigating life, and the earlier you can begin teaching your child to use their Strategy, the better they will understand how to respond to the things life sends their way now and into adulthood. Most adults must decondition from how they have been taught to respond to life, learn to make aligned choices, and stop people-pleasing.

One of the biggest elements of deconditioning in Human Design is to learn to wait. All energy types have an element of waiting built into their Strategy, even the Manifestors. As you read on and perhaps feel the wish to be another energy type because it seems like they have it so much easier/better or anything else, remember: You have the perfect design for you and when you embrace it, you will have everything you need.

With our children, we have a lot of work to do to release the societal conditioning of how we are "supposed" to parent. How we expect children and parents to be, and how we tell people they should approach the world, their jobs, and social interactions all need to shift. We must stop telling people how to be themselves and allow them to have their own processes while honoring who they are. These children come through us, but they are not ours. We do not own them. They are gifts entrusted to us to help them navigate this world. They were not sent here to become mini versions of us, but to be their own individual people with unique gifts to share with the world. The moment we can see that, the more expansive their worlds become, and the better able we are to learn from them. More control does not make a healthier child. Punishment for who they are does not make them become what you want them to be. Maybe on the surface or in your presence, they act the way you want, but in their hearts, they know it is not safe to be themselves around you. Imagine what you will miss out on by not allowing them to be their authentic selves.

Energy Types

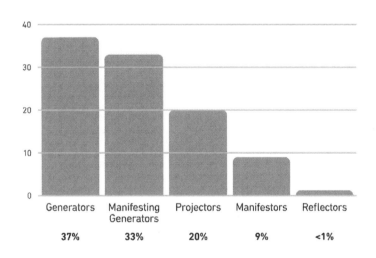

ENERGY TYPES BY PERCENTAGE OF POPULATION

Generators	Manifesting Generators	Projectors	Manifestors	Reflectors
37%	33%	20%	9%	<1%

There are four different energy types in Human Design. Though you may have heard about five, there are actually only four different energy types: Manifestor, Generator, Projector, and Reflector with a subtype of the Generator known as the Manifesting Generator.

The energy type is related to aura, which is the energy that flows around the physical body. As you move through the world, it interacts with other auras. You've probably had the experience of meeting someone new, or even someone you know, and the feelings you got from them were just different. Maybe they felt intrusive, asking you things that you didn't feel comfortable sharing, and you wanted to disengage and get away because you felt exposed. Or perhaps they were so energetic it amped you up or excited you, or, if it was too much, it left you feeling anxious. And there are those people who, when around, see you, respect your unspoken boundaries, thus sharing space with them feels comfortable. That's their aura or energy field that you're sensing. When someone is aligned, their aura feels different than when they are living in the not-self. If you read through these energy types, and feel as if the chart is wrong, consider where you may be in the spectrum of living in a heavily conditioned life versus living an aligned life.

Our auras enter the room before we do. Knowing what your energy type is and how it interacts with other people can help you understand so much more about the responses you or your child receive when interacting with the world and each other.

The energy type of the Manifestor has an aura that is big, bold, and beautiful, and its ability to initiate can at times feel intense. Though this aura is often described as closed and *repelling* in Human Design, I think it's mostly just misunderstood both by the person who lives it and the people around them. Can you imagine someone who is designed to create new things in the world and take inspired action—their aura must be impactful to break through with new ideas!

We live in a society that uses the word *manifest* for everything that we want, while the Human Design meaning is literally about creating and initiating or taking action. What a Manifestor does when they initiate does not always come to completion through them. They often hand it over to others like the Generators to continue the energy they set into motion. The Projectors oversee and help guide the energy, while the Reflectors are taking the temperature of the whole operation and reflecting back to us how well we're doing overall. Manifestors are here to learn about their impact on others; however, they still must wait until their "inner creative drive" tells them it's time to take action. They do not just dream up something in their mind and then make it happen. They may dream it up, but they also must wait until they get the physical sensation (the inner creative drive) and have the energetic resources to take action. This physical pull can be described as an inner drive that cannot be stopped. They cannot explain why they need to manifest this thing, but it must be done, or they can become angry if stopped, which is an emotional signature of the Manifestor.

The energy type of the Generator and Manifesting Generator has an aura that is open and inviting, bringing people and opportunities to them. Because they are here to respond and not initiate, their aura brings them everything they need. Even Manifesting Generators are here to respond as they are a Generator energy type at their core. When aligned, they are energized and spilling over with lifeforce and workforce energy and can be energizing to be around when they live their lives in alignment with their Strategy. They learn more about themselves through what their aura brings to them throughout their lives.

The energy type of the Projector has an aura that is focused and absorbing and is here to learn about *others* more than *self*. They connect with one person at a time and connect deeply, which is why they need to be invited to do so. If a Projector tries to connect with you deeply without your permission, it can feel obtrusive and exposing. But once you invite a Projector in, they will see you and recognize you in a way other energy types do not.

The energy type of the Reflector has an aura that is reflecting and sampling as they check the environment and health of their community. They are here to become wise. They are sampling the people and environments around them and reflect what they are sensing in their community by adapting to and becoming like their environments.

The four energy types will feel different when you interact with them. As you read the descriptions, I bet you will have people in mind who fit these descriptions, and perhaps you even see yourself or your children in them.

In the next section, we'll break down the four energy types, their characteristics, and corresponding Strategies in more depth. If you have not already gotten a copy of your child's Human Design Chart, you can do so at www.geneticmatrix.com.

Make sure after you read about your child's energy type, that you also read about your own energy type and notice how similar or different they are and how you may be bringing your energy type Strategy or ways into your parenting. Allow yourself to imagine what it might be like for your child who has another energy type and consider how you might be able to shift your ideals of how they should behave, learn, or just *be* according to what is correct for them. If your energy type is the same as your child's, remember that they have other key aspects that will differentiate them from you, making them appear very different from how you experience your own energy type.

Manifestors

Non-Sacral Energy Type – Approximately 8-9 Percent of the Population

Purpose: To initiate and bring new ideas into form.

Strategy: To wait for their *inner creative drive* (the feeling that tells them to take action and is often seen as irrational to other people) to tell them to take action, and then to inform those who will be affected.

Signature Emotion: Peace

Signature Not-Self Emotion: Anger

The Manifestor does not have a defined Sacral Center and is identified by having a motor (ESP, Root, Sacral, or Will Center) connected to the Throat Center by a defined channel. This definition may go through another center, such as the G Center or the Spleen Center, or have a direct motor center to Throat Center connection. Having a motor connected to the Throat Center gives them the power to manifest - to bring things into reality without the help of anyone else. They can take action on their own and are the kids who often just dive into things without warning.

The Manifestor is here to have new ideas and get things started, which means that these can be the children who dream up exciting challenges and learning opportunities. It's important to let them follow those ideas as long as they're not threatening their own or anyone else's safety.

Most of the world is taught to think that they're here to be Manifestors, but the reality is that only about 9 percent of our population are. Ironically, while the Generators are trying to be Manifestors, most Manifestors are raised by Generators and conditioned to work, work, work, which is not correct for their energy type.

When a Manifestor, who does not have a defined Sacral Center, is raised with Generators and conditioned to push through and keep going, even when they don't want to anymore, it can shut down their gift of initiation. They cannot easily fulfill their purpose of initiating if they are tired. It is through initiation that they bring new ideas and concepts to the world. Because they are not here to work like a Generator, and instead follow this need to initiate through their inner creative drive, they need to approach life and work differently than 90 percent of the population.

Manifestors are not here to just work, work, work.

They are designed to wait for their inner creative drive to tell them it's time to act and follow that feeling. Manifestor kids are driven by this urge to create and explore in a way that cannot be turned off easily and will often push the boundaries as children while bringing new ideas to life. They are the kids who spontaneously set up a lemonade stand on a summer day, but rather than setting up at the end of the driveway, they decide to sell lemonade and snacks from a floating lemonade stand at the lake for the boaters to stop by and get refreshments.

However, just because a Manifestor has a great business idea doesn't mean that they'll do that work forever. When they feel their excitement or drive diminishing, they will need to retreat, gather more energy/resources, and wait for the next inner creative drive to tell them what's next.

Manifestors can be great at starting new businesses, selling them, and moving on to the next thing. As children, they can be great at starting new things, getting other people excited about them, and then moving on to the next thing. When they're operating in alignment, their goal isn't even about the final outcome, but rather about fulfilling their inner drive to create when the time is right for them, and they have enough resources.

Suppose a parent of a Manifestor continuously tells the Manifestor child "No" when they dream a new thing up. In that case, it will either teach them to suppress that inner creative drive and people-please or teach them to find new, often sneaky ways, to do what they want to do anyway.

Here is where the parent must make a choice. Either try and parent your Manifestor by suppressing this drive and shut down this aspect of them that is so special, and risk them never really feeling like themselves, or teach them to inform. When you teach them to inform you of what they want to do, you can screen their ideas for harmful things and let them learn about life by experiencing it when it is safe. Even if you can see ahead of time that it won't work out as they think it will, they need to be allowed to follow their inner drive if it's not harmful.

The parenting challenge is to let your Manifestor child follow their inner creative flow and powerful initiation abilities without over-parenting them.

Reacting to their initiating abilities by trying to control them, setting firmer boundaries, saying no to everything, and generally overpowering them, can lead them to use the anger they feel to fuel finding another way to do what they want anyway without telling you.

Parents, these children are here to teach you about surrendering. Learn to work with their natural way of being and not try to over-control them if you want to experience a more easeful flow in your relationship. The relationship will still have its challenges, as every parent-child relationship does, but you can encourage their natural abilities and still be forewarned of what they're going to do if they learn to inform.

The world needs for Manifestors to understand their unique abilities and to avoid becoming people-pleasers. What can you do to allow your Manifestor child to step into their power, without being dangerous? When you let them realize their *appropriate* power and allow them to experiment by following their inner creative urges, they will experience their emotional signature of peace.

By the time a Manifestor becomes an older teen, they won't need you in the way other energy types do. They've sort of raised themselves at this point and figured out how to take action on what they want/need. Because they can take action on their own, they usually do, and their informing becomes more of a courtesy to you unless you try to control them and limit what they can do. If you try and suppress their inner creative urges, you will experience their signature not-self emotion of anger. Try asking your Manifestor teen what their plans are and ask them to inform you if their plans change, which gives them space to know that you're not trying to control them but want to know their whereabouts as a parent who cares about them. Give them an appropriate level of trust and find a way forward that keeps you in the know of what they're doing and allows them the freedom to explore their world. If you have a Manifestor teen approaching graduation, rather than asking what colleges they are going to apply to or where they're going to get a job, try asking them, "What do you think is next for you after high school?" "How will you make that happen?" "What have you found out about what it would take to make that happen?" Asking them open-ended questions allows them to dream, consider, and see what stirs their inner creative drive that tells them what's next.

Communicating with a Manifestor

Manifestors need to be asked open-ended questions, rather than yes/no questions, and given positive reinforcement.

Let them remain open to the possibilities by asking them open-ended questions and providing positive feedback when they've come up with a great idea or way of doing something. For example, if you know they like trying new foods, rather than asking "Do you want pizza for dinner?" try "What would be fun to have for dinner tonight?" Replying with "That's a fun/great/interesting/creative idea!" can help them feel good about following their inner creative drive.

They are always coming up with new ideas, so listen to their ideas and ask questions that help them to think through the consequences and possibilities of what might happen, rather than just saying no immediately, or help them follow the idea through in a safer way. For example, if they tell you they want to start a fire while camping at age ten, rather than saying no immediately or shutting down the idea because they're too young, you can take that opportunity to teach them to respect fire and how to be safe with it. Or sign them up for a class on fire safety where they can learn about fire and how it can get out of control very quickly and must be respected.

If they come up with a new innovative way of doing something at home that you wouldn't have ever considered, praise them for their idea. Just take care to consider if you're praising their work for the sake of working and doing what they're told without question, versus praising them for their innovative ideas.

Manifestors in School

In a group activity in school, they may play the role of initiator coming up with ideas for what the project could look like, sketching it out, and then involving others to take the project and keep moving with it. They may struggle with bringing it to completion if their creative energy wanes. It's not that they're trying to get out of doing the work, but rather their portion of the job involves a different kind of work than the often-labor-intensive part. Engage their imagination to keep them inspired.

If your Manifestor has taken on a big project like a senior paper, a college degree, or organized a committee or group to help others, for example, make sure they are allowed and encouraged to have downtime after getting the ball rolling or turning in the paper. This helps them to keep their inner creativity flowing and teaches them to work correctly for their energy type by allowing them to nourish themselves with downtime after a big push. Getting out in nature, unplugging from devices, or even just digging into a great book can provide ways to unwind. Maybe they like to practice yoga, do spiritual work, play soccer, or hang out with friends. Depending on what stage they are in, notice what they need. They feel best when allowed cycles of rest between initiation cycles.

Manifestors and Homework

Getting your Manifestor to do their homework may be challenging if your Manifestor is not in the mood to do homework. After being attentive all day at school, they may need a break before they can dive into their homework. Taking in all the Sacral energy in a classroom can be exhausting. As a parent, rather than setting a structured schedule for what you want them to do, try giving them a window of time to get things done, and let them decide in what order they will do them. Let them know you're available within that window of time to help. But if they do not get their work done, nagging them or doing the work for them won't help. They need to learn the consequences of their actions and understand that there are specific parameters they will need to operate within. You can remind them they have some control over how the work gets done and that you'll be there to support them when they need it. It can be hard to let your child learn through the consequences of their actions, but it is much easier to learn with lower consequence tasks earlier on than when they are in their teens or out on their own. Your Manifestor child does not need to be micromanaged, but they do need to be informed of the expectations just as much as they need to inform others of things that will affect them.

Manifestors and Work

When it comes time for a Manifestor to get a job, they will likely do best to find a job that allows a more flexible schedule or even shorter work times if possible. This will enable them to rest when needed instead of conditioning them to work through their whole lives trying to be a Generator and burning out by age forty or fifty. Manifestors who have been pushing hard all their adult lives to work, work, work, can find themselves failing in health, burning out, aging faster than their peers, and losing their zest for life. Manifestors can be great at starting companies and selling them, which keeps them fresh in creating and initiating by avoiding burning out on day-to-day monotonous work. The truth is, any energy type can do any job, but they must approach it in a way that works for them. Understanding their unique attributes allows them to find a job or start a business that encourages their energy to flow rather than become draining.

The Manifestor's Signature Emotions

Manifestors and Anger

The not-self signature emotion that lets a Manifestor know they are out of alignment is anger. It is important you help your Manifestor child understand that anger is a normal feeling which is part of their process, but they need to use care in where they direct it. When they get angry, consider what would be helpful for them. Do they need to be alone for a few minutes (or more) so they can process what they are feeling? Do they need to go for a walk and move their body? Do they need to yell into a pillow? Have they been stopped from initiating something? Emotions are essential and should not be stuffed down because they are unpleasant. Manifestors also need to be taught to be responsible with how they treat others when they feel emotionally charged. As the parent, remember that anger is usually the sign that your Manifestor's inner creative drive was interrupted. If you know where they're feeling blocked, is there a way to navigate it? Is there a compromise?

Manifestors and Peace

When the Manifestor is operating within their Strategy and informing (and is informed) and allowed to follow their inner creative drive, they can feel their signature emotion of peace.

The Manifestor Strategy

Manifestor Children - Ask and Inform

The Manifestor child needs to be taught to inform you of what they want to do, but informing doesn't come naturally to them, so they need to learn this Strategy. Teaching them to ask helps them learn to let those who will be impacted by their decisions know what they intend to do and because Manifestors often dream up some exciting stuff, you, as a parent, will be happy to know what they plan on doing before they do it!

Teaching them to ask can sound like "Please let me know before you go over to your friend's house, so I know where you are." "If you decide to do something else, please check in with me first." It doesn't mean that you always have to say yes, but it teaches them to inform, and you get to know where they are and what they're up to rather than having to alert the neighborhood watch to help find them because they decided to follow a path through the trees to see what was there.

Because the Manifestor must make decisions on their terms, you need to ask them to do things in a way that informs them of what you need them to do, while also allowing them some freedom of choice. "If you want to go to Michael's house, I need to know by 10:00, so I can take you there" is an example of informing them that if they want something from you, they need to inform you what they need, and as the parent, you get to set some parameters around it. You, as the parent, do not need to say yes to everything they dream up or at the time they dream it but try to empower them to ask/inform and be polite about it.

Having the big ideas and being allowed to follow them (within reason) are essential to their signature emotion of peace, so be careful not to shut down this drive in them by constantly telling them no. Teach them to be polite when asking. For a Manifestor, their love language is for them to hear you say "Yes" and "Let's try it and see what happens" more often. It helps them feel recognized for their ability to have big or new ideas, to trust that they can offer something important to the world, and to know their ability has value.

It is also important for you to inform your Manifestor as well. If you're going to leave, take a trip, move, bring someone new into your home, or anything that will impact them, you need to inform them. Just as you want to know what to expect from them, they want to know what to expect from you.

Adults - Inform

As your child grows and becomes an adult, they will shift from asking permission to do something, to just telling you what they're going to do, unless you've told them no so much that they hide it because they think you won't approve. Their aura is big and bold, and when it moves, people around them feel its presence and absence. If a Manifestor aura leaves the room suddenly without informing, we want to know where it's going and when to expect it back. Help your child understand that they impact others even when they're just doing their own thing so that when they reach adulthood, they have an easier time following their inner creative drive without encountering resistance and feeling anger. Informing is not about obtaining permission for the adult Manifestor, but for them to feel less resistance when they're ready to take action.

Parenting the Manifestor as Another Energy Type

Projector Parent and the Manifestor Child

Though you are also a non-Sacral energy type, your energy needs may be quite different from a Manifestor. If you are a Projector who has no motors defined in your chart, the energy of the Manifestor child in your life may feel overwhelming. You might need some extra breaks in your day from one another, especially if you are the primary caregiver when they are home all the time. Remember that you will need downtime at the end of the day to discharge other people's energy, and your Manifestor will need rest at the end of the day also - see the sleep section in Chapter Eleven about Manifestor sleep needs.

Your Manifestor child may appear to be able to dig in and get things done, and at first, may even seem more like a Generator in their initiation phase. However, if the project is long and you start to see their energy wane, this is an opportunity to discuss their energy needs. You likely know as a non-Sacral energy type that when you push yourself beyond your energy limits that you'll need to rest after. Help your child understand that this is a natural ebb and flow of energy for them and that it does not mean that they are quitters or can't finish things. It means they are here to start things, have new ideas, and change the way we work, but it does not mean they always have to finish those jobs. Help them learn to know when enough is enough.

As a Projector, you may be able to see that the way your Manifestor child is approaching things is not the most energy-efficient or easeful way of doing things. Be careful how you approach them, as the Manifestors are not here to be guided. If you can see a better way of doing something, consider an approach of "I have some experience with what you're doing that I could share with you if you're interested." This is not telling them how to do it but informing them that you are a resource if they choose to engage your help.

Reflector Parent and the Manifestor Child

This combination can be challenging in that the not-self emotion of the Manifestor is anger, and it can feel intense for a Reflector to be around that energy, especially if they are living in conditioning, and taking in and holding other people's emotions as if they were their own. To avoid this feeling, a parent may try and please them to keep their anger from becoming overwhelming.

Your Manifestor has at least one motor defined which can feel very powerful and overwhelming at times. As a parent, when you feel energetically overwhelmed by your child, you can emotionally beat yourself up over the fact that you're not more patient or understanding and need a break from your child. I want to tell you that it is okay to not want to be around your child 24/7 and that breaks from one another are okay, good even. If you don't have family around to help, hire a babysitter or make a trade with another parent to get breaks. You need your downtime to discharge the energy you pick up from others, especially when they have a powerful aura and defined motor energy like a Manifestor.

Reflector parents, you will feel what your child is feeling (make sure you don't take it on personally). Remember to sample their energy field, learn what you need to know, and help them to navigate back to a place that feels good for both of you rather than just taking it on as your own.

When your Manifestor is angry, you will feel it. You can let them know you feel what they are feeling and ask them what they need to move forward, or if they have an idea of something you can do together, that would be fun. Use their initiating energy to make more fun times.

Generator/Manifesting Generator Parent and the Manifestor Child

When you have a renewable life force/workforce energy, as Generator/Manifesting Generator energy types do, it can be hard to understand how someone else could not have that same drive and work ethic you do, especially when they have these big ideas and dig into them enthusiastically. If Generator energy type parents raised you, you likely learned your work ethics from them and the conditioning they gave you, and this is what you know. You may feel like your Manifestor is lazy. They're not! They're just here to work differently and their work is not the same as the work you're here to do. Create an opportunity to learn from one another and lean into a new way of parenting.

You may not understand your Manifestor easily because your energy operates quite differently. Still, the more you open the dialogue with them about what they are called to do, how they feel driven, and how they know when they need to follow their creative drive can help you see what kinds of jobs around the house they could help with. Learning their strengths helps you and lets them see what they are good at when they're given the opportunity. It helps them feel confident. Don't we all feel like we just want to contribute something that makes us special in our own way? Long-term physical work is not what your Manifestor is here to do, though while they are in your aura, they can probably work a lot longer and harder than usual. Be careful to understand that this is not sustainable for them. If you're cleaning their room with them and then you leave the house to run to the store and tell them to finish up, you may come back to an unfinished room because when you left, your borrowed Sacral energy left with you. When they borrow energy, they can amplify it and work hard for a while, especially when they're younger, but we want to teach them how to work for *their* energy type, not *your* energy type.

Manifestor Child Story

With only 8-9 percent of the population being Manifestors, we don't generally have many of them in our lives, or more likely we don't know that we know many in our lives as they are often conditioned to live as Generators, dimming their magic. I have found through running charts that I have at least two in my family. I recall a memory from my childhood of a cousin who was two-three years old, and I was about twelve. I was outside playing tetherball at my grandmother's house out in the country. The road she lived on was rural, and cars generally drove a minimum of 40 mph down this road, and on either side was an irrigation ditch. One of those was full of fast-moving water and was several feet wide, so I'd been charged with keeping an eye on my cousin while outside. This little Manifestor LOVED horses. In fact, I've never met anyone who loved a horse more, and the neighbor across the street happened to have a couple of horses. In what seemed like a split second, she was gone. We called for her and immediately searched the yard. Adults got involved in the search, and the worst was immediately feared by all involved. My grandmother was especially distraught as a cousin of hers drowned when he was a child. Just about the time we were freaking out, someone spotted her. There she was across the street petting the horses. She had navigated the driveway, avoided two irrigation ditches, crossed the road, and was visiting the horses. She was perfectly unharmed. I now know that she was just following that inner drive to initiate and do. She saw something she wanted to experience and just went after it. This is the Manifestor child in action. (I see it. I want it. I do it.)

Young Manifestor children need guidance around what is safe and not safe because they will try things without regard to their consequences. However, there must be a dance with this where we don't shut them down completely and, instead, allow them to learn to trust that there is something there for them to follow and that it is correct for them to do so. Nourish their inner creative drive and curiosity to see where it takes them and how they uniquely contribute to the world.

Parenting as a Manifestor

Are You a Manifestor Parenting a Manifestor Child?

How were you raised as a child? Were you stopped from following your creative drive? Do you people please? Were you allowed to explore and try new things or were you shut down? Did you hide the things that you tried from your parents? How did they respond to you? Do you have a pattern of people-pleasing as an adult?

Consider how your own experience as a Manifestor child affects how you parent your children. Were you controlled by your parents, and has that led to your being more controlling of your child(ren)? What would you like to have experienced differently as a child, now knowing as an adult that you're a Manifestor? This can be an incredible learning opportunity for you to parent your child the way you wish you had been parented–by Type. You can reparent yourself through your parenting experience with your child as well.

Manifestor Parent and the Sacral Energy Type Child

When parenting a child with a defined Sacral Center, you need to exhaust your child's Sacral energy through physical exercise. This is especially important when they are young so that you can get them into bed and asleep more quickly and allow yourself downtime. It's best if you allow yourself at least thirty minutes in bed lying down and unwinding so that you can fall asleep easily. You are not designed to wear yourself out and then fall into bed and immediately sleep like a Generator. This *extra* time in bed is important for you and is not really extra at all.

Manifestor Parents Need to Inform Their Child

As a DO-er and not a natural delegator, you can struggle to navigate telling your children (who are looking for you to lead them) what they need to do, and you can often end up just doing it for them. Consider a child who is learning to tie their shoes and insists on being the one to tie them when you're running late. A

Manifestor parent is likely planning on just tying the child's shoes and getting out the door, but the child is at the stage where they need to do it themself. As the Manifestor parent starts to tie the child's shoes, the child fights and insists on doing it themself. The Manifestor parent now feels the not-self signature emotion of anger because their initiating flow was interrupted, making them later than they already were. Now the parent and child are upset. The child is upset both because they can't do it themselves and because you're upset with them. In this case, try informing your child that you'll need to tie their shoes this time because you must get somewhere on time, but next time you'll plan more time to let them do it themselves (and then keep your word).

Putting It into Action

As a Manifestor parent, you need to inform your child(ren) about what is coming and what you need them to do to make things run smoother. If you're raising Generator or Manifesting Generator children with defined Sacral Centers, and you already feel tired, the less resistance, the better. And in the case of Generator kids, be sure to ask them yes/no questions to get their Sacral motors moving.

In the example of shoe tying, just because you can do it for them doesn't mean it's the best thing for them. Empower your kids by informing them what you expect/need before becoming frustrated that things aren't moving as quickly as you'd like.

Generators

Sacral Energy Type – Approximately 70 Percent of the Population

Purpose: Workforce builders. To find proficiency in their work, by responding to what life brings them through their Strategy.

Strategy: To wait for something to show up in their external reality and then respond through their Sacral response.

Signature Emotion: Satisfaction

Signature Not-Self Emotion: Frustration

Generators represent roughly 70 percent of the population and include Manifesting Generators. Generator energy types have the Sacral Center defined (colored in), and no motor connected to the Throat Center in their chart. They are here to learn about themselves through the work they respond to in life, guided by their Sacral response. Being here to work does not mean that Generators are here to do all the grunt work that nobody wants to do, though that is a theme that is often conditioned into them. They can be conditioned to take up the slack for other people because they know that the job needs to get done, and they can find the energy to do it. If Generator children are rewarded when they do the grunt work, they can begin to feel like they're only worthy if they are doing for others, leading to lifelong patterns of people-pleasing and ignoring their calling in life.

Generators are here to interact with life by *waiting* for life to bring them things to *respond* to. These could be opportunities to network, play, work, create, perform, travel, or move. They do not have to go looking for life, as life will come to them. The difficulty for most adult Generators is that they've become conditioned to go out and make things happen and push with their energy rather than waiting for life to bring them opportunities to respond to. This conditioning begins in childhood. Responding is how the Generator accepts the offer to engage their energy in their next right thing, through their Sacral response, which takes patience when they've been conditioned to operate more like a Manifestor. They must have faith that the Universe will send them what they need—and it will! But waiting for it to show up can feel scary when they've been told their whole life to be in the driver's seat and that they must be the one to make their dreams happen. In Human Design, we are each the passenger in the vehicle (body), and our Magnetic Monopole (located in the G Center) is what drives our vehicle along the road of life. When we are living in alignment, we are watching life happen while we are living it, rather than trying to make it happen.

If a Generator does not wait for things to respond to and continues to push and initiate, they will find themselves entering commitments incorrectly, and their energy will not be right for the task. Though they will likely be able to find the energy to keep doing the job, their joy will suffer, and they can experience their own form of burnout. Unlike the non-Sacral energy types, they will generally not burn out to the point where they can't do anything, but they will lose their zest for life along with their purpose and drive. There is a rebound energy effect when a Generator is not using their energy correctly, and they can have a decline in energy and feel burned out. When their energy drops, they stop pursuing the things that interest them. If this happens, this is a critical time for the Generator to look at their life and see where they have been saying yes when they want/need to say no. If they have been people-pleasing, it means learning to set good boundaries around their time, energy, and working on self-worth. Teaching your Generator child to use their Strategy and Authority can keep them from reaching a point of burnout later in life.

If this has happened to you, you can start by re-learning how to use your Sacral response, which is the unh-uh (no), uh-huh (yes) response when asked a yes/no question. Once you've responded with a yes (or uh-huh) from your Sacral (if you don't also have Emotional Authority), then you can proceed with taking action about what you responded to. If you have Emotional Authority, go to Chapter Six and read more about waiting for clarity on a decision before taking action.

When we ask Generator kids to explain themselves or rationalize their why behind their yes/no, response, we condition them to use their minds to make decisions rather than letting their Sacral guide them with what is true for them. They then grow up to be adults who have a hard time saying no because they feel like they must justify it, and it's easier to just do what's asked of them by people-pleasing.

Communicating with a Generator - How to Work *with* the Energy of Your Generator Child

When parenting a Generator child, you must learn to ask them questions that they can respond to rather than just telling them what to do. Because they respond to what you're asking them to do through their Sacral, you need to make sure you're asking yes/no questions. The Sacral is ultimately answering the question, "Do you want to do this work?" "Do you want to use your energy for this?"

You can get a Generator child to take action and move forward if you ask the right yes/no questions, for example, when you see they are frustrated with making a sandwich, yet they have quickly dismissed your offer to help. You can ask questions like "Do you need help?" or "Do you know what you need right now?" or "Do you need to do it on your own?" It's a little like that game where you think of something, and the other person has to ask you questions about that thing to get a better idea of what it is until they gather enough information to guess it. See Appendix for more specifics on how to ask these Sacral-response questions to your Generator child.

Initially, this process can be frustrating for the parent if they've been used to telling their child what to do and were raised to believe that parents talk, and children listen. But once you get the hang of it and start understanding what they need generally, your questions quickly improve at getting to the heart of the matter to get them moving forward again. Remember, you know your child best, and though it will slow you down at first to begin asking these types of questions, you will see your child develop confidence in knowing what they want/need in the long run, and you will learn how to get them to take action and make forward progress, empowering them to understand their truth and stay connected to it as they go out into the world.

Generators in School

In school, your Generator child is more likely to be the one doing the work in a group project. They may see that the work needs to be done and do it when others are not and end up doing more than their fair share. Their teachers may rely on them more because they know they will get the work done. Now, this is a gross generalization because there are lots of other elements that come into play in the chart, but if you notice this tendency in your Generator child, this is an opportunity for you to help them understand that just because they *can* do all the work, it doesn't mean they *should*. They can also become frustrated when learning something new, as they have a stairstep learning approach that can lead to frustration when they hit a plateau and it feels like they can't get any better. It's important to understand whether they truly want to quit because they don't like doing it anymore, or if they are just frustrated that they are not improving as quickly as they'd like to.

Generators greatly benefit from physical ways of moving their body and energy, so extracurricular activities where they can burn off some of that energy may be helpful. If they are not having enough opportunities to use up some of this energy throughout their day, sitting in class may become difficult for them. They may fidget, lose focus, be distracted or distracting, and have a harder time concentrating. If this is the case, see if you can find more opportunities for them to move their bodies and encourage them to physically move and play at break times.

Generators and Homework

When it comes to struggles with getting your Generator to do homework, remember to use yes/no, or this/that Sacral-response questions. You need to give them something to respond to. Rather than saying "You need to get your homework done" or "When are you going to get the project done that's due on

Friday?" try asking "Do you want to get your homework done now or after dinner?" You might also try "Will your project be done and ready to turn in Friday morning?" If the response is no, then follow up with "Do you know what needs to happen to make it ready by Friday morning?" "Do you know what's stopping you from getting it done?" A project that gets delayed until the last minute can be a result of feeling overwhelmed around getting organized. If they have an undefined or open Root Center (more to come on centers in Chapter Eight) the pressure can either cause them to speed through a project just to get it done and be free from the pressure, or it can alternatively lead to paralysis from the overwhelming amount of pressure they feel.

I'll leave you with one more thought about Generators and homework: What are the expectations that this child feels over what they need to do? Generators can often be rewarded for doing the work that nobody else wants to do, or they'll overwork to feel recognized if they learn that when they go above and beyond, they get praise for it. This can lead to always putting that same amount of pressure on themselves to feel good about the work they are doing. If they have an open Will Center, they can also struggle with feelings of worthiness. As parents, it's our responsibility to be mindful of how we communicate our expectations of the work they do so they don't adopt a mindset of working, working, working, even when they don't want to, just to please the adults or other people in their life.

Also, make sure before they sit down to focus on their homework that they've had enough physical movement that day. This will help them to concentrate better. If they've been sitting in class all day and come home and are expected to get right to their homework, they may struggle.

Generators and Work

The work that your Generator child grows up to do should be work that they enjoy. Even if the work they do for a job is not the most joy-filled, they need to have some sort of work, volunteering, or hobby that brings them joy. They are here to become skillful in their work when they enter into it correctly through their

Strategy (to wait to respond to something that shows up in their external reality like a job offer or suggestion from a friend). The work they enjoy may not be the work that pays the bills, but it does pay them high dividends to their energy banks and their satisfaction in life, which is their signature emotion.

Help Them Understand Their Sacral Response Process

Listen to the questions that your Generator child asks and ask them questions in return to help them get to their truth and inner knowing. They need your help to get to their knowing through yes/no questions and to help them get their minds out of the way. Ask them if they would like you to ask them a series of questions to help them uncover their truth. You can even turn it into a game–the yes/no game. If you begin with the line of questions and they are not ready for it, their Sacral will not engage because they're stuck in the conditioned mind, and they will become frustrated with you and the process, so you'll need to warm up with easy questions first. The younger they are, the faster they generally move through the questioning, as they have less conditioning involved in their process. See the Appendix for more about how to ask Sacral questions.

For Generators with Emotional Authority

If your Generator child is emotionally defined, make a note of the questions you asked that were particularly relevant so you can ask them again later in the day or over the next few days or weeks, depending on the situation and the weight of the decision. The bigger the decision, the longer they will need to wait for clarity if they have Emotional Authority. If you find that one or both of you are becoming frustrated or upset during the questions, take a break, and let them know that you need to get clear to be most supportive in their process. Clearing the emotional field by taking a break will teach them not to make decisions when feeling emotionally charged.

On Saying No as a Generator Parent

When the Sacral response is no, it can be difficult for a conditioned Generator to say no and feel like they let another person down. At this point, there is a sense of duty conditioned into them about helping others and pleasing people. Saying no to someone else is often, in the long run, just as beneficial to the person asking as it is to the Generator. If they've been giving a parent, sibling, or child money to help them out because they feel bad for them and their luck, they need to take a step back and consider if they're helping them or if they're enabling them and are creating a dependency. If, as a Generator parent, they're cleaning up after everyone in their home, are they teaching their family to be self-sufficient so they can one day take care of themselves?

Every circumstance is different, and I don't presume to know yours, but I ask you to consider why you're doing for others constantly and if you have room left over for you and your interests? How are you taking care of yourself?

When you say no, it doesn't have to be harsh or rude, but it needs strength. You must be confident in your decision so that you don't waffle and cave in when the pressure comes. Those who have been on the receiving end of your people-pleasing will apply pressure for you to continue with your pattern. That is why a solid connection to your Sacral response is essential. It can help you remain connected to your truth as you communicate your decision. When you hear interjections or pleading, or you begin to feel sympathetic to the other person's needs/wants you can check in with your gut and ask, "Do I want to do this?" And, if it's a no, kindly but firmly decline. This could sound like, "I know you've been used to me doing all of your laundry, but I know you're capable, and I'd like to teach you how to do your own laundry so that I have some more time for the other things I like to do too." "Because I can't" and "Because it doesn't feel right to me" are also perfectly good reasons to say no. Don't get lost in the pleading to change your mind. It's not your mind that we're talking to. When the Sacral says no, it says *no*. Period.

Do you ask your Generator child to change their mind when you think something is good for them? Do you ask them to stick out the piano lessons for the year when their Sacral is saying no? Consider where you might be conditioning your

Generator to say yes from their mind when their Sacral says no. Observe, reflect, and consider why it's so important for you to have them complete this. What are you teaching them? Again, this is not a judgment. We all condition our children by just being ourselves, but we can become aware of how our conditioning is passed on to our children and what the story is that is driving our decision.

Generators Are Here to Respond

Although the world speaks to us as though we are all Manifestors, the truth is most of us and our children are not. How many times have you heard in your life "If you want it, just do it! Go after it! Make it happen!"?

Imagine if even 10 percent of the Generator energy types shifted and lived more in line with the Generator Strategy (which is to wait to respond to something that shows up in their external awareness). How much more easeful could life become? Do you relax a bit when you think of waiting for life to bring you things to respond to, rather than going out and making it happen, or do you feel stressed at the thought of not having control over it all?

The Generator's Strategy is to *respond* to life. Something must show up in their external reality for them to respond. Rather than following every whim they have in their minds, they are designed to have life bring things to then respond to with a yes/no decision. Don't misunderstand: They can think up ideas and creations, but they need something to respond to, to take action. How great would it be to grow up knowing you don't have to go out and create every opportunity for yourself, but when you sit back and listen, life will bring you the opportunity for everything you need? Wow! Can you imagine the immense relief of pressure you'd feel? The more people learn to lean into the experiment of living their design, the more freedom we all have to be present in our lives and allow Divine timing to bring us what we're ready for. Now imagine that your Generator child(ren) learned this from a young age and didn't have to decondition from the pressure to always do and make things happen.

Asking a Generator the Right Kind of Question for their Energy Type

Knowing that Generators are here to respond, we can learn that as parents or caregivers, we just need to ask the correct type of questions to get them to turn on their Sacral response and the best questions to do so are ones that can be answered with a yes or a no. No long explanation is needed. You could also use a "this or that" option. Limiting the choices allows them to connect into their Sacral with a yes/no to the choices, rather than asking "What do you want to wear today?" which can lead you to wait for them to try on forty-seven outfits and end up frustrated, while you're waiting to get them to school. See Appendix for how to ask Sacral questions, but here are some examples of questions you could ask your Generator for them to respond to:

- "Do you need a hug?"
- "Do you want a hug?"
- "Would you like to go to the park after lunch?"
- "Do you want the red pants or the blue pants?"

Let Them Experiment

Letting Generators try things to see how they work and what is involved in different tasks allows them to understand what they like and don't like, deepening the connection to their yes/no response. It's a much bigger mess to let them help you bake cookies or make dinner than it is to do it yourself and share the results with them, but they get so much more out of the doing than the watching. Don't forget to let them help with the clean up too! Learning the effects of a decision can be just as important as completing the original task.

Getting a Yes from a Generator When you Need to Keep Life Moving

When Generators are told to do things that their Sacral responds *no* to, they can get frustrated. But sometimes, as parents, you need to have them put on their shoes and get in the car, even though they don't want to. Rather than get into the power struggle of shoes or no shoes, and being late to school, turn it into a question they can respond to. Here's an example.

- "Do you want to see your friends today?" Yes.
- "Do you think they'll let you into school without shoes where your friends are?" No.
- "Would you like to put on your shoes and go see your friends at school?" Yes.
- "Can I help you?" No.

The Generator's Signature Emotions

Generators and Frustration – When a Generator Child is Experiencing Excess Frustration

If your Generator child is getting frustrated often, take a step back and see if there is some place where they feel as though they have to do things they don't want to do, and whether this is something you can let go of. If it's not, you can use yes/no questions to lead them in the direction you need them to go. This is not to manipulate them, but to encourage them to see another side of the decision that would benefit them rather than the limited view they may currently have. For example, if they have an assignment to create a vision board and they just really don't like to draw and paste pictures onto a poster board, they can easily end up frustrated. Consider if there is another way to approach the issue. Questions you could try in this scenario are, for example:

- "Are you frustrated with this project?" Yes.
- "Is there another way you could do the assignment that you would like better?" Yes.
- "Do you want my help?" No.
- "Do you know how you'd rather do it?" Yes.
- "Can you tell me?" Yes, I want to make it on the computer instead.

Frustration is the sign that your Generator is going against their design. Are they trying to initiate? Are they saying yes to please other people when they really want to say no? Are they waiting for something to respond to, or are they trying to force a response? They can also experience frustration when they are learning something new. As they reach a plateau in their learning, they may get frustrated and want to quit. You can use Sacral questions to see if they truly want to quit and are done with learning, or if they're on the edge of their next breakthrough and need help getting unstuck and moving forward again.

Generators and Satisfaction - When They Wait to Respond, They Find Satisfaction

When your Generator child learns to wait for something to respond to rather than to initiate, and then enters into it correctly *through* their Strategy, they will feel their signature emotion of satisfaction. Just as important for them, is the need to use their Sacral response to say no to things they do not want. Satisfaction for the Generator can be described as contentment. Consider when you've eaten a meal that wasn't too much or too little, it was just right. It was satisfying. Satisfying isn't an extreme dramatic or showy feeling, it's more of a grounded, content feeling.

Your Generator and Their Energy

The total number of motor centers defined in their chart will impact how much energy they have and how they express it. Even though the Sacral Center has consistent power, The Will, Emotional Solar Plexus, and the Root Centers all have energy that pulses in waves or operates in cycles. Depending on where they are in their pulse or cycle with any other defined motor centers, you may see more or less energy from your Generator child. The Sacral can be coerced to turn on through responses to the right questions, while the other centers have cycles that they go through. The Emotional Solar Plexus has waves that it operates in, the Root Center has pulses of being either on or off, and the Will Center has cycles of pushing through a commitment and then needing a cycle of rest before committing to the next thing. Overall, a Generator child generally has a lot of energy whether they have one center or all four defined in their birth chart.

If a Generator child wants to quit something (a lesson, a class, a group, or a friendship), ask them yes/no questions to help them get clear on what is problematic for them. Sacral questions can help with clarity on whether they want to quit or if something about the situation is not working for them. Do they want to quit the activity? If not, is there someone there they have a conflict with? Is it too loud? Does something make them uncomfortable there? Do they feel like they're not progressing? Often Generators and Manifesting Generators will hit plateaus where they feel like they are not getting better at something and want to quit. Then, suddenly, they'll have a period of growth and level up in what they are doing. Help them learn not to quit before they get to the good parts and ask them Sacral questions to find out if they truly want to quit or if they're just frustrated because they haven't mastered it yet.

Parenting the Generator Child as Another Energy Type

Manifestor Parent and the Generator Child

Even though you have a motor connected to your Throat Center, you don't have the staying power of Sacral energy to keep pushing all day long. If you were raised by Generators, you may unconsciously fall back into old patterns of working too hard for your type because of the Sacral energy you are surrounded by in your home. Make sure you're taking time to rest and finding ways for your Generator child(ren) to expend enough physical energy to help them rest at night and get to sleep easily. If you don't get enough sleep because your Generator keeps popping out of bed at night, it can lead you to have a shorter temper and your emotional signature of anger showing up in your parenting. You also need to have enough time for yourself to discharge other people's energy at the end of the day. Proper rest allows you to have the energy to follow your inner creative drive and experience your signature emotion of peace. And, of course, inform them of what you need from them, as well as what you plan to do, and you'll feel your not-self emotion of anger less.

Projector Parent and the Generator Child

A Projector is perfectly designed to help guide a Generator's energy. Learn to ask the right yes/no questions, and you'll feel like you've just unlocked a secret to parental success!

As a non-energy type parent, your Generator may seem like they are always bouncing off the walls with energy. Get them outside and let them burn off some of their energy every day and they will sleep better, study better, and pay attention better in school. Their bodies need to move every day. Unlike you, who needs to unwind for thirty minutes while lying in bed before sleep, your Generator needs to physically wear out their Sacral energy so that they can sleep well at night.

Reflector Parent and the Generator Child

Everyone's energy can feel like a lot to take in for a Reflector, but Sacral energy can be powerful. This may help you feel motivated and able to power through your parenting, household duties, and work but remember that it is borrowed energy. You may need frequent breaks from their Sacral energy, especially if you have more than one Generator in your house. Help them find physical activities to wear them out so they can get to sleep easily and sleep well. As mentioned with the Projector parent of a Generator above, your bedtime routine will be different from your Generator's. Be mindful to help them get enough physical exercise to be able to rest at night. You will need time alone to discharge the energies you pick up every day, so make sure to find space in your day for yourself so that you can show up as the parent you want to be and show up for your own needs too.

All Non-Sacral Parents of Generators - Finding Enough Energy to do it All

A non-Sacral parent with a Generator child may find that because their child has higher energy to release in the day, the time they spend playing with their child far outweighs their other household tasks. If you're able to, hire some help for the other tasks. If hiring help is not an option for you, you might see if you have any neighbors or friends who would consider a trade of some sort that doesn't require as much physical labor, like trading your house cleaning for help with organization or tutoring their child, bill paying, or accounting support. What are your strengths that you'd be willing to make a trade with? Get creative and experiment with what works for you.

Generator Parents and Children of all Energy Types

If you are a Generator parent, it can be easy for you to fall into the pattern of picking up after your kids all day long doing their laundry, cleaning their rooms, doing all the cooking, and the rest of the cleaning too. Maybe you like doing these things, and it's how you show your love. If so, I would gently ask you to ponder the question, "Where did you learn that that was how you show your love?" And "Is teaching your children that this is how to show their love the message you want to give them?"

It can feel incredibly good to care for others and be rewarded for it but understanding what a gift it is to have someone help you with those things only comes from understanding the depth of that work. I'm not suggesting that you make your kids do all the chores in the home but consider a healthy amount of work for your child to contribute based on their age, abilities, and energy type. As a Generator parent, you have the energy to keep working, even if you don't love what you're doing. If you notice you're feeling frustrated, it's a good time to reflect on the things you are saying yes to that you don't want to be doing and see how you can navigate the chores or tasks differently.

Generator Parent and the Projector Child

As a person with a defined Sacral Center, you have consistent access to workforce/lifeforce energy while your Projector does not. They can get things done more efficiently with you around them—sometimes even quicker than a Generator/Manifesting Generator! Because your Projector child takes in and amplifies your Sacral energy, they can use it to get through the tasks at hand more easily. If your Projector child has a defined ESP, Root, or Will Center, you may notice that they do better at completing tasks when they're working on their own some days more than others. Remember that what they are learning as children can set a lifelong pattern of how they approach work. If we're thinking of the long game of life, not just the present moment, we want to set them up with sustainable work habits. Projectors need to be taught sustainable ways to work with the energy they have and be allowed time to rest and not overdo it. This starts with following

Strategy (to wait for the invitation), rather than pushing with their energy to force their way through projects, jobs, relationships, and to use their inner Authority, which we'll cover in the next chapter.

As mentioned in the Generator section, as a Sacral energy type parent, you don't need to do everything for your non-Sacral energy child. Teach them how to take care of their responsibilities in a sustainable way, rather than doing everything for them. Rather than a rigid schedule, consider a weekly task chart where they can choose to do what they have energy for and when they'd like to do them as long as they get the tasks done within the week.

You may have an entire family of Generators and Manifesting Generators, when you have a Projector child come in and disrupt the whole family dynamic. I see this often in my practice with clients where parents don't understand their children, especially the Projectors. The Projector child may not be interested in the same things their outgoing physical, high-energy family is into. When parents can see their child for who they are, rather than who they think they should be or wish for them to be, in order to fit into the mold that already exists within their family, they have an opportunity to give that child a gift that no one else in their life can replicate. No matter how seen a child feels by their peers, when a parent starts trying to see their child and stops trying to fit them into a pre-sized box, they give their child confidence to be themselves, freedom to feel secure in who they are, and they become someone to lean on when life gets hard for the child. Children are so willing to forgive parents because, at their core, they just want to belong. No matter how hard you've tried to change your Projector child in the past and have been rejected, your child wants to give you another chance. Show them you're worth taking that chance on.

Generator Parent and the Manifestor Child

Remember, your Manifestor child doesn't have sustainable energy like you do, so make sure to allow them the cycles of rest they need after big projects, sports games, or high interaction events. Proper rest allows them to have the energy to create and initiate. Make sure to inform them of what changes are happening, what you need from them, and then leave some space for choice in their response.

Putting it into Action

Whether you or your child is a Generator, neither of you should be stuck doing all the work that nobody else wants to do all the time. We all need to learn to be responsible for ourselves and that includes our children. Whether Sacral or non-Sacral energy types, children should be able to do age-appropriate chores¾cooking, cleaning, laundry, managing money, helping others¾that help them learn to care for themselves. If we all do our share, we lighten the load for everyone and teach our children that we are all capable and responsible for ourselves as well as contributing our unique gifts to our family or community.

Generator Parent and the Sacral Energy Type Child

As mentioned above, teach your child to take care of their responsibilities but remind them they don't have to take on all the work no one else wants just because they have the energy to. Teach them to grow up and be responsible but not to martyr themselves taking care of others.

Generator Parent and the Non-Sacral Energy Type Child

A non-Sacral energy child (unless they are amplifying your Sacral energy, which should only be for short periods of time) does not have the same capacity for physical work that you do. This does not mean that all the work should fall on you as the Generator. Even non-Sacral energy types can do their own laundry, play sports, hold jobs, etc. Energy type is not an excuse to do nothing or be catered to, but non-Sacral energy types won't be able to sustain the energy to complete tasks in the same way you, a Generator, can. What other tasks could you get them to help with? What are their strengths? Are there other types of work they could help with around the house? If not, just remember that without your defined Sacral Center in their auric space, their ability to work will only last for so long and you may come back to find them napping, reading, or involving themselves in a totally different project than what you gave them. Also, make sure to let them have some downtime after a more physically demanding task, like yard work for example.

Projectors are great at guiding, advising, mastering systems, and working one-on-one with people. Manifestors are great at having new innovative ideas, and Reflectors are here to show us what is going on within the family or community. Reflectors can do what other kids are doing, but they can also provide you with great insight into a group of kids to know what the emotional field is like and how things are working within the group.

Manifesting Generators (Generator Subtype)

Sacral Energy Type - Approximately 35 Percent of the Population

Purpose: Workforce builders. To find proficiency in their work, by responding to what life brings them through their Strategy.

Strategy: To wait for something to show up in their external reality *and* inform those who will be impacted by their actions.

Signature Emotion: Satisfaction

Signature Not-Self Emotion: Frustration and Anger

Though the Manifesting Generator shares some of the qualities of both Manifestor and Generator, it is a subtype of the Generator energy type. I often see adult Manifesting Generators trying to act more like Manifestors (which has a lot to do with conditioning) and acting from the mind rather than their Sacral response. Because they can do things quickly and simultaneously and because they also bore quickly, they tend to try and manifest more. They are *not* Manifestors, though, and thinking they are may leave them feeling frustrated and angry.

Manifesting Generators are often self-conscious of being called "non-committal," "flighty," or of being told they "Don't know how to pick one thing and stick with it" because they have been told these things their whole lives. Society says (though this is a changing thought, thank goodness!) that we need to pick a career, go to college, get a good job, work until retirement, and then have fun. Boo. That sounds terrible to a lot of Manifesting Generators, and a lot of other energy types too! By the time they are old enough to retire, their ability to do a lot of the things they wanted to do when they were younger may be gone. Maybe they made investments that didn't pan out, and now they're left having to work longer than expected. There are no guarantees in life. The Manifesting Generator exemplifies that life is to be lived fully and sometimes at warp speed. They have many different interests and try lots of things. They often have many different careers in their lifetime and can be fond of new experiences, or they can have a larger focus that holds their attention, but they explore all different angles of it.

In their true alignment, Manifesting Generators work as Generators but with the added benefit of moving through the steps of a process quicker. They help us learn where we can take shortcuts. Imagine two teens deciding to prepare meals for their families (I know, most of us are thinking great fantasy, right? However, if you have this kid, please send them to my house). One child is a Generator and one a Manifesting Generator. Each teen has three different dishes they are cooking. The Generator starts with the first one and gets it going to the point where it's time to start the second; they prepare the next dish and finally move on to the last dish. The Manifesting Generator is in the kitchen with all three dishes going simultaneously, which probably looks a bit chaotic from the outside, but they have a process going on, and to interrupt them will throw them off; they need to be able to work their madness. Ironically both the Generator and Manifesting Generator will likely finish at about the same time; however, their processes to get there are vastly different. There is nothing better or worse about either method but understanding how your child works can help you understand why they do what they do and how to support them best. If you are a Generator parent and have a specific cooking method, for example, it may take some letting go to allow your child to find their process. And the learning process of cooking with a Manifesting Generator approach can mean a few burned dishes, but that's how we learn, right? We get our hands in there and experiment to learn. If, as parents, we get upset that they're burning everything or insisting they just need to do one thing at a time, we teach them to hate cooking and that their way isn't "right." Surrender to the process and they will find their way. Also, don't forget to have a fire extinguisher on standby just in case!

Manifesting Generator children may want different routines, toys, and lots of choices for them to keep busy. If you put them in the same area with the same toys every day, they will likely be fussier than if you change it up for them often. However, don't rule out that they may have a favorite toy they always want to take along for comfort or go through phases where they want one thing for a while, then suddenly drop it and move on to the next constant thing. Remember, they have Sacral energy, so plenty of playtime will help them with both nap time and the ability to sleep at night.

The Manifesting Generator is figuring out the quickest or most efficient way to do things and will dive in with both hands and start experimenting. While it may be frustrating to you as a parent to have six Lego sets scattered around the house, they are probably dancing between them all, building a little of each one at a time. Sitting with one set and working start to finish sounds oh so boring to a Manifesting Generator. Or maybe they start a Lego set and then decide to run around the yard or put on a movie while working on the Lego set. The point is, they are doing many things often at the same time.

Manifesting Generators are busy, busy bees. They like to have their hands on multiple things at one time. They get bored with just doing one thing at a time. They will probably jump from one thing to another often in life. These are the children that want to take a class like ballet, for example, when they're five, so you sign them up, buy them the appropriate leotard, shoes, and a month or two into classes, they declare that they are done with ballet and want to learn ice hockey. From a parenting perspective, this can feel frustrating because you've just invested in ballet, and like many adults, have also been conditioned through childhood that "If you start something, you need to see it through or finish it." I would ask you to take a step back and consider where that voice comes from if this sounds familiar to you. Do you recognize the voice? Can you visualize a situation where you were told just that? If you can, perhaps there's an opportunity for you to also do some healing in this area; from feeling like you must finish what you start, even when it doesn't feel right for you anymore. Before quitting, make sure to ask your child yes/no Sacral questions to be sure they're quitting for the right reasons and not just out of frustration they haven't mastered it yet.

Communicating with a Manifesting Generator

Manifesting Generators are frequently viewed as wishy-washy but jumping from thing to thing can be correct for them if taught to follow their Strategy and Authority. However, what often happens is that Manifesting Generator children are conditioned to stick with one thing and see it through to the end, making them frustrated and angry because they aren't following their Strategy and Authority. They become conditioned to try to be something other than what they are. Suppose you have a Manifesting Generator child and they have decided that they are done with a sport or project, and you keep making them participate. In that case, you're likely spending a lot of energy and effort on making them continue, and let's get honest: Is that really how you want to spend your time or teach your kid to be? It's also important to note is that their Sacral needs to tell them to quit, so ask them Sacral questions (see Appendix) to see if their Sacral is done with this specific task/class/event. Sometimes they don't want to quit, but something about the class or event is not working for them. Use the Sacral questions to help get to their truth of whether they really want to quit or if they just need an adjustment, or perhaps they've reached a plateau and want to give up before they get to the next level. Their learning is a stairstep process, meaning they ascend in their learning until they hit a plateau before ascending again to the next plateau. If they are not clear on whether they truly want to quit or are just frustrated with the learning process, they might quit before they actually want to, and later regret it.

So back to these little busybodies. Your little Manifesting Generator, who just started ballet and now wants to ditch it for ice hockey is listening to their inner cues of what is correct for them. When they learn all that they need from the class/task/environment, they will move on to the next thing. They are taking in all the deliciousness of the world as children, trying lots of things to see what their interests are. Therefore, their two short months in ballet are not a waste, but a learning experience for them, and they're getting a lot out of it. If you can, let them try lots of things and they will be happier children for it. Note: This does not mean that you must go out and invest a ton of money every time they have a new calling.

As a parent of a Manifesting Generator, it would be a good idea to invest in used or borrowed equipment and to trade or share with other parents to keep costs down, as well as consider the environmental impact of potentially using things for a short amount of time.

All their experiences give them their unique worldview. They may try many different things that seem random, but to them, each experience is a thread in the tapestry of the life they're weaving. It's like going to 31 Flavors and sampling all the ice cream flavors versus always ordering the same flavor. They're here for the experiences, and you get to enjoy the ride with them.

As your Manifesting Generator becomes a teenager and enters high school, the pressure to figure out what they want to do with their life will be put on them, leading to stress and anxiety, especially if their Root or Head Centers are undefined or open, as these are pressure centers in the chart that can create feelings of anxiety or nervousness. Check their chart to see if these centers are defined or undefined/open, and then read more about them in Chapter Eight. This is another place where parent/family conditioning can heavily come in. Your experience of how you were parented influences how you parent. Whether you did or did not go to college, for example, can impact the pressure you put on your child because of what your idea of success looks like. I invite you as the parent or caregiver to take a step back and consider why you want this for your child and if it's something that your child also wants. Sometimes there may be a condition of financial support that the child must go along with, like graduating college or taking a particular path, in order to reap the rewards. Again, gently and lovingly, I invite you to consider why you feel like you know what's best for them. This wisdom you have gained throughout your own life can be an example for your child. Were you given the freedom to choose your path? If so, what did you learn by trying? Where did you struggle, and what did you learn from those struggles? As parents, we so often want to protect our children from struggling or being hurt by making what we consider "bad" decisions based on our life experience; however, most of us learn best by acting and seeing how the world responds.

When the college, career, or job talk begins, open the conversation with yes/no Sacral questions. Consider that if you were not given a choice to learn through your own navigation, how your life would have been different with such choices? You can encourage your Manifesting Generator to explore lots of different things as they grow up which will help them see what piques their interests.

Manifesting Generators in School

Your Manifesting Generator child will likely have lots of interests in school, change directions frequently, and speed through things, often having to double back and correct the steps that they missed along the way. This is a normal part of their learning process. They are learning where they can skip steps and make things more efficient, but to do that, they must be given the chance to do it their way and learn where they can and cannot afford to skip steps.

Manifesting Generators and Homework

Manifesting Generators will have similar concerns as the pure Generators in that they need to get their Sacral energy engaged in the activity they are doing. If they're struggling with getting homework done, try some Sacral response questions – see Appendix for details. Make sure they've moved their bodies enough throughout the day during school or after, so they will be able to sit down when it's time for homework. And lastly, know that they may shift between projects or assignments rather than completing one and then moving on to the next. They may need breaks to do something completely different or ask for snacks or other distractions while working. Use your curiosity and observe them, notice their patterns and experiment with them to figure out how they work best. Forcing anyone to learn, study, or research *your way* doesn't help them learn how they work best, so let them know that you'll help them experiment to figure out their best way of getting things done.

Manifesting Generators and Work

When it comes time to find a job, they will likely try lots of different types of jobs or they may work in very different businesses. This is part of the process to help them figure out what it is they like to do. They can be very quick at what they do, and they have the energy to do the work, so if they find something that holds their interest, they have great potential to excel at it. If they jump around in different careers, it does not mean that they are flighty. It means that they are a Manifesting Generator doing life just the way they are designed to.

The Manifesting Generators' Signature Emotions

Manifesting Generators and Frustration and Anger

Manifesting Generators can feel both frustration and anger as their not-self emotions. This is their signal that something is out of alignment in their life or they're feeling blocked from taking action once they've decided to do something. They can also feel these emotions when they've entered into things incorrectly (by not using their Strategy and Authority) and what they're trying to do isn't turning out as they thought it would. If they learn to respond from their Sacral yes/no inner truth without feeling forced into things they can experience a signature emotional response of satisfaction.

Manifesting Generators and Satisfaction

The Manifesting Generator experiences their signature emotion of satisfaction just as the Generator does; by waiting to respond to what life brings them through their Sacral response rather than trying to initiate. It is important for them to only say yes to things they truly want to do; however, once they do, they have one extra step which is to inform anyone who will be impacted by the decision of what they are going to do. This step helps them avoid being stopped in their creative process and feeling the not-self emotions of frustration and anger.

Manifesting Generators Strategy - Responding and Informing

The Manifesting Generators' Strategy is similar to the Generators' Strategy in that they must wait for something to show up in their external reality to respond to, however Manifesting Generators have one added step. Once they've said yes to something, they need to inform others about what they are going to do in order to proceed with ease. They are learning to inform, not to check for the okay status (though when they are young, this is an added benefit for a parent if they are about to do something unsafe). They need to let others around them know what they will be doing, so that they have fewer interruptions when doing their thing. As young children, this could look like a parent asking, "Do you want to play Candyland?" the child replying "Yes!" and then asking the child, "What are you going to do?" to get them to inform you that they are going to play Candyland. This helps reinforce the idea of informing before they act. As they grow and inform others of what they are planning on doing, it helps them to not be interrupted when in a creating process. We are not training Manifestors or Manifesting Generators to ask permission so they become dependent on other people to tell them it's okay, but rather to help them understand that their path will be less restricted in getting where they want to go if they slow down a beat to tell others what they are going to do.

Like the Generators, you need to ask them questions in a way that their Sacral can respond, with yes/no questions. Because they have a connection from a motor center to the Throat Center, they can act quickly once they have responded with a yes from their Sacral. Like the Manifestors, they do not need other people to be able to act, but they *must first respond* to something in their external reality before taking that action. A Manifesting Generator child can move quickly *once they respond*, so teaching them to inform you of what they intend to do can help you as a parent, while also lessening the frustration and anger they experience when they have to slow down or get stopped in the middle of their creating.

Parenting the Manifesting Generator as Another Energy Type

Manifestor Parent and the Manifesting Generator Child

As a Manifestor, you do not need anyone else to initiate. To manifest an idea, when you get your internal creative signal to create or do and you have the reserves, you can take action quickly. Your Manifesting Generator can also take action quickly and doesn't need anyone else to start a project; however, the difference between your energy types is that they must wait to respond to something in their external environment before taking action to enter into the task or work correctly. This may at times be frustrating for you, but if you can slow down and ask them Sacral response questions, they will have something to respond to and you can get them moving quickly again and keep up with you.[1] Remember that part of their process is to figure out which steps they can skip, so they often must go back and repeat steps in a process as they learn. Try and hold compassion for them as they go through their stairstep learning process. However, while you need cycles of rest after you've manifested your creative vision or task, they do not. They do, however, need to move their body enough throughout the day so that they can sleep well at night. Make sure you help your Manifesting Generator get enough physical activity, so you can have your downtime before sleep and also get good rest. And always remember to inform them of what will be happening or what you will be doing when it affects them. This way, you will move through life with less resistance.

Projector Parent and the Manifesting Generator Child

As a Projector parent of a Manifesting Generator, you will notice that your child has a lot more sustainable energy than you do. For you to be able to get your much needed time at the end of the day to unwind and be in your own aura and to clear the energies you've picked up throughout the day, you'll need to make sure they have physically moved their body enough to be able to sleep easily. You may also find yourself upset that you can clearly see how they could do something more efficiently, but they won't listen to you. Remember that they are learning through their doing, and often have to go back and correct steps, which is all part of their process. You can let them know that you have some experience with the subject and let them know that you're a resource if they should want any suggestions, but do not force your suggestions. Instead, try using Sacral-response questions. Give them something they can respond to with a yes or no, or a simple choice between

---

[1] See Appendix.

two things. As much as you like the time and space to talk and process to find your answers, your Manifesting Generator just needs something to respond to with their yeses and noes.

Reflector Parent and the Manifesting Generator Child

Though you will need plenty of time to rest and reset as a parent, I believe that this combination can be really fun for a Reflector parent. Manifesting Generators are always doing, and often do many different things simultaneously. As a Reflector, you are here for the experiences of sampling different auras and communities and your Manifesting Generator child can help you find many different environments to adapt and try on.

Your Manifesting Generator will move faster than you when it comes to making decisions. You need to wait a lunar cycle to make big decisions, which can be challenging, as you may feel a lot of pressure from your child to make faster decisions. Remember to utilize Sacral-response questions to understand your child's needs and navigate parenting in a way that doesn't leave you exhausted. Find the support systems that you need whether it's hiring a babysitter or swapping childcare with another parent. And if you're not already great at it, learn to accept help when it's offered, so you can make sure you're taking care of your needs too. Allow time for your Manifesting Generator child to expend all the energy they need to in the day, so you can get your restorative downtime at night. When your child is very young, you may find co-sleeping difficult as you need time alone when sleeping to discharge all of the Sacral energy you've taken in, including that of your Manifesting Generator child.

Manifesting Generator Parents

Like the Generator parents, you are not here to be your child's parent-maid. Just because you can do the work yourself doesn't mean you should. Avoid people-pleasing to find praise, particularly if you learned to people-please as a child to feel valuable. You are valuable just because you exist. You do not have to prove your worth through how much you do for others.

Manifesting Generator Parent and Non-Sacral Energy Type Child

As a Manifesting Generator, you have lots of energy, and the ability to do multiple things at once. Your non-Sacral energy type child does not possess the same energetic qualities as consistently as you do. It is important to understand that the Projectors, Reflectors, and Manifestors all play different roles and will do things differently, but this does not mean they can't do anything but sit on the couch all day either. The challenge for you will be to resist doing things for them because you can do it quicker, or you've found the "best" way to do it. Allow them the space to find their way of approaching work and be sure to ask them open-ended questions, rather than the yes/no questions you respond to best. It may take time and patience to learn to let them have the space to talk and figure out what they need to say.

Your biggest challenge with parenting a non-Sacral energy type will likely be around their energy or what you perceive as a lack of motivation. Your non-Sacral energy child is not lazy; they just have a different level of energy than you do and need to approach life differently. Expecting them to be like you, have energy like you, or multi-task like you probably won't work for them. When they live with you, they take in your Sacral energy and amplify it, so it can look like they have just as much or more energy than you do, but one of the kindest things you can do as a parent of a non-Sacral energy type is to listen when they tell you they're tired. Help them listen to their bodies and know when it's time to rest. Teach them to get in bed before they're tired and to allow themselves time alone to discharge other people's energy they've picked up all day.

Manifesting Generator Parent and the Sacral Energy Type Child

As a parent of a Generator or Manifesting Generator, you will want to make sure that you are solid in your ability to respond to questions through your Sacral response so that you can help your Manifesting Generator child learn to engage their Sacral response as well. If you are a parent of a Pure Generator, you'll need to also be patient in their learning process as it will be different than yours. One process is not better than the other, they are just different, and you need to learn to navigate how to honor their way and let them learn by doing – even if it feels like you know a much better, faster way.

Putting it into Action

Manifesting Generator parents, remember that not everyone will be able to keep up with you or shift gears quite as quickly as you. Like the Pure Generator energy types, you are not meant to do all the work that no one else likes to do just because you have the energy to do it. Share responsibilities and have patience in letting your children learn through their process, as aggravating as it may be. Sit back and watch while they do something that could take you a fraction of the time and experience the world through another view as they learn and find *their* way.

Projectors

Non-Sacral Energy Type - Approximately 20 Percent of the Population

Purpose: To guide.

Strategy: To wait for an invitation for the big things in life, and to wait for the right timing to share their insights with others after being recognized.

Signature Emotion: Success

Signature Not-Self Emotion: Bitterness

Projector children are here to be wise about other people. As they grow into adults, they need to be recognized for their ability to help guide and potentially advise others as they begin their careers. Even as young children, they have the gift of seeing how systems could be improved, however, they need to wait for the invitation to offer their guidance for it to be received well. Waiting can be challenging in a world where people talk over one another and doesn't allow space to ask for help. As parents, it is your job to help your Projector child feel seen and recognized for their abilities and talents. Because a Projector does not have a motor center connected to their Throat Center, they need to wait for the right timing to be recognized and invited to share their thoughts and wisdom.

Projectors are experts at understanding other people but can have a bit of a blind spot when it comes to themselves, which is why they must have a group of trusted individuals for them to talk to and bounce ideas off of. If they have a Mental Authority, this is doubly true. Talking to trusted people in their life is not necessarily to get advice; in fact, it rarely is, but instead, they speak so they can hear themselves process the decision they are working out. Asking an open-ended question about their decision is often much more effective than giving them advice. An example of this type of question could be "What led you to that decision?" or "What do you think will happen next?"

When a Projector child (or adult) does not feel recognized, they can become bossy and bitter. They begin to force their help on others; after all, they can see a better way of doing something and can't wait to share it with you because they know it will help you so much! When they are recognized for their ability to guide and are invited to do so, this will be a success, which is the signature emotion of the Projector. Success is knowing they have value, have contributed something useful, and have made the world a better place in their own way. If they do not wait, they will either be met with defensiveness or told they're bossy or ignored altogether. This can lead them to feel bitterness which is the signature emotion of a Projector out of alignment.

Right Timing and Waiting for the Invitation

Waiting for the right timing can be hard for a child to learn, especially as they get older if they haven't been taught this from a young age, but it can be done! Projectors of all ages feel much less bitterness and pain when they realize that waiting for the right invitations can bring them success.

Ask for their advice, thank them for their insights, give them space to be heard, and any of the neediness or bitterness that can come from an unrecognized Projector can fade quickly with a routine of letting them know they're seen. This will help them grow up knowing that recognition and invitations will come, and they don't have to try and force their way, repelling people from them, leading to fewer invitations.

If a Projector has an open or undefined Throat Center, they will need time to be heard every day. Set aside a few minutes a couple of times a day and ask them what's on their mind. You can even set a container of time but give them your undivided attention for those few minutes and let them know you are fully present. You are rewarded with a happier Projector and some time to yourself after when you give them this time first. I often notice that my Projector kids get more needy and interruptive when I haven't given them this time. Once I make a point of spending ten minutes listening to them, they are happy to go about doing other things independently. Sometimes we take a walk where I leave my phone at home and ask them to tell me what's new in their world or how their friends are doing. Asking a Projector for their input on something specific you know they're good at will give you bonus points if it's sincere. If it's not, don't bother, they'll see right through you.

Projectors who are not recognized or invited to share their insights can become loud, talk over other people, or become a family clown to try and get attention. On the flip side, sometimes in a big family, they can get quiet and almost disappear, feeling like no one sees them at all.

I like to tell young Projectors that waiting for the invitation is like waiting to spend your money on something great. You've been saving up your money for a great toy, one that costs $100, and you have $80 right now. You walk into the toy store and see that there are lots of other toys for less and you could spend your $80 right now and get something, so you buy several things that add up to $80. Initially, you are excited. You saved your money for so long and now you have these new things, but after a few hours you start to realize that you didn't really want them, you wanted the $100 toy and then you get upset and feel bitter that you spent all your money on something that didn't even come close to the toy you wanted. So, now you must start saving all over again. But the goal seems so big now that you don't even want to try anymore and any money you get, you just spend immediately, feeling this bitterness that you'll never get the $100 toy you wanted.

Now, imagine that you walked into the toy store and realized those toys weren't right for you to spend your money on because what you wanted is the toy that cost $100 and you've been saving for it, so you decide to be patient, because you know it'll be worth the wait. When you walk out of the toy store you find twenty dollars on the ground, and no one is around to claim it. It's like it just fell out of the sky and was put there just for you. Because you waited and were patient, you ended up getting the toy you wanted, much sooner than you expected, because you knew to wait to invest your money in the thing you really wanted.

Projector invitations are the same way. If they try and share their guidance before they have been recognized and invited, they walk away feeling like the kid who just spent all their money on the toys they didn't really want–they feel regret. They spend their energy on giving advice that isn't received well. But if they wait, and just focus on doing their own thing, knowing that the invitations will come, they will be rewarded with enough energy for the right invitations when they come along. The less they try to force the invitation, the easier they will come to them. When they can sit back and be patient and focus on their personal development or skills in the things that interest them, the invitations will come.

Invitations and Parent Help

Speaking of invitations, the Projector child may need your help in facilitating invitations for parties, playdates, and maybe even getting their first job. This parental support does not indicate a failing parent or flailing child. When the Projector tries to put themselves out there like a Manifestor, Generator, or Manifesting Generator and take action if they haven't been invited, they can repel invitations with their aura. It's not personal, but the Projector feels so deeply into the other that it can feel intrusive or off-putting to the different energy types when not invited. Imagine how you feel when someone you don't know asks you how much you paid for your car, house, jacket, shoes, or TV. If this is not a person you usually share that kind of information with, it feels intrusive. That's the kind of energy that the Projector can put out if not invited, or when someone you just met says, "I noticed that you don't like confrontation, why is that?" "Ewww, get out of my aura. Stop looking at me!" is the feeling it gives the other person. So, teach your Projector children that the correct invitations come when they stop trying so hard for them, and to just be themselves. When they are in their Projector-ness, they will attract invitations because they become irresistible when they're just minding their business, not seeking invitations.

If Projectors try to generate an invitation by asking to be invited, it usually doesn't work. They may get an invitation, but it probably won't feel like they hoped it would when they are at the event. The other person usually feels that they are fishing for an invitation or leading, and it will turn off the other person to their energy. It is best to let your aura speak for you, and you'll find that you get more invitations if you release the expectation of receiving invitations.

Projectors will find their group of people who recognize them and appreciate them, but it won't be through the Projector pushing their way in. For the invitation to be correct, the correct people will find the Projector and invite them into the relationship.

Projectors need invitations to the big things in life – relationships, friendships, events, jobs, partnerships, groups, etc. They do not need to be invited to go to the grocery store or for everyday life things. However, it can be a fun experiment for a Projector to sit back and see how many invitations they receive on a regular day, to everyday things.

Invitations can be formal, but they can also be energetic. When a Projector tunes into how the people around them feel, they can sense when invited energetically. They can also feel when that invitation has ended. A child will not always have words for these things the way an adult would but listen to your Projector child when they tell you that Suzie doesn't want to be their friend anymore. There may not have been words spoken as such, but they can feel the energy shift and that the friendship has changed. Forcing them to go be friends with Suzie will cloud their understanding of the invitation as it goes against what they know to be true. If this continues through childhood, they can reach adulthood not understanding the significance of the invitation and feel very misunderstood and left out.

Speaking of Invitations and Life...

While most kids grow up and become independent and want to take control of their birthday parties and such, a Projector may want to but may still need your help in the inviting process. Because it can be repelling for a Projector to send out the invites to their own party, having the invite come from a parent or recruiting a friend of theirs to help plan and/or invite other friends can make the party more successful. There is nothing more heartbreaking than watching your Projector child plan their party, hand out the invitations at school, and then have no one show up, even those who said they'd be there.

When it's time for them to get a job, they may need your support by connecting them to a job opportunity. Recognizing what your child is capable of and helping them find the right opportunity—even making the first connections to help them find a job—can be correct for the Projector parent. Where they invest their time and energy must feel rewarding for a Projector, so it's important that where they work makes them feel recognized and valued.

If I had one wish for what a Projector child grew up knowing, it is this: *You are enough, and not all people are for you, just like you are not for all people, and that is perfectly perfect. Your energy is a precious resource that you must be careful to share with just the right people for you. Others will see what you are capable of and will want to be near you but listen to that inner voice that tells you if these people and their intentions are right for you. Be patient. Your time will come. The less you do to try and create the invitations, the more successful you become in life.*

Communicating with a Projector

In contrast to the yes/no Sacral-response questions of the Generator and Manifesting Generator, your Projector will need to be asked open-ended questions and allowed the space to verbally process their thoughts. Start questions with things like "What do you think would happen if...?" or "What should we do today?" "How do you think we could make this better?"

Projectors in School

School can be overwhelming for Projectors who are taking in a lot of energy from all the people around them. They are designed to take in the energy field of one person at a time, so being in a classroom full of approximately 70 percent defined Sacral energy can be a lot. They need time after school to unwind and discharge the energy they've picked up all day. They might even want/need a nap. In contrast, the energy they pick up throughout the day can also amp them up and they can appear hyperactive, in which case a little dancing or movement to shake out some of that energy can be helpful.

Projectors and Homework

Pressure can be an issue for Projectors because they take in all the work energy through their undefined/open Sacral Center and amplify it. This can lead them to be super achievers and doers or eventually wear them out. If kept up at a high pace, they can easily burn out early in life. If they have a lot of other open or undefined centers in their chart, they can be even more sensitive to the energy from other people. If your Projector has an open or undefined Head Center or Root Center, which are pressure centers, they can put a lot of pressure on themselves to get things done. Check your Projector's chart for these centers and see if they're open or undefined. If so, read more about those open/undefined centers in Chapter Eight and how you can support them to manage the pressure they feel. A Mental Projector, for example, takes on energy in six to seven of their nine centers and can get overwhelmed by the pressure to get things done. They also take in the emotions that others send out through their emotional waves (see Emotions Chapter Seven and Emotional Solar Plexus Chapter Eight for more information on emotions) as well as the amped-up fears from an open/undefined Spleen Center. Look for the defined centers in their chart to know what is consistent for them and recognize that everything white in the chart is variable for them and help them to navigate the fluctuating energies.

Homework for Projectors is often one of two scenarios. If they have a defined Root Center, they do tasks at their own pace, in their own time, based on their energy. In contrast, if they have an undefined/open Root Center, they may hurry up and rush through it to be free of the pressure or procrastinate until the last minute and cram to get it done (sometimes under your prodding). With their open Sacral Center, they may also have a hard time knowing when to quit and need your guidance as to when enough is enough and they need a break.

Projectors and Work

Projectors aren't here to work a traditional Monday to Friday, 9-5 job. Projectors are here to guide. This does not mean, however, that they cannot work a full work week, but it depends on the position they have and if they were recognized and invited into it. Most Projectors that I work with and know in my personal life who work a full-time job have either burned out using their energy incorrectly or have adjusted to make their work fit their energy. Many work for themselves and have learned to schedule their downtime first, manage their calendars so they don't overbook, and develop good boundaries around their energy. Burnout for Projectors who are pushing their energy usually happens around age thirty. If they do not correct the pattern that led them to burnout, it can keep repeating, so it's important to teach your Projector child early on that they need to work differently than 80 percent of the population and that it is normal for their energy to be quite different from other people in their lives.

Pushing With Their Energy

If a Projector does not feel recognized or doesn't receive the invitations they think they should, especially when they look around and see what their friends are up to, it can lead a Projector child to push for the attention they desire. Unfortunately, the more they push, the more repelling they become and the fewer invitations they receive.

I have seen this in remembering my childhood and in observing my children's. The more they want to be included and try to share thoughts or insights or add to the conversation, the more other people avoid them. Then, ironically, when they pull away and do their own thing, they find people approaching them with invitations.

They Need to Talk

A Projector never has the connection of a motor center to the Throat Center, (that would make them a Manifestor) so they need to be invited to share. Giving them space to talk once a day at least, can give them an outlet so they don't end up talking over you all the time. They will also need to talk to hear themselves process their thoughts and ideas. Ask them thoughtful open-ended questions (see Appendix for examples) to help them get to know themselves more profoundly but avoid giving them too much advice. Let them problem solve and gain confidence in their abilities. They see things differently; they have a 40,000-foot view and can offer you a new perspective if you invite them to share what they see.

Energy and Sports

Because they do not have a defined Sacral Center, sustainable physical energy can be a challenge for them, unlike the Generator energy types who need lots of physical movement, but do not let that deter the Projector from accepting their correct invitations. Olympic Gold Medalist, Serena Williams is also a Projector. This reinforces that any energy type can do anything; they just need to approach it differently for it to be sustainable, and they need to enter into it correctly through recognition and invitation. Projectors may be at higher risk for injury and burnout when they push too hard using borrowed Sacral energy. This is not to say they cannot be good at sports or enjoy them but listening to their body and its needs will be important. Don't be surprised if your Projector child who plays sports is found napping after a game or event. Any energy type can be anything they want in life; however, they may need to approach life differently in specific areas like sports.

Energy Projectors

A subtype of the Projector is the energy Projector, defined as a Projector with one or more motor centers defined (Emotional Solar Plexus, Will, or Root Center). These three motors operate in pulsing rhythms, so the Projector's energy can vary significantly from day to day. Combined with their open Sacral Center, depending on who they are around, they may feel like they can keep going and do more than a Projector who does not have defined motors. While this is not borrowed energy because they have this energy consistent within their defined motors, it is not like having a defined Sacral Center. If a Projector is conditioned to believe that this energy is sustainable, they will eventually burn out and create a lifelong pattern of *doing* that they try to live up to. This may lead them to feel like they aren't enough when they realize they can't physically keep up anymore, especially if they have been praised for all the work they've done up to that point.

Projectors with a Lot of Openness in Their Chart

Projectors often have a lot of openness or undefined centers in their chart which means they take in a lot of energy through their open/undefined centers and amplify it, and they can appear to have a lot of energy. As an informed parent, you get to help them realize that this feeling of energy is not entirely theirs and that they need to pace themselves and learn to schedule regular downtime to avoid burnout when they're older. Because this is one of the most common areas of conditioning for the Projector, the more you can do to help them see that they need regular rest and to work in a way that their energy-needs are recognized and supported, the better you set them up for adult life and long-term success.

The Projector's Signature Emotions

Projectors and Bitterness

The Projector's signature emotion that tells them they are off track is bitterness. This allows them a signpost to watch for so they can course correct. Most Projectors feel bitterness when they are either not feeling recognized and invited or when they are doing too much and need more downtime or time alone to discharge and reset from the energy they pick up all day. A lot of their observing and learning about the *other* is integrated into wisdom when they have time alone to reflect, so this downtime is also an integration period.

Projectors and Success

Success is the emotional signature of an aligned Projector. When they can live by their Strategy to wait for recognition, and to only respond to invitations that are correct for them through their Authority, the Projector feels success. Success is not necessarily about money or notoriety (though those things can sometimes come with success), it is more about living an aligned life where they feel good, recognized for their contributions, and they don't feel the need to try and force the invitations. They learn to wait for people to be attracted to them and call them out for their contribution of guidance. Success is being at peace with who you are and feeling contentment in your life Strategy, knowing that when you surrender to the process, life will bring you all the invitations you need.

Projector Sleep

If your Projector child is hyper at bedtime, you've likely missed the magic window of getting them into bed when they were ready to start winding down, and now they've revved back up and are wired. Try backing up their bedtime fifteen minutes every couple of nights and having them lie in bed and read a book or read to them. You could also let them listen to audiobooks or invest in one of those lights that project stars or images onto the ceiling and let them use their imagination until they fall asleep. (If they have a defined Head/Ajna, this may be calming or stimulating, so it's important to experiment and see what works). I will admit that even though we've kept TV out of our kids' bedrooms, we found that our Projectors benefited around age ten or so by downloading a show to their iPad and watching thirty minutes some nights before they turned out the lights making it possible to go to sleep while lying down in bed relaxing. Sometimes they don't want to talk about things and even reading a book is too much, so allowing them to watch a show can be used as a tool to help take them out of any worrying thoughts swirling through their minds so they can wind down for sleep. The content of the show matters (so something lighthearted works best), and then we remove their devices from their room. Having them download the show keeps Wi-Fi off so that it is not overstimulating their bodies and we have them use NightShift on their iPads so that the color of the light emitted from their devices is not as sleep disruptive.

Note: This does not work for all kids, so you need to discover what works for yours, but the point is to remain open to the possibilities of what does work for you and your kids, not necessarily what the "current guidelines" say is right. Those who create the guidelines mean well but don't live with your kids or know how they respond. The guidelines are designed in a general sense for all and are not personalized for your child.

Projector Newborn/Toddler with Motorized Parents

If you have a newborn or toddler Projector that you are co-sleeping with and your child wakes or screams all night long, or fusses all day from being tired, it may be that your energy is too much for them. I know this can be crushing for a parent who has dreamed of co-sleeping with their child but consider either putting them to bed in another room or taking turns with the other parent (if available), so there is less energy in their sleeping aura. The same is true for naptime. If you can have them nap in a room away from the other defined motors (ESP, Root, Sacral, Will), they will rest better and be happier babies. It can be too stimulating for them to try and relax with motorized energy around them. Remember, this is not personal; it's just the energetics of your designs coming together. When everyone gets to sleep, the whole family is happier.

Projector Teens and Bedtime

When you have a teen Projector, how you've taught them to manage their energy will determine how much they understand their own needs. If they have been raised as Generators, they may try and go and go and go until they just can't go anymore and then find themselves wired when it's time to sleep. This pattern can carry over into adulthood. I have worked with many adult Projectors who have had lifelong patterns of staying up super late and then being unable to sleep. Shifting that pattern can be difficult.

Many teens also have a habit of sleeping with their phones in their rooms, turned on, and even under their pillows. I beg of you to remove them from underneath their pillows at a minimum. Their brains are still developing and are so much more susceptible to the effects of radiation from cell phones. Nighttime is when our bodies go into a rest, digest, and detox phase which lowers their internal defenses and leaves them more susceptible to bodily disturbances from the signals being emitted. Every ping of their phone also releases adrenaline, waking them up and alerting them in the way an emergency would. This is then followed by a flood of dopamine when they see the likes, comments, and other rewards from social media, creating a vicious cycle of bad habits with rewards. Now combine these effects with a Projector who is already sensitive to energy surges, not getting enough sleep, and feeling left out, and it can be quite a recipe for teen agony.

Other Energy Types Parenting the Projector

Generator/Manifesting Generator Parent and the Projector Child

It is important as a parent with a defined Sacral Center to be aware of how you are conditioning your Projector child to work. Because they do not have consistent access to Sacral energy like you, they need to find ways to get their work done that does not burn them out, by listening to their body's signals saying they need rest. You may notice this shows up in them as irritability, crankiness, or apparent laziness, when they simply need to take a break. A child who plays in organized sports such as football, for example, may be able to leave it all on the field, and then want to come home and nap rather than go celebrate a win. It is important to also realize that they won't be able to always keep up with your renewable energy, and you may have some parent work to do around deconditioning your own ideas of how work must get done to allow them to work in a way that is correct for them.

As mentioned in the Generator sections, as a Sacral energy type parent, you don't need to do everything for your non-Sacral energy child. Teach them how to take care of their responsibilities in a sustainable way, rather than doing everything for them.

Manifestor Parent and the Projector Child

As another non-Sacral being, you understand that energy comes and goes; it is as not consistent for you as it is for a Generator or Manifesting Generator, and that is okay. You are playing your part in the fabric of society by initiating. Your Projector child is here to learn to wait to be recognized and invited to guide, not to work a physically demanding job every day of their life. If your child is a *no motors*

Projector, they take in your motor energy and amplify it in your presence, leading you to believe they have a lot more energy than they do. Still, just like you, they need downtime to regenerate, discharge other people's energy, reset, and come back to themselves at the end of the day. They may also love napping as a Manifestor does, or they may be the child that gives up napping at two. Each child is different and understanding their true needs versus their conditioned needs will make all the difference in the world when raising them.

The flip side of amplifying your motorized energy is that they may take it in and feel overwhelmed by it or become especially sensitive to your not-self signature emotion of anger. It will be important for you to communicate with them that you are not **angry** at them but rather frustrated that you weren't able to use your energy in the way you wanted.

Because your Projector child will never have the configuration of a motor center connected to the Throat Center as you do, they will build up pressure in their Throat Center as they take in energy all day. If you are apart for most of the day, when you come back together again, you allow them access to your motor center to Throat Center connection which allows them to relieve the pressure easily. You may find them to be chatterboxes when you come back together until the pressure is relieved and they feel heard. If you are at home having a conversation with someone else and your Projector child walks in the door, they may even try to insert themselves into your conversation (even if it doesn't concern them).

They are listening, wanting to guide, and feeling the pressure to speak, so some boundaries around what that looks like in your family may be helpful. It is also critical if you have a child with an undefined or open Throat Center that you give them time each day to just speak and relieve that pressure, and if you can give them time regularly, they talk over you less and less. This is also a great tip if you're taking them to grandma's house or a family gathering or somewhere where there will be more people. On the drive, ask them things about their life, how they're feeling, their favorite animal, and why. Depending on what stage they are in, ask them age-appropriate open-ended questions to let them relieve that pressure, and you'll find you have a different child at your event. They will be more patient and wait to be invited to play with cousins or other kids if they have been recognized recently.

Projectors are here to be wise about other people. They watch and learn and try to correct, advise, or guide, and as a Manifestor, you don't like to be told what to do. Your Projector needs recognition for their contribution and to feel recognized when they give good advice. Remember they need to be invited to share, and if they aren't invited, they will start sharing even when not asked because they can't help themselves; however, it won't be received the way they'd hoped. The invitation is the ultimate form of "I see you and what you contribute" to the Projector.

It is also important for you to inform your Projector of what you plan to do, so they know where to expect to feel your energy, as well as understand how it will affect them. When you act suddenly without informing them, it can feel unsettling. This can lead them to ask you lots of questions about what you're doing, what you're going to do, and so on, which can lead to your not-self emotion of anger being expressed. Learn to inform your Projector child of what you're doing so they can feel settled and less inclined to interrupt your process.

Projectors can also be the children who see the inconsistencies of parenting and call you on them. When this happens, it's essential to recognize your child and acknowledge what is happening while setting clear boundaries around what you expect from them. Here's an example: You have a Projector child whose bedtime is 8:00 and occasionally you don't enforce a strict bedtime. When you try to enforce the bedtime again, they will call you on your inconsistencies. You have to own up to it and then assert your position with something along the lines of "Yes, I've been inconsistent with bedtime lately; however, your bedtime is 8:00, and that is when I expect you to be in bed so you can get enough rest to have a good day tomorrow. Now, get to bed, and thank you for bringing that to my attention."

Reflector Parent and the Projector Child

Since you are both non-Sacral energy types, you may find that you can have more downtime than if you had a Sacral energy type child because you both need the downtime; however, because neither of you have a defined Sacral Center, when you two are together, energy or lack of energy, may be an issue. If your Projector child has other motor centers defined in their chart, you may notice cycles of energy that come and go. You both like and need open-ended questions which can allow for the ability to follow curiosity and go deeper into subjects without realizing how much time has passed. Other energy types living with you will determine how you both handle your energy. Be conscious of your downtime needs and those of your Projector child as well. Your Projector likes to guide and can become bossy if they don't feel recognized and invited, which you may reflect back to them as a Reflector. Your Projector, if they have a lot of open centers in their chart, can be quite sensitive, even more so than you with all of your centers open. This is because you have more of a Teflon aura that doesn't allow others' energy to stick to you when you are aware of how your energy works, unlike the Projector who tends to take it all in and hold onto it more. Be mindful of the emotional space between you two and who you're around. If your Projector is emotionally defined, be sure to get familiar with their emotional wave(s).

Projector Parent and Children of all Energy Types

You need to take care of yourself. You need to make sure you have downtime and are meeting your own needs so that you can be a patient and compassionate parent, rather than a burned-out and bitter parent who reacts before thinking and does not take time to respond thoughtfully. As a Projector parent, you may find it is harder to have your children listen to you than it seems to be for other parents. The Projector's energy does not work well when they try to yell and command, and your gift is in learning how to ask your children questions based on their energy type. Generator energy types need yes/no Sacral questions, and Manifestors, Projectors, and Reflectors need open-ended questions and space to talk.

When offering guidance to your child, offer a statement of recognition about what you're seeing and ask if they would like your suggestion. If not, do not push. They will usually come back and ask for your help, but if you push, they won't. An example of this would be a child who has a stack of notes all over the place on different loose papers stuffed in pockets and books. Maybe you think to yourself *They should just put them all in one notebook, so they don't lose them.* Rather than telling them that they must do it your way, show them recognition, and then offer a suggestion such as "I see how carefully you've been saving all of your notes. They must be very important to you. I keep mine in one notebook which makes finding things easier for me. If you'd like, I can show you my method of organizing notes." You've recognized their care with something important to them, and then offered another solution, and then leave it if they don't say yes right away. You're planting seeds so that they know you are a resource if they would like help. Also, keep in mind, their way might be working perfectly for them, even if you don't understand it.

Projector parents—you cannot do it all. You cannot keep up long term with the pressure of Pinterest-worthy parties for every event on top of everything else, and you shouldn't try if it's not your thing. Do what works for you and your family and know that it is enough, and that you are enough.

You are designed to take in the energy of one person at a time, so Projector parents of multiple children may find it challenging to take in the energy of all their children at the same time. Try giving them one-on-one time at different times in the day to have access to you to talk, especially if they have an open Throat Center. It will also be essential for you to have a trusted group that you turn to in order to process your parenting and other conundrums that come up in life. I have found that life coaching is beneficial for Projectors, especially if you find a good coach who can hold space for you, ask good questions, and allow you to process and come to your own conclusions verbally, instead of advising you on what to do.

Projector Parenting and the Sacral Energy Type Child

You must be clear about your Sacral child's energy and your energy versus what you are amplifying from them. It's easy to run on borrowed energy for a while, years even, but when a Projector crashes, they crash hard. Life tells them, "You're doing it wrong" and shows them how much they need to slow down. A crash does not have to happen to you, but it is essential to be aware of it as a Projector. Projector parents need to fill their cups first to have something left to give their children that isn't filled with bitterness, resentment, or irritation. When a Projector is tired, they can become bitter if they do not get the rest they need.

For you to get your rest, you will need to make sure your Sacral energy type children have been worn out so they sleep easily and well at the end of the day, and are not wired and tired the next day. Send them outside to play, take them to the park, schedule playtimes with friends, take them to the skate park—whatever allows them to expend energy and lets you conserve energy while they expend their Sacral energy. Of course, have fun with them too and join in when it feels good, but don't forget to get their playtime in even when you're tired so you don't have a sleepless night because they're having one.

Reflectors

Non-Sacral Energy Type - Approximately 1 Percent of the Population

Focus on Who You Are BEing, Not How Much You Are DOing

Purpose: To reflect the health/status of the community.

Strategy: To wait through a lunar cycle before making a big decision.

Signature Emotion: Surprise

Signature Not-Self Emotion: Disappointment

Reflectors are rare: less than one percent of the population. Unlike the other energy types, Reflectors are not here to learn about themselves or other people as the three other energy types are. They are designed to flow in and out of each day in more of an experience of wonder at what and who they will experience that day. Reflectors need to be in the centers of their communities, so they learn from, and experience, lots of different people. With all the undefined/open centers in their chart, they take in everything around them and offer a unique view of their world because of that. When they are trying to adapt to the other 99 percent of the population, they can live a very difficult and painful life; however, when a Reflector is living in alignment with their energy type and not trying to be something they are not, they can live magical lives.

While Reflectors are here to take it all in, they are not here to identify with it. Their identity is flexible, and it changes based on who they are spending time with. Because they are reflecting what is around them, they can reflect their community's health and show them where there is an opportunity for growth. If you are lucky enough to have one of these rare energy types in your circle, pay attention to them. It is not always easy for them in this world, and a lot of Reflectors are conditioned to live a life that does not honor their gifts. Most of the

Reflectors I know have struggled with self-esteem, confidence, friendships, and more, never feeling like they lived up to everyone else's expectations of them. The greatest gift you can give your Reflector child is the freedom to be themselves, which is ever-changing. Unlike the other energy types who have cycles that revolve around the Sun, the Reflector is the only energy type who is deeply connected with the moon. As they reflect the moon's lunar cycle, it is important for them to feel the changes through all the gates as the moon transits through them over a twenty-nine and a half-day cycle before making decisions for themselves.

When I first learned about the Reflector in Human Design, I thought, *How cool! The rarest energy type! I wish I were one!* This is pretty much my whole life; if it's rare or unusual, I like it more. When I started learning more about the Reflector energy type through people who knew a little about them, it began to sound like an awful burden to bear, to be a Reflector. When I'd run a Reflector chart I would think, *Oh, that poor misunderstood, open to conditioning, sensitive human.* I didn't fully understand how unique the Reflector is and how critical they are to our communities. No, it is not the easiest of energy types to be in a world filled with conditioning and society's pressures to "get it right" in every aspect of life such as having the "right" job, being in a relationship with the "right" person, raising your kids "right." There is so much projection about how everyone else seems to think we should all live our lives and behave, but when you find a Reflector who understands and lives their design, you know you have someone special in your life.

I want Reflectors to know from a young age that they are special. They are different and unique and have so much to contribute to the world by just being themselves. They don't need to try and fit in—they will when the circumstances are correct. When they are not, they will stand out and signal to the community that things are not right. And I don't mean that from an our-society-says-this-is-right kind of way, but a "right" way of being in a healthy community where everyone feels good, seen, heard, useful, valued, and loved in whatever way is meaningful to each individual. When they stand out and behave in a way that the community or family doesn't like, it's essential to investigate what, from the community or family, they are reflecting.

The environment is critical for Reflectors. If it does not feel comfortable, happy, or peaceful, they will not be comfortable, happy, or peaceful. When a Reflector child is unhappy, it is important to look beyond the child (if their needs have already been met) to see who around them is unhappy. What are they asking their community to heal?

The unhappiness from others does not have to appear outwardly because Reflectors can feel what is going on within the other person. Parents often think they're good at hiding what they're feeling from their children. They're not. Children see right through parents' masks. They are so much more connected to feelings than adults are. If there is conflict in your relationship with them or another person in the house, your Reflector will definitely feel the conflict, and reflect it.

All That Openness

When we talk about the open centers in the chart, they all are significant in different ways. An open Emotional Solar Plexus amplifies the emotional energy and nervousness around them. The open Root Center takes in and amplifies pressure and adrenaline. The open Sacral Center takes in and amplifies workforce energy. The open Spleen takes in and amplifies instinct but also fears. The open G Center takes in and becomes who they are around and feels off when their environment is off. The open Throat Center takes in and builds the pressure to speak. The open Ajna Center takes in other people's ideas and anxieties and pretends to be certain of them themselves. The open Head Center takes in the pressure to be inspired and figure out who is inspiring. Most people have some of these centers open, but at least two out of nine are defined in 99 percent of the population. Now consider that the Reflector has zero of these centers defined; they take in all of the energy and can amplify it from those around them. If you as a parent are worried, your Reflector child will take it in and amplify it and may appear worried themselves, or they may become worried about you. If you have a defined Root Center, they take in that pressure and amplify it, and it can make them feel a lot of stress to get things done quickly. The same goes with the other centers. They do, however, have a unique aura that reflects a certain amount of the energy from others, allowing them to sample the energy of everyone but not necessarily take it on in the same way say a Projector with a lot of open centers would. The Reflector aura has been described as a Teflon aura because they sample the energy around them and don't let it stick when they are operating in alignment.

About That Waiting...

Though Reflectors don't need an invitation or something to respond to, nor do they have an inner creative drive, they do have their own process to approach opportunities, which also has a waiting period. Reflectors need to wait full a lunar cycle, 29.5 days, to make decisions. I know you're thinking, *That's insane! No one can wait that long to make a decision!* One of the biggest things you need to know about Reflectors is that they cannot be rushed to make decisions. They need time. Waiting through a full lunar cycle allows the Reflector the opportunity to feel various elements of definition from the people in their life who can "flavor" the way they feel about a decision in addition to the movement of the moon through all 64 gates during this time. They also need time to retreat, sit in their own aura, and know what is true for them after talking decisions over with people in their life.

Think of the wise Sage who has wisdom from their life's experiences–everything the Reflector experiences gives them wisdom, as does the moon energy as it transits all 64 gates in a lunar cycle. They have a grounded presence that is not to be rushed because they've learned that few things in life are that urgent. In their own way, the awakened Reflector is the Sage within the Human Design System who we turn to when we need to know the truth and what is essential. This is not necessarily handed out through advice, but by them just being in their *being-ness*, we find our own truths when in their presence.

The waiting period gives them time to talk to others about their decisions, which is important for them. Having a parent or someone with an aura familiar to them to bounce their ideas/thoughts off of helps them immensely. Letting them talk it out without offering advice (unless asked) is one of the most beneficial things that a parent or friend can give them, and they will gravitate toward the people in life who allow them space to do this. These children need not be rushed when they do not know what they want, as this will train them to make hasty decisions and not trust the waiting process for their truth to come forth. Remember, environment and their sense of feeling are everything to these children, so if you've just forced them into a decision they didn't want to make, and it wasn't the right one, they will not be happy children and are likely to blame you for their decision. Sometimes with a big decision it may take several lunar cycles for them to reach clarity, which may take a lot of patience from parents with other energy types.

Reflectors in School

Your child is taking the environmental temperature of every setting they are in. If they are acting out in class, volunteer if you can, and see how the other students are behaving. Whose energy are they taking in and reflecting? They can easily take on the environment they are in, so if what you're seeing from your child feels like a sudden change, inquire about their friends, for example, whether they're sitting next to someone new in class, or what has changed in their environment. Are they trying to behave like the other energy types, pushing themselves beyond what feels good to them? However, because Reflectors are so adaptable, they also get along quite well with multiple people and interests.

Reflectors and Homework

Depending on the environment at home, motivation could be an issue for your Reflector child. If they are left to themselves to do their work, they may lack motivation and energy. If they live in a home with Sacral energy types, they may have more temporary energy to work with, but may become overwhelmed by everyone's energy, especially after being at school all day. Consider the environment they are working in if they struggle with getting their homework done.

Reflectors and Work

Just like all the other energy types, a Reflector can do anything they want to do when it comes to their work. The job opportunities they are given need time for them to reflect on and to decide if they are correct for them. They need to be able to take time to figure out if it is right for them or not. There is no need to worry about missing out by waiting so long to decide. If the opportunity is correct, it will still be there once they've gotten clarity, even if it takes a whole lunar cycle or more. If it's not, it likely was not the correct environment for them. Burnout can be an issue for Reflectors if they are not aware of their energy type and how it operates, especially if they are not taking enough downtime to discharge the energy they are taking in all day long, so proper rest is a must for this energy type.

The Reflectors' Signature Emotions

Reflectors and Surprise

Surprise is the signature emotion that tells a Reflector that they are living in alignment. Surprise reflects not that they are trying to *do* anything but rather that they just are be-ing the reflective community member that they are designed to be. They are surprised by what life brings them and that each day and each person are different. Their surprise is more of a delight than something startling, when living in alignment and in the correct place. They have the ability to find the people in life who are aligned with their energy type and Strategy and who don't just go along with what everyone else is doing; those people offer them a beautiful surprise.

Reflectors and Disappointment

When they see that their community is missing out on the opportunity to live up to their capabilities and potential, they can feel disappointment. Feeling how unique everyone around them is but seeing them continue to strive for a life of sameness, leads to their signature not-self emotion of disappointment.

The Reflector Strategy – Wait a Lunar Cycle; Don't Make Transitions Quickly

While your Reflector child can adapt and take on the environment they are in, life transitions can be hard for them and may take at least one or more lunar cycles. Because they like having reliable auras that they know around them most of their time, transitioning to a new school or even class can take a while for them to settle into it. Joining a new team or adding someone new to the home/family can also take time to transition.

Their open Head and Root Centers, which are pressure centers, push pressure into all the other open centers in their chart, and the pressure can feel enormous for them until they can learn to sample other people's energy and not take it all on as their own. This pressure can lead them to rush through things to be "free of the pressure" or shut down and not do anything, becoming paralyzed with overwhelm. It can also lead them to feel pressure to be sure, to lock into an identity, or force with willpower that they do not have consistent access to, for example.

If they are struggling with making a decision, it may be helpful to ask them how they feel in their surroundings. With an open G Center, location is vitally important for them, and if they are not in a place that feels good with people that feel good to be around, they will struggle with decisions even more.

They Need to Talk

As they enter the teen years, they may need those late-night talks more than other children as there is a lot of growth happening and social interactions they will need to process. When they get home from an evening with friends, and you want to go to bed, they may need to process with you the events of the evening. Knowing this ahead of time can allow you to mentally prepare so that you can patiently support them even when you're tired. Non-Sacral energy type parents may want to get a nap in if they anticipate a late night talking with their Reflector. Alternatively, they may just want to close their bedroom door and be alone after all that socialization.

Challenges in Social Settings

Because they connect to other people so deeply and feel everything through them, being in classrooms all day may be challenging. They may come home and want to sleep after school. This is not because they are lazy but because they need the downtime to regenerate and release all the energies they picked up throughout the day from their peers and teachers.

Friends

If they find a close friend that they enjoy the feeling of being around, they may want to spend a lot of time with them and perhaps only them. They like the consistency of having certain auras around that they know. A new person is always a new aura to understand, so they may gravitate toward the people whose auras they know best, even if they aren't the healthiest for them.

Other Things to Note

If you have a defined G Center, you have a strong sense of who you are. If you asked the people in your life who know you best to describe you, you would hear similar descriptions of yourself. Your Reflector child will have an undefined/open G Center and all other centers as well. Therefore, it can look like your child has no idea who they are and go whichever way the wind blows, but this is who they are designed to be. They adapt to their community. If your family has a strong identity, this may be difficult for you to accept when they are no longer in your family's aura and seem to change when they move out. Suppose you have known your Reflector child to be devout in religion or fanatical about sports or academics like everyone else in your family. In that case, you may notice that when they do finally leave the nest (and I say that lightheartedly because they sometimes need a gentle push out of that nest), you may see them change into someone you don't recognize. They may decide they don't love sports or identify with that religion or have decided they don't want to go to college. They are becoming their own person, and their identity is designed to be someone who tries on lots of different things. They may try on lots of things for the rest of their life, or they may find something that feels good to them and stick with it, at least until something else comes along that excites them.

In my life, I have witnessed Reflector children, especially when young, become easily influenced to go along with the crowd to try and fit in, sometimes drifting from group to group, and unfortunately falling victim to bullying, pressuring, and adrenaline-seeking activities (hello open Root Center!). I've also watched Reflector children who seem to struggle with life while living at home, and then, once they get out on their own, find people that support them and make them feel good about who they are and thrive in the correct environment. Reflectors give us an honest window into ourselves so if you're troubled by what you see in your Reflector, this is an opportunity to look within yourself or your family to what wounds may need tending.

The Teflon Aura

The Reflector is undefined or open in every center in their chart; it's what makes them a Reflector. When I first learned about Human Design, I thought that the more defined centers you had, the better, but this is not true. It is a common misconception when people first learn about Human Design and needs to be cleared up. Someone with lots of definition in their chart is no more advantaged than someone with little to no defined centers. Often when someone new to Human Design sees a Reflector chart, which is rare—only 1 percent of the population—that person may think, *Oh, how hard their life must be.* But even with all their openness, they have a special element to their aura, making it have more of a Teflon quality. If you've ever cooked in a Teflon pan you know that things don't stick to it. The Reflector aura is designed to have a similar quality. Reflectors are designed to experience things through others—their energy, identities, emotions, ideas, and more, but they're not meant to attach themselves to those qualities as if they were their own. Reflectors are their own people, and though they are here to help show the community's health, they are not here to lose themselves completely in it. When living in alignment they are a screen allowing emotions, thoughts, ideas, and more to move through them, but not to soak them up like a sponge and hang onto them.

Health and Your Reflector

Because your Reflector takes in the other energies so easily, they can mistake others' health issues for their own if they are not aware. The Spleen Center relates to the immune system. Because of the Reflector's openness (this applies to anyone with an open Spleen Center), they can sense when others are not well, which can make them great healers and helpers, but they must not identify with what they pick up from others as their own. Remember they are here to sample, not take on, the energy of others. If you as the parent have a defined Spleen, you may have a harder time getting your Reflector to go out into the world without you, because your defined Spleen helps them to feel good.

They Need Lots of Time Alone

Due to their sampling aura where they take in other people's energy all day long, your Reflector needs to have a good amount of alone time. This may feel strange to you if you are a people person, extrovert, or a defined Sacral being. It may look to you from the outside that they are just depressed or anti-social because they want to be alone so much. Still, you must give them ample time alone to discharge the energy they pick up from everyone throughout their day, particularly if they are in school or working a job that involves many other people around them or that is over the phone or internet. Reflectors take in all the energy from everyone on a video call, so while a class with fifteen kids can give them energy during the call, afterward they may need a nap to release all the energy they took in from the other students. Throughout their school years, they may continue napping long after other kids have given up napping.

Other Parenting Types with Reflector Children

Generator Parent and the Reflector Child

Generator parents can struggle to understand the relationship with their Reflector child because their energy types are so different. I am so happy to be able to share about your Reflector child with you, particularly if you're new to learning about Human Design. Most Reflector parents have struggled with their Reflector children, often in really challenging ways. As parents, we want the best for our children, and Reflector children can have a hard time if they do not understand how they are designed to be different and what their superpowers are. I have personally watched Reflector children in Generator families struggle, as well as endure social bullying/drama, addictions, interaction with the wrong crowd, and struggles with unworthiness or isolation. With more understanding of how they are designed to be different, your child doesn't have to have those experiences.

Reflector children can struggle if they do not understand how wonderfully different they are meant to be. Learning they are different from other kids can be challenging for them, especially at first, because as kids, we just want to fit in, make friends, and be part of the societal norm to feel accepted. And because they reflect the community they are in, they can fit into any group. However, the group they are in can influence what they do, how they behave, how they dress, what they like, and more. Other kids may tell them that they are copying them, or just trying to be like them, which is not the motive of the Reflector. They really can't help but take on the identity of the people they regularly surround themselves with because it's how they are designed, yet if you plunked them into another group, they would quickly adapt to the identity of the new group too. When your Reflector becomes a teen and starts dating, they may easily become just like the person they are dating because that's who they are being influenced by.

Reflector Mood

Without other people around, Reflectors can relax, sit in their energy, and follow their inspirations quite contentedly, and because they are not feeling other people's emotions, they may appear very emotionally neutral. Not happy, not sad, just neutral because they do not have an emotional wave. They can however, experience what it feels like to have a temporary definition in centers and channels through other people and planetary transits. There may be times when your Reflector experiences emotions and behaviors that feel out of character for them in their neutral states; it might be helpful for you to check the planetary transits that are lighting up different gates in the Human Design Chart. You can check daily transits for free or you can download one of the Human Design apps that includes the transits so you can have that information at your fingertips.[2] Remember, anywhere another person or a planet defines a gate is where your Reflector will feel its energy (that is not consistently available to them) as the planets move or the people around them change. This creates a temporary definition of not only the gates, but, if the gates create a channel, it will also temporarily define centers in their chart and affect their energy and self-expression.

Manifestor Parent and the Reflector Child

Since you do not have a defined Sacral Center, you may be able to understand the Reflector child's need for rest better than a Generator inherently can. However, Manifestors can still have a lot of definition in their chart, giving them fewer areas where they are taking in energy and information from the other. I invite you to tap into the feeling you have after ending an initiation phase when you feel the need to rest, so you can better understand that your Reflector needs that level of rest and downtime on a regular, daily basis. As a Manifestor parent, you need to inform your Reflector child what is happening and what you expect from them so that they have time to prepare themselves for what is to come. They do not make decisions quickly (unless your defined Root Center is putting pressure on them

---

[2] "Just Now Chart," Jovian Archive, Discover Your Design, Live Your Life, accessed on 12/17/2021, https://www.jovianarchive.com/Just_Now.

and they're hastily doing things to relieve themselves of that pressure). Do not expect them to initiate like you or be as driven as you are. If your Reflector child is behaving differently, consider what is going on in your own life first as they reflect whatever is going on around them.

Make sure to inform them of any changes that will affect them, and even informing them of your day-to-day interactions around your home can be helpful. Because you have a powerful aura, they will want to know where it is and what it will be doing. Children's auras are not mature until the age of seven, so they will feel comfort and familiarity in knowing where your aura is, especially with a lot of openness in their chart, until then.

Projector Parent and the Reflector Child

As a Projector you have at least two defined centers in your chart, which gives you more consistency in some energy centers than your Reflector child. Remember that your Reflector child is reflecting the health of their environment, so your emotional state, as well as the relationships of others in your home, will be highlighted in your Reflector child. Any behavior or emotion that doesn't seem to make sense from your Reflector child is an opportunity to step back and consider where these emotions are coming from and where there is an opportunity to shift. Additionally, if you are a Mental Projector or have very few centers defined in your chart, you may be more sensitive to other people's energy than your Reflector with their Teflon aura. You're more sensitive to taking in energy of others into your open centers and can more easily hold onto it (unconsciously) longer than your Reflector when they are living in alignment with their energy type.

Remember that Reflectors need time to make decisions and do not act quickly when they are waiting out their Lunar Authority. They will need to process their thoughts with you and have you help them find their clarity. As a natural guide you do not need to give advice, but rather hold space and support them as they find their truth.

The Reflector Parent

You probably already know that you're a little different from most people at this point in life. If you are the parent of a Reflector, you have unique insight into what you need to do to nurture them well; however, I have yet to see a Reflector child of a Reflector. If you are one, please reach out to me; I want to know more. You are more likely to have a Generator energy type child or a Projector or maybe even a Manifestor. If you are a Reflector parent trying to raise a Generator, you now know that their energy levels are much higher than yours. While this can be overwhelming, it can also make you dependent on your children if you're not aware of the energy exchange. Because their Sacral energy is renewable every day, being around them allows you to feel motivated to get more done. If you've stayed home with them, you'll notice that when they go to school there is a significant shift in your motivation during the day while they are away. And when they move out of the house, if you don't have any other Sacral energy types in your home, you may notice the energy shift even more. While this can feel like you don't have the energy or motivation to do things the way you have been, it can also allow you the downtime you need to understand your energy without the presence of another person. You can always find other people to be around if you need a little motivation or energy by doing something as simple as just sitting in a coffee shop to get your work done.

If you have a Generator child who has not been able to get enough exercise in the school day, they may need to have some outside time or some way of moving their bodies so that they are not just buzzing with energy when they get home, as you will likely find this overwhelming after experiencing the absence of their energy all day.

If you work outside of your home and are around people all day while your child is at school, you will need to make sure you find time for yourself to discharge the energy you've been picking up all day so that you can be a present and patient parent to your child(ren). You need to make sure your needs get met so you can be the parent you want to be to your child(ren).

CHAPTER SIX

AUTHORITY

Do what you feel to be right – for you'll be criticized anyway.
~E. ROOSEVELT

Authority is an internal process for making decisions. It is a way to connect with your innate knowing of what is true and correct for you as an individual. It does not come from the outside or anyone else. It empowers you to make decisions that feel right for you and to anchor into as you navigate life. Ideally, we would all live according to our Type, Strategy, and Authority but we're all being conditioned to give our authority away all the time. We give it to society, the media, doctors, leaders in our communities, religions, and more. I am not saying that you should ignore any of these sources completely but do notice where you might be giving your power away. For example, when you feel like something is wrong and you go to your doctor, and after an examination and tests, they tell you that you're fine. But you walk away still feeling off, and you take no more action, you're giving your power away. You're letting the doctor be the authority of you. And while a doctor is an authority through their training and experience, you are the one living in your body, and I believe you know your body more than any test or any doctor who tells you you're "perfectly healthy" when you have that nagging feeling that something isn't quite right. This same type of scenario plays out over and over in our lives, and we become so accustomed to giving our power away that we don't even see how often we do it anymore. As a parent, your Authority is used to navigate decisions every day. For example, your child's teacher says that Bobby has a behavior issue, and he might need medication to manage it, but you know that he hasn't been getting a lot of physical playtimes lately and you feel that internal parent radar go off. You take him to the doctor, and they diagnose them him ADHD and suggest medication to alter his behavior. Is the teacher or the doctor the correct authority in this scenario? Perhaps, as an external Authority—someone who offers their experience or training as the voice of information for you to take into your inner Authority and feel into whether it's correct and true for you or not. Have you had a conversation with your child about what's going on? Have you listened to your parental knowing that says, "This seems aligned with what I have sensed" or "No, that's not my child" after gathering information? That nagging feeling that something is off is likely your Authority trying to get your attention. Especially with medical decisions, if it doesn't feel right, get another opinion.

I know that these are both very emotionally charged examples of giving your authority away. Still, we must look at the stuff that matters and not just live in a world where we allow others to decide for us or use our minds to rationalize why something might or might not be true. With the example of the doctor who declares you "perfectly healthy," as soon as you walk away, your mind starts getting involved. Your mind says, "I went to the doctor, and they did an exam, tests even, and everything was great, so I must be healthy. I guess I can ignore this feeling that something's not right." And you rationalize your way into ignoring your knowing because "they have a degree" or a lot of experience and you don't have that kind of experience in this area. Knowing comes in many forms, not just in the ways that are most praised in our current society.

I want to acknowledge that there are situations where people have exerted their power over others, and that is different from not using your Authority. That is abuse, and it is not okay, not your fault or responsibility, and is not connected to Authority. Authority is inner guidance to help move you along the path that is correct for you and is not about anyone other than you.

We can't control all the things that happen to us, but even in the crummiest of situations, we have the power to choose how we will respond. Viktor E. Frankl's

Man's Search for Meaning is a deep and profound excellent example of how we have the power to choose how we will respond to what life gives us.

Learning to trust your Human Design Authority helps you take your power back at home, work, in friendships, and in family dynamics to follow what is correct for you. When people feel threatened, insecure, or hurt, they can try to exert control over others. Let's create a world where we do not feel the need to exert power over one another and allow ourselves to be our own authorities.

Every Human Design Chart has an inner Authority, which is a way to make decisions that are aligned with their truth. Some decisions are body-based, some are centered more around verbal processing, and some simply take a longer time. They are determined by definition or lack of definition in the BodyGraph centers, but all can be felt through a deep connection to self.

When multiple centers are defined, they follow the following order for determining Authority in the chart:

INNER AUTHORITY HIERARCHICAL ORDER

	Authority	Energy Type
1.	Emotional Authority	M / G / MG / P
2.	Sacral Authority	G / MG
3.	Splenic Authority	M / G / MG / P
4.	Ego Manifested Authority	M
5.	Ego Projected Authority	P
6.	Self-Projected Authority	P
7.	None or Environmental or Sounding Board Authority	P
8.	Lunar Authority	R

M- Manifestor I G- Generator I MG- Manifesting Generator
P- Projector I R- Reflector

Disclaimer about Authority

I trust that you will read the following information and use your judgment on what is correct for yourself and your child. Any information about making decisions should be considered with parent awareness and depending on the level of the decision, potential impact to both the child and family, and anyone else involved. Encourage your children to communicate with you and keep an open dialogue so that you can know what is going on in their lives. Authority through childhood is meant to help the child become empowered in their own decision making, and like when you teach them to ride a bike, you keep one hand on them and follow along closely behind until they're ready to ride without you holding on. Teach them to be confident about making their own decisions, just as you teach them to be confident in their abilities to keep themselves upright on a bicycle before you let go.

A Note About the Mind as an Authority

Your mind is never your inner Authority, as it is too easily conditioned, especially through the open centers, to do what it perceives will please others, like parents for example. When you understand your Authority and use it to guide you, your mind can, however, be helpful as an *outer* Authority for others to find their knowing or truth, by providing a more objective view of the situation. By being able to reflect to someone their thoughts and considerations or sharing information, you can help them to get clear on the decision they need to make. The mind is great at processing information and therefore helpful to others when we are grounded in our own Authority, but we cannot rely on our minds to access the innate truth or wisdom that we possess for our own decision making.

When you try to make decisions from your mind, you make decisions from the conditioned or not-self. Your openness in your chart feeds into the mind and conditions it to make choices from a place that is not your truth. You must drop down into your body wisdom to access your truth. Even with rarer Authorities such as the Mental, Lunar, or Ego Authorities, a final piece clicks into place that is about a feeling in the body, a knowing or sensation that lets you know it's true for you. Sometimes with the Mental, Lunar, or Ego Authorities, it's about hearing your decision out loud that allows your body to feel the resonance in it, and you feel aligned. The mind will always try to compensate for what it is not; therefore, it cannot make choices that are aligned with your truth.

It is not easy to shift from making decisions with your conditioned mind to making decisions with your Authority. It can take time. In Human Design, it is said that it takes seven years for one deconditioning cycle. This does not mean that you will not see any changes for seven years. It simply means that the longer you live according to your design and trust your Authority, the more benefit you will see in living your life on your terms, in an aligned way. While the mind can begin to comprehend the idea of Authority, it does not trust that the body can make the correct decisions and will try and speak up and tell you that it knows best. I invite you to lean into curiosity and start with things of small consequence, such as what to have for dinner, or whether to go see that new movie you've been hearing so much about as you begin using your Human Design Authority. As you gain confidence in your abilities, over time you'll work up to using it for decisions with bigger impact such as whether to take that new job offer or end a friendship that no longer feels correct. As you, the parent, become solid in your Authority, you become an example of living authentically for your child.

There is however a certain amount of surrendering that must happen to trust that your mind is not the best at making decisions for you. If you like to feel in control and have a hard time relinquishing it, this may take longer for you. The beauty is that the more we surrender to the body, the more we realize life is a beautiful thing to watch happen to us, and ironically, we often end up feeling more in control through choosing to surrender.

I know how trying to take control of anything you can in a situation where you feel powerless can feel temporarily empowering. Eventually, as we wake up to ourselves, we realize that this perception of control limits our life and our ability to bond and be with the people around us.

Letting go of control does not mean letting go of boundaries, however. Boundaries around your time, money, energy, health, and more, and are important for you to know, understand, and enforce in your life. Boundaries can change over time, and I would encourage you to let them. When you grow and learn more, you'll notice that a boundary that once helped protect you is now holding you back, and you'll know that it's time to adjust that boundary.

You can feel when a boundary is too strict or too loose once you've connected with your Authority. As you begin experimenting with your Authority, you'll get it "wrong" (if *wrong* is even a thing). You'll make choices that turn out to be incorrect for you, and that's okay. It's part of your learning process. You're not expected to always get it right. Some of our best lessons come from getting it wrong, but fear of getting it wrong can keep us from even trying. Don't miss out on life because you're afraid of getting it wrong. The only right way is your aligned way. What feels true, authentic, and right to you? Listen to your body, and it will help show you the way. And remember, "It's ALL just an experiment" as my mentor Kate Swoboda often says during coach training.

Emotional Authority

Emotional Authority applies to roughly 50 percent of the population and is determined by having a defined Emotional Solar Plexus in the BodyGraph. With this Authority, the child does not make decisions that are correct for them spontaneously. They need time to ride out the highs and lows of their wave to get clarity. A child with Emotional Authority can say yes in the moment to playing with a friend, and then when getting to the friend's house they complain, don't want to play with that friend or want to go home. This can feel confusing to the parent that is doing this for their child; they said they wanted to play together, efforts have been made, and now they no longer want to.

If they say no to something when they are feeling low, they can later throw a tantrum that they wanted to do that thing and they didn't mean it when they said no earlier. With this Authority, there is no truth in the now, meaning it takes time to experience the waves of emotion that come with emotional definition in the chart to get clarity around a decision. If they can ride these waves and feel consistent about the decision through the highs and lows, they'll feel, over time, if this decision is correct for them or not.

The Emotional Waves

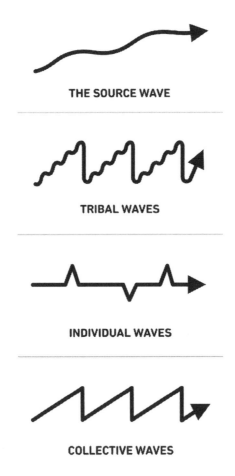

THE SOURCE WAVE

TRIBAL WAVES

INDIVIDUAL WAVES

COLLECTIVE WAVES

You'll want to look at your child's chart and see what channels they have connected to the Emotional Solar Plexus (ESP). They may have more than one channel, which will give them one, two, or all three wave types.

Emotional definition comes from the defined channels connected to the Emotional Solar Plexus. The ESP has the potential to be directly connected to four other centers, which will create definition in both the ESP and the center(s) it's connected to. The channel that is created between those centers (due to the gate definition on either end of the channel) will tell you a lot about the type of emotional wave(s) you experience. The wave type is determined by the Circuitry that the channel is in either Tribal, Individual, or Collective.

The Tribal Wave - Channels 37-40, 59-6, and 19-49

This wave has small undulations that ratchet up a notch at a time to a point of emotional outburst, explosion, or clarity. Children with this wave have a fairly balanced emotional appearance, until they don't. This wave is concerned with need and touch, so a gentle hand placed upon a child's back or shoulder or a hug when they've had a hard day is enough to help take their emotional intensity down a notch if they haven't exploded yet. They don't need to hash out how they feel necessarily, but just allow them their process. This wave can also come back down after they've reached a point of clarity without an explosion.

As someone who carries this emotional wave, I can tell you that as a child I was emotionally fine and tolerant until something tipped me over the edge and I blew up, got roaring mad, and then within thirty seconds was over it. Unfortunately, the people around me were usually not over it that easily. My mom has an undefined ESP, and my dad has a defined ESP. When we argued, my mom would get to a point where she would draw a hard line and say "enough" and just stop talking, walking away. It could be hours later or the next day, and then things would seem like nothing happened, which always left me confused. But seeing it through the lens of Human Design, I can see how this may have been her just recognizing what she needed and allowing space to stop the escalation of emotion and clear the air to reset. It felt like I was being punished with the silent treatment when I just wanted to talk it out, blow it up, and deal with the thing causing the issue. When an argument didn't result in an explosion of sorts, I can see now how I kept prodding trying to make the blow up happen, so I could reset and not feel so emotionally charged. I knew that I wouldn't feel better until the intense feelings were over, and I felt the pressure to get to the other side of the wave. I sure wish we had known then how it could have been explained through this emotional wave that I have defined in my chart. On the other hand, my dad and I both have a defined ESP; however, we have different waves. We could yell and blow up at each other and say terrible things through the emotional intensity and then walk away feeling mad. I would reset and move on, while he would seem to stay disappointed in me for a while as I didn't live up to his expectations. After some time, we'd try again and end up back in a disagreement over something and then need another break again. This was a completely different experience than with my mom and her undefined ESP. I felt like I had to be careful with the arguments with my mom while with my dad I felt like we could throw emotional intensity back and forth at one another more easily. Neither one of us knew about this emotional wave and how it was affecting our behavior. Add in some teen hormones and I am sure he thought I was a real pain in the ass, as I thought of him at the time. No matter what configuration you and your child have, understanding the ESP, waves, and how they work together can provide a lot of compassion and understanding for what each other's needs are, allowing you to navigate your relationship in a healthier way.

The Collective Wave - Channels 36-35, and 41-30

This wave is concerned with desire and is built upon expectations that, when not met, lead to a big drop in emotions. It is better for people with this wave to live in more of a state of curiosity than to build up an expectation of what will happen. When they allow themselves to build an expectation and it is not met, the wave that has been slowly building with anticipation of the desired outcome comes crashing down and they can feel the low of their wave until their wave begins to shift again.

This wave is a slow build where it begins at the low part of the wave and gradually climbs higher and higher feeling more and more excited and then has an abrupt crash in their emotions. The length of this wave is individual, meaning that each person who carries this wave will have a different amount of time that they spend in the different parts. I cannot stress enough the importance of not getting stuck in identifying your child with the emotion they experience. It is simply an emotional wave that they ride, and they do not need to judge themselves or overly identify with it. If you can learn to avoid language that identifies them by the highs or lows, they will learn that *they* are not identified by those highs or lows. The more they identify with the emotion, the longer they may spend time in that part of their wave. Consider helping them when they wake up feeling low with the reframe from "I'm so sad and low today, what's wrong with me?" to "I feel sad today and that's okay. How can I take it a bit easier today?" For younger kids, maybe that's just more snuggle time, a hug, watching a show with you, or reading books quietly, drawing, or anything that allows for going more inward creating space to process the feels that they are having. For older kids, talk to them about not identifying with the feeling by saying "I *am* sad" but rather "I *feel* sad today." The more they identify themselves with that part of their wave, the more time they will spend down there. To be clear, this is not about bypassing the feelings but acknowledging them, giving the child space to feel them, and not making it wrong to feel the lower vibrational emotions. Of course, there are many factors to this and if you have a child who has very low lows or stays in them, seek professional support for yourself and give them the support they need. The earlier we can teach our children these lessons about their emotions the more resilient they can become and see emotions as just a thing they experience rather than who they are (the emotion).

It's important to understand that some days will be down days and it doesn't mean there is anything wrong with them or anything needs fixing, but that it's one part of the emotional wave. It also does not mean that you should not seek help with your child's emotional health and assume it's just Human Design at work. We are complex humans and Human Design only tells part of their story.

The Individual Wave - Channels 12-22, and 39-55

Though this wave is concerned with passion, it is even keeled most of the time. This wave can have higher highs and lower lows with its variations than other wave types and can vary greatly from person to person as to how long they spend in their unique highs and lows.

As with the Collective wave, it is however, important to understand that some days will be down days and that it doesn't mean there is anything wrong or in need of fixing.

While this wave can feel extreme at the times it dips or crests, these times are usually shorter, which means that they don't spend a lot of time in either the high or low, and a new day can bring a whole new outlook.

Emotions are Chemical and Mechanical Interactions, not Personal

From a purely mechanical aspect of Human Design, people with a defined Emotional Solar Plexus have an emotional wave that they ride, and sometimes it's high and sometimes it's low. The important part of this when thinking of it as an Authority is that they ride through their emotions while waiting for clarity on a decision and checking in when they're at the high, the low, and somewhere in the middle. Do they feel the same way about the decision they're making at all points? You can imagine how their decision to say yes to a game, friendship, or a toy when they're on the high of their wave and happy about everything in life may seem great! But the next day if they crash down to the lower part of their wave, they may not feel as excited or aligned about that decision and regret it.

You as a parent or caregiver can help them by checking in with them on bigger decisions such as spending all their savings on a toy they just saw, by making them wait a couple of days. Ask them when they are feeling happy and excited, versus pouty, sad, and frustrated, and then again when they've come back to a neutral emotional state and see if they still want to spend ALL their savings on that one toy. By encouraging them to examine their decision during the high, low, and neutral parts of their wave, you can help them understand the process of waiting out the wave for clarity.

Putting it into Action in the Baby/Toddler Stage

One way for you to understand more about what is happening as a parent is to know which waves your child(ren) carry and then keep a journal with their moods, and when they're old enough, ask them to tell you how they feel. At this stage, you'll just be watching and noting and if you feel like tracking their moods, you can write down their moods regularly to see if there are any patterns. There is no need to provoke them, but just observe and take notes if you find it helpful.

If there are multiple waves, it may be a bit trickier to track but even just knowing that your child has normal ups and downs based on their design can help you as parents and caregivers to not overly attach meaning to them.

Putting it into Action in the Elementary School Age Stage

At this stage, you can begin asking them how they feel. If they tell you they feel a particular emotion or if you notice a strong emotion, you can ask them to hold up their hands and show you how much they feel that emotion—is it a little bit (hands close together) or a lot (hands farther apart)? You can keep a journal or even just make a note on a calendar in your phone or where convenient for you. Over time you'll see a pattern emerge about roughly how long the highs or lows last or how often they experience them. Another thing to take note of is if they are well-rested or not, which can affect their emotional wave, especially if they are a non-Sacral energy type who is pushing too hard with their energy.

FEELINGS

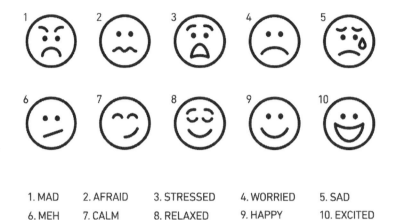

| 1. MAD | 2. AFRAID | 3. STRESSED | 4. WORRIED | 5. SAD |
| 6. MEH | 7. CALM | 8. RELAXED | 9. HAPPY | 10. EXCITED |

As they get older you can show them this chart and ask them where they feel their mood is that day. They may find it fun at this stage to rate where they are, which also opens an opportunity for them to share more about how they are feeling and let some of it out in a more controlled way rather than holding it in and exploding in frustration, bitterness, anger, or disappointment. You can cover the names of the emotions at the bottom of the chart so they can focus on the faces rather than the names if they can already read them. Society tells us every day that we should be happy, and not sad, so taking the labels away can help them share their truth a little bit easier.

Putting it into Action in the Teen Stage

If you've been talking about emotions throughout your child's life in Human Design language, this won't be so weird for them. You can begin asking them in the pre-teen stage when they are feeling high or low, and where they are in their wave. Ask them to rate it with a number as to how high or low it feels. Offer them a scale of negative five, for the lowest low, to positive five, for the highest high, with zero being neutral. If they have a big decision to make about school, college, a large purchase, a job, a relationship, etc., help them to navigate their wave until they are in an emotionally neutral place before making a big decision. For emotionally defined people, there is no truth in the now. Clarity only comes with the passage of time; ask them to at least sleep on it a night before deciding. The bigger the decision the more space it should be given to experience the different feelings throughout the wave.

And remember, *they* are not their emotions. They simply are human beings who get to *feel* many different emotions.

About Spontaneity

Having a defined Emotional Solar Plexus can be a wild ride when you don't understand it. It can feel like you're spontaneous and living in the moment! It can be a real rush! When you're in the high part of your wave, you make decisions that can push you higher in your wave because there is a thrill. The problem comes the next day or so when your wave turns and as it comes back down, and those decisions you made in the moment leave you feeling regret, remorse, and possible embarrassment. If you know that you have an emotional wave that operates in this way, you can be more mindful when you are presented with decisions, allowing yourself the time you need to get clear before making a decision.

Sacral Authority

The Sacral Authority is exclusive to the Generators and Manifesting Generators, who are the only energy types with a defined Sacral Center. This Sacral definition gives them a consistent workforce, life force energy, and is the Authority for Generators/Manifesting Generators when the Emotional Solar Plexus (ESP) is **not** defined in the chart. The Sacral Center is also important even when the ESP is the Authority because it is the Generator's and Manifesting Generator's inner compass helping them to know what is true and correct for them in the moment. It bypasses the mind's conditioning to get to the truth of the matter when it has not been conditioned out of them.

Generator and Manifesting Generator children will need your help staying connected to this powerful inner compass. The Sacral speaks through sounds more often than words and can sound like "uh-huh" or "unh-uh." When you ask your Generator and Manifesting Generator children questions, ask them yes/no questions so that they can access this part of themselves. You can also try either/or questions.

Open-ended questions are great for the non-Sacral energy types but only leaves the Sacral energy types working hard to rationalize or explain their answer. It muddles their clarity on whether they want to say yes or no, taking them back into the mind as it tries to find the "correct" answer.

Practice asking your child with Sacral definition yes/no questions from an early age, and they will never have to re-learn what it's like to be able to access their inner truth without getting their minds in the way (see Appendix for how to ask Sacral questions). Much of my work with adult Generators and Manifesting Generators involves helping them reconnect to their Sacral response. As parents and caregivers, you have an amazing opportunity to help your child stay connected to their Sacral response, and they can benefit from this inner compass all their lives, keeping them on their path of inner truth. What a unique gift you are giving them!

Putting it into Action in the Baby/Toddler Stage

At this stage, ask simple yes/no questions. "Do you want peas? Do you want to go to the park? Do you want to play with blocks?" Rather than asking "What should we play?" or "What do you want to do?" ask them yes/no questions. Keep the questions sweet and simple and know that they are telling you their truth at that moment, but as things change and shift through the day, you can try those same questions and get a different answer. This does not mean that they don't know what they like or don't like. They are getting in contact with what it is they want to invest their energy into right now, in this present moment. If they say no to blocks three days or even three weeks in a row, don't give away the blocks; just know that they don't want to play with them right now and something else is turning their Sacral motor on.

Developmentally around the age of two, children start realizing their autonomy and practicing the word *no* more. If they are allowed to say no to the things they don't want (or you can find creative ways to get them to say yes to eating their vegetables without force), they will feel empowered. Use of the word *no* won't hold as much weight to the parent/caregiver anymore, so when they say no it doesn't have to be about you. Your child saying no does not have to be a power struggle. This is a developmental stage where they are beginning to recognize that they are individuals and can make some of their own decisions and we can empower them through choice.

Putting it into Action in the Elementary School Age Stage

As your child starts school, there may be an adjustment period where they are expected to conform to what the class is doing or what the assignment is, and if their Sacral says no, they can be labeled a problematic or resistant child. It is important to open a dialogue with your child's teacher, if possible, for them to ask your child yes/no or this/that questions. In fact, wouldn't it be great if all teachers understood that 70 percent of the population has Sacral definition and needs to respond with yes/no answers? Imagine if our school systems could allow children to learn in a way that was supportive of their Strategy and Authority. We're not there yet, however you can still arm your child's teacher with information that will help them succeed with teaching your child.

When your child's teacher can't support your child this way it can be a difficult situation. Most of our school systems are designed for one style of learning–which is linear and logical currently, and a lot of children don't learn this way. When we teach a child that there is only one way to learn correctly, we tell them it's wrong for them to be themselves, and what they can hear is that they are not good enough, smart enough, or capable enough. You can reinforce to them at home the importance of listening to their yes/no and teach them that there are still places in their life where they are allowed to practice autonomy. And if there is something they are being asked to do at school they really can't get behind, you can use Sacral questions to understand what is bothering them about the situation. For example, some children hold so much empathy for animals that any activity that involves learning lessons on real animals (including reptiles and insects) can be too much for them. While on the outside, it may appear that this child is just stubborn or doesn't want to participate, on the inside, they may be feeling very upset about the animal, which is why they don't want to participate.

If you're a homeschooling parent, you can utilize this information to help you navigate when and how to help your child learn without having to go to battle every day. Understanding your child and their needs and working with them rather than trying to make them fit into a societally conditioned box will help them to feel empowered, love learning, and know that you're on their side. As a homeschool parent for the last five years, I had to decondition what it meant to school at home. I attended public school and learned that there were certain things taught in particular grades. When it came time for me to homeschool my children, who attended public school for a few years, I had to learn to let go of those ideas and realize that the whole reason we were homeschooling was so that we could learn what we wanted at our own pace and in our own way. Taking the same school system and replicating it at home may not give you the experience you're hoping for because the system that public school offered was not what your child needed, and the location/environment wasn't the only issue.

Putting it into Action in the Teen Stage

This can be a difficult time if your child is asserting their independence or is in a rebellious stage. This is probably a good time for more questions such as "Can you do this?" Or "Would you please do this?" or "Do you want to do this or that first?" type of questions rather than "Do you want to?" Another thing to note is that when they are tuned into their Sacral and you ask them a question, make sure that you're ready to hear the answer. Asking if they like your clothes, new couch, or anything else you're proud of or fond of, might not be met with the enthusiasm that you're hoping for.

Turn your Child's Sacral Motor On!

See the Appendix for more information on Asking Sacral Questions.

Splenic Authority

This authority is a stark contrast to the Emotional Authority. The Emotional Authority needs time for clarity, while the Splenic Authority is the opposite and provides instant in-the-moment knowing. These are children who will be able to make quick decisions easily and be sure of what they want *in the moment*. The only caveat with this is that because the Spleen is about safety and security and is constantly scanning for new information, it can change quickly. If it senses new information that feels as if it might compromise safety, their decision can change. The Splenic knowing is a whisper telling them to trust or not, to go or not, whether it's healthy or not, and is based on whether it feels safe and correct. It's more of a whisper that says "Stop" or "Don't," rather than "Yes!" Because it's in-the-moment knowing, the Splenic Authority will not repeat, so asking repeatedly for an answer does not help your child get clearer. As a parent, it may be confusing because their answer seems to change depending on when you ask them, but remember they are constantly taking in new information to base their decision upon. When I think of this Authority, I think of big cats or other wild animals that use their senses to know if it's safe or not. The saying "it made the hairs on the back of my neck stand up" would be appropriate to convey the subtlety of this inner knowing.

Imagine you have a child who has Splenic Authority, and you invite them to go get ice cream with you, and they say yes. Five minutes later, their sibling walks in, and you invite the sibling to go with you, and unbeknownst to you, earlier in the day, they had a fight, and the sibling was picking on this child. Now your Splenic Authority child decides they no longer want to get ice cream. On the surface, it feels frustrating as a parent because you're ready to walk out the door, and just five minutes ago, your child was excited about ice cream, which they love. Now, they'd rather stay home, and they seem unhappy. Their Spleen is taking in the information that this sibling picked on them, and it doesn't feel safe or enjoyable to go get ice cream now. Because the Spleen is all about instinct, safety, and security, it sees this as a potential threat, and it now decides that it's not a good idea to go get ice cream with this sibling. Maybe they talk privately and work it out, and in another five minutes, everyone wants to go get ice cream again. This is the in-the-moment Splenic Authority in action. It's spontaneous.

If your Splenic Authority child does not want to do something like go to school or play with a friend, ask questions. What about the situation feels like a threat to their safety or security? There may be other things at play in this situation, but it's a place to start.

Suppose you have an Emotional Authority or another Authority that needs time or verbal processing to make a decision. In that case, you may feel inclined to ask your child repeatedly if they are sure of their decision because you have a hard time understanding how they can be clear of their decision this quickly. This can unintentionally make them question their own decisions and stop trusting themselves to make good choices. When a Splenic Authority child decides in the moment, you can trust that it is true for them in that moment. Too much questioning can make them disconnect from their truth and begin answering from their conditioned mind as they begin second guessing their inner knowing.

Putting it into Action in the Baby/Toddler Stage
Ask them once for their yes or no. Avoid asking them repeatedly if they want the toy, the food, the attention, etc. If they say yes, give them what you offered. If they say no, try and honor that or look for an understanding of what may be stopping them from saying yes. If you can dispel any fears that are coming up for them, they may change their answer.

Putting it into Action in the School Age Stage
Teach them to trust their instincts, respect their inner knowing, and listen to the little whisper of a "no" or "stop" that they may hear. Building upon the baby/toddler stage, help them by trusting what they feel in the moment is true for them. If they say no to something like a family event, ask them more about it to see

how their safety or security might feel threatened. Is there a particular person there that makes them feel uncomfortable? Do other kids bully them? Is there a family member that they don't feel good being around?

Putting it into Action in the Teen Stage

At a time where social and peer pressures are high, if you've been able to teach your child since childhood that they can trust their instincts, they should have a pretty strong foundation at this point to listen to and trust. If you're new to Human Design and your child is already a teen, don't fret; now is a perfect time to teach them that they can trust their inner knowing. Help them find ways to practice with it on a smaller level and ask them how they feel about situations before moving forward with decisions. They may hear that inner voice but stuff it away because their conditioned mind is getting involved in the process and talking them out of their truth or knowing. Teach these children the importance of listening to that feeling or voice especially when driving a car, getting into someone else's car, or being in a social situation that doesn't feel right. If they feel it's not right, it probably isn't. Encourage them to wait to drive the car until the feeling passes, even if it makes them late, or not to go to that party even if all their friends are all going, and if the people them give them a bad feeling, to leave and return to people who feel right to be around.

Ego Authority

The Ego Authority belongs exclusively to either the Manifestor or Projector energy type.

The Ego Manifested Authority

A Manifestor can manifest what they are called to create or do without support from anyone else and can act on their inspirations. This Authority can feel very powerful and even somewhat egotistical to others as it comes from the Will Center, which is also known as the Ego Center. It comes from a place of "I want this," "I want to do that," and is very "I" driven. The Will Center is related to the energy of "What do I want?" and "Do I have the resources to take this on?" Even though the voice can sound like "me, me, me" the Will Center correlates with the heart chakra and has a tribal element to it. The motivations behind "I want" and "I need" are bigger than the individual "I" in its purest form.

The Manifestor is designed to significantly impact others, so when it speaks from the Ego Authority, it can feel powerful and lead the Manifestor to become conditioned to filter what they say, so others receive it better. This conditioning quiets the Authority of the Ego Manifestor as they try to make themselves small, to want for nothing, and to people-please instead because that seems to make everyone happier.

The challenge is for them to stand in their Authority and power by continuing to say those "I" statements and to make sure they're informing those who will be impacted by what they intend to do. So perhaps rather than "I need a car" which can leave those around them wondering if they are asking for money for a car, try add in the informing: "I need a car. I'm going to get a job and save money so I can drive myself to school."

The Ego Projected Inner Authority

The Ego Projected Authority belongs to the Projector and is a rare Authority as it only occurs in Projectors that have the Will Center and the G Center defined through the Channel 25-51. Projectors must wait to be recognized and for the invitation. When they respond to the invitation, they respond from a place of "I do (or do not) have the energy/resources for that." They need to be selfish and ask the questions, "What's in it for me? What do I want?" in response to the invitations they receive. Waiting for invitations can feel like they take forever to arrive. During the waiting, it's important that they refine their craft, learn a system, and become a resource for something in order to receive the invitations that are right for them, to be recognized, and to respond. Waiting for correct invitations can sometimes take a while. It's important with all the open centers in their chart that they don't act from the conditioned mind, jumping into things they do not have the energy for or have not been invited into. You can help your child understand this Authority by asking them questions such as "How do you think it will be beneficial to you if you say yes or no?" or "Will you be passing up an opportunity for something you need if you say no?" or even "Why do you want it?"

Children with Ego Authority

The child with an Ego Authority will speak from the voice of "I want" and "I need," and our societal conditioning tells us to make sure that this child knows that they need to share their resources and that it's not all about them. But the child doesn't see it in the same way as the conditioned adult does. It is not coming from a place of greed but rather a sense of *knowing* that "This is what I need for myself" now. It's not an "I want it" because I want to possess and own all the things in the land; it doesn't think that far in advance. That would be the Strategy of the mind.

Putting it into Action in the Baby/Toddler Stage

When they begin speaking, listen to your child as they will use the language "I want" and "I need" to communicate their needs and tell you what is correct for them. They may lean in and grab things when pre-verbal, to communicate what they want and need. Teaching them not to grab at things can begin to quiet this connection for them. However, asking "What do you want/need?" when they lean to grab for something can reinforce that they want or need that thing and deepen their connection to their knowing.

Putting it into Action in the Elementary School Age Stage

At this stage, we can deepen the communication of how they ask for what they need. Socially, they may need to begin to learn to communicate their needs in a way that doesn't feel so harsh to others by informing if they are a Manifestor. A Projector, on the other hand, needs to learn to wait for an invitation to respond. Rather than grabbing and taking, while saying "I want" or "I need that," consider phrases like "I like that toy, may I play with it?" "I would like to have that toy." "I want chicken for dinner, can you make that?" These phrases soften the needs with the consideration of others, rather than just taking what they want.

Putting it into Action in the Teen Stage

This age becomes very self-centered already as they are finding their autonomy and trying to separate themselves from their parents while finding their own identity. Their words can hurt. Remember, as the parent of a child with an Ego Authority, this is not personal when they are always saying "I want" "I need." This Authority can present more of a challenge, especially when it comes from an Ego Manifestor child, who can already feel intense for the parent at times, but if you work with the Strategy for their energy type you can learn to navigate this together.

Self-Projected Authority

The Self-Projected Authority is exclusive to the Projector energy type. It is determined by having a defined G Center connected to the Throat Center *without* a defined Emotional Solar Plexus, Will, Sacral, or Spleen Center. Because the G Center is about identity, love, and direction, when it is connected directly to the Throat Center, they speak the truth from their core, especially the Channels 1-8. Because they have so many open energy centers in their chart, they are open to a large amount of conditioning, so it is important for them to not filter what they say in response to the invitations they receive. By listening to their voice without filtering their response they get to hear their truth rather than their conditioned response. This Authority is often a verbal processor, so allowing them space to hear their truth, through a trusted person who can just listen is very helpful. Often, the person listening doesn't have to do much more than hold space to process and let them hear themselves. Let them process and allow the truth to flow out of them. They will know what is correct for them when they hear it come out of their mouth. They must not let the mind get involved in their decision-making by filtering what they say. Let the G Center speak spontaneously and freely to find their truth.

When Responding to an Invitation with this Authority

If you or your child have this Authority, good questions to ask or encourage are, "Does this decision make me feel more like me or less like me?" "Is this the right direction for me?" "Will I feel good when I get to the destination that this decision will take me?" And of course, there is no certain 100 percent knowing, but the more you learn to trust this inner guidance, the more reliable it will become as you learn from when it has led you to truth and when you let your mind lead you. This Authority is navigating their invitations through the filter of "Does this make me feel more or less like my authentic self?"

Putting it into Action in the Baby/Toddler/Preschool Stage

This is a Projector child, so inviting them to talk and speak freely is important once they develop the language. From a young age, ask them questions about what they feel would make them happy. For example, ask how they feel in different places, or whether something gives them joy or sadness. It's not that you're going to get substantial verbal responses, but you're subtly helping them recognize what they should be asking themselves when they make a decision. If they grow up hearing that how they feel about their decisions and surroundings is important, they will learn to trust their Authority more and more. As they get older, they will be better equipped to understand the difference between making self-aligned decisions and making conditioned people-pleasing decisions for their life.

Putting It into Action in the Elementary School Age Stage

Again, this Authority is about asking what they feel or sense about the decision they need to make. "Do you feel good about going to your friend's house?" "Do you feel comfortable there?" This is not about getting super-specific in why they feel a particular way about a decision because that trains them to get the mind involved and explain what they feel. You want them to trust that the things they feel are true and correct for them without justifying them. It also means as a parent, you need to step back and allow them to decide *and* allow them to understand the consequences of that decision (within reason for their age). Show them you recognize that they are doing what they feel is best for them in that moment. Remember, Projectors need to feel seen and recognized.

Putting it into Action in the Teen Stage

Having regular check-ins with your child about the decisions they are making or need to make can be supportive to them at this stage if they're willing to talk to you. Sometimes the parent isn't the person a child turns to for advice or support. If they don't turn to you, help the adult they are turning to understand that it's essential for them to be able to talk and to hear themselves when they talk. Having a person they can talk to without having to filter themselves, can help them get to the truth a lot faster. A child often has preconceived ideas of how a parent will react and will filter what they say out loud, which can shift their decision making to the mind—not a reliable place to make decisions for the self from.

Mental Authority

This is another Projector Authority and can be a bit more challenging because it doesn't have a single specific place it lives in the body (like the Sacral or Splenic Authority with their gut response or inner voice or whisper). This Authority has no centers defined below the Throat Center but can have either the Head and Ajna, the Head, Ajna, and Throat, or Ajna and Throat Centers defined.

This Authority filters information through its open centers, determining if the environment feels correct or not, and if the person feels correct. If the environment or the people they're with feel wrong to them, then the decisions they make while in that environment will not be correct for them at this time. That same environment may be okay for them at another time as something may shift in that environment, such as a person may come or go, or an item may be moved or removed. Environment is everything when this Authority is deciding, so if your child struggles with decisions, consider where they are when they're trying to decide. Because there is so much openness in their chart, the Mental Projector deeply takes in the person they are with and is essentially looking for the people in their life who feel good to be around to make their decisions. Through their open centers, they can become very wise about who feels grounded in their own timing (Root Center), who listens to their intuition over fear (Spleen Center), who is confident in who they are (G Center), who has a high sense of self-worth (Will Center), who is inspirational (Head Center), and who can speak and be heard (Throat Center). Once they identify the people in their life who feel grounded in these areas, they can turn to them to help them verbally process their decisions.

When They Don't Turn to The Parent for Support

These kids need people in their life that they can use as sounding boards and may have different people for different areas of their lives, which may not be you, their parent. This can be difficult when your child wants to talk to someone else about big decisions in their life. It's important to remember that they need to talk to someone who can help them process without telling them what to do, which can at times be challenging for a parent because we want them to turn to us for the big stuff. Try to hold compassion for their process and gratitude they have someone, or multiple people in their life they feel comfortable with, to assist with their decision-making process.

Location Matters

This Authority heavily relies on the place and people around them, so if a decision requires relocation, it would be wise to go visit the place first before committing, to make sure it feels correct. If your child struggles with deciding, ask them if they'd feel more comfortable in another room or outside or if they need a change of scenery to get clear. If the decision is not coming, don't force it, and try asking again about the decision while your child is in a place that is happy and feels good to them.

They Need to Talk It Out

The best thing you can do to empower someone with this Authority is to let them talk. They are what you might know as a verbal processor. They gain clarity about a situation and how they feel about something by talking it out with others whom they trust. It does not mean that they are looking for you to tell them what to do. They will come to their conclusions if you just let them talk, asking them a few good probing questions to get them to think about their answers along the way. If you try and tell them what to do or what you think they should do, they will likely not turn to you for this sounding board support often because it's not what they need. If they ask you point blank, "What would you do?" then share your perspective of what you would do if you were in their position, but it's important to also make it clear that you are not them and that you support them in finding what is correct *for them*.

Putting it into Action in the Baby/Toddler/Preschool Stage

If trying to get your child to decide which shoes they want to wear or what they want to eat is a struggle, look at the surroundings. Is there pressure exerted on them to decide? Are they distracted by toys? Can you take them to another room to ask them about it? Is there someone in the room that stresses them? These kids can be easily overwhelmed by too much pressure.

Putting It into Action in the School Age Stage

Again, this is about the environment, so if your child is struggling to decide something, change their environment. Look around. Who is in the room? Do you have a defined Root Center exerting pressure on them? Do you have a defined ESP and they're picking up on your emotions of stress, frustration, or concern?

These kids may feel unsure of their decisions with this Strategy at this age, so helping them understand that some places are better than others for them can help them learn what makes an environment good for them or not, and when timing is right for decision making. Teaching them not to make decisions when they don't feel great will help them learn early how to navigate this to make decisions with greater confidence as they get older, when they will have more significant consequences. Ask them what feels good to them in a place or with people around and what does not feel good. Ask them about their decision and what they think they should do. Here are some example questions for this Projector Authority to begin with:

- I'm curious what/if/how/where/how you'd feel if ...
- What would you do if you got that opportunity?
- What do you think that class would be like?
- How would you feel if you gave your favorite toy away?

Remember, this Authority is exclusive to the Projector, so make sure to ask open-ended questions.

Putting it into Action in the Teen Stage

Reinforcing the lessons taught when they are younger about being in a place with people who feel good to make decisions is essential. If they did not grow up knowing about this part of themselves, then you may need to have more conversations with them about why they made the decision that they did *after* the fact, dissect what felt good or bad about it, and how they knew it was the right decision for them. If they don't know, this can be a good opportunity for you to help them understand that the feelings they get from certain people or places can be instrumental in them knowing what is correct for them. Stay curious and help them learn to look at it as an experiment and play with making more minor consequence decisions with this outlook. They will need to talk to someone they trust about their choices, not to get advice from them (Parents, this is the part where you step back, become a good listener, ask good questions, and refrain from going into advice-giving mode.) so they can hear themselves and their thought process. They will come to their own decisions that feel correct for them if you give them space and support to do so.

Lunar Authority

The Lunar Authority belongs exclusively to the Reflector. Reflectors have no centers defined. One of the crucial things to remember is that Reflectors are here to BE, not to DO. Once a Reflector realizes that they are not here to work like a Generator, initiate like a Manifestor, or guide like a Projector, they can allow themselves to settle into their role as a Reflector. If they can do this, it can take the pressure off them to try and keep up with the other 99 percent of the population who are designed differently.

So, What Exactly Does It Mean to Wait for a Lunar Cycle? Do You Mean Like a Whole Month?!

Yep! Reflectors need to give things time. The bigger the decision, the longer it can take them; however, once a Reflector gets clearer on their process and their knowing, they may be able to come to clarity in a shorter amount of time depending on the level of decision. Still, they do their best with big decisions when they wait at least the full twenty-nine and a half days of a lunar cycle so that they can experience definition in all the different gates of the chart as the moon moves through them. They need to talk to other trusted people in their lives about their decisions during this time to gain clarity and reflect on their decision while experiencing the definition of all 64 gates throughout the month.

It can be helpful for you as the parent to get familiar with the gates of the Human Design Chart and track the moon changes through the month to understand what energies are influencing your child as they navigate life and bigger decisions.

Putting it into Action in the Baby/Toddler Stage

This stage is more about you and what you observe about your Reflector child. How do the auras of the people in your home affect them? Consider the environment when your Reflector baby is unhappy, uncomfortable, or moody, versus happy and content.

Putting it into Action in the Elementary School Age Stage

Take a step back and help them make their decisions with enough space and time (when possible) so that they can begin to understand that it's okay for them to take longer to make a decision. Encourage them to wait until it feels right to decide and not rush. The correct opportunity will still be there when they decide if it's meant for them. Teaching them not to rush decisions will help them in the future. Practice patience in letting them feel into their decision.

Putting it into Action in the Teen Stage

As they reach their teens, they will feel peer pressure to make decisions through their open centers. Because they are influenced by how other people feel, they may make incorrect decisions for themselves based on who they are around and how much pressure they feel. They may try to avoid feeling other people's emotional response by going along with everyone else and deciding in the moment rather than taking their time and waiting for clarity. Remind them when you can that they must take their time with decisions. Their design regularly needs more time than any of the others to make decisions, and that's okay. Look around their friend group to see who is influencing their decisions, whether helpful or hurtful, and help them navigate finding people who feel good to be around and who positively influence and support them.

CHAPTER SEVEN

EMOTIONS

*The most beautiful things in the world cannot be seen or
even touched, they must be felt with the heart.*
~HELEN KELLER

Emotions seem complex, yet when looking at the mechanics of them through Human Design, they become simpler and less personal.

What we do with the emotions we experience and how we choose to identify with them gives them power. When you learn more about the mechanics of the emotional wave that roughly 50 percent of the population is sending out into the world, you can understand the emotional soup we all live in and learn to separate yourself from what someone else is feeling and what you are experiencing.

If you have a preschool or older child, or if you've ever been a child (yes, that means everyone), you'll probably recognize the phrase "You made me angry!" or "You're making me sad," and so on—but the words we choose to use matter. No one can *make* you anything without your permission. A child who says such things is experiencing an emotion, but they are not that emotion. Therefore, we must teach them to separate "I am angry" from "I am feeling angry." This distinction can be a game-changer both for you, the parent, and for the child who is learning to identify who they are, as they're learning to separate themselves from their parents and others or are trying to fit in with other people.

Imagine a child who experiences regular emotional extremes who overhears "He is just an emotional child" or "She has anger issues" or "He's just a sad child." We learn who we are from the people who raise us. We assume the things we hear about ourselves are true and don't begin to question and reason what we are told until around age seven.[3] Consider that seven years is a full conditioning cycle in Human Design–they've already learned a lot about who they are. The words we use to talk about our children matter. They hear everything. Even when we realize that not everyone has that same opinion of us and that maybe our parents don't know everything, what they say about us still holds a lot of weight. We still hear their voice in our heads as we repeat the stories we have believed are true of us until we're able to shift that story. We are always seeking acceptance from our parents, even if they are the worst human beings we know. We always want to know that we belong somewhere, that someone else knows us, and that we're not just floating around out here on our own. How we grow up learning about emotions can make all the difference in our lives as we grow.

So, let's break this down from a Human Design perspective. Roughly half the population creates the emotional waves that are sent out into the world, and the other half are the emotional empaths that deeply feel those emotions. The emotional waves have three basic patterns that they follow and can be either Tribal, Collective, or Individual. These terms relate to the Circuitry that the waves are located in, within in their BodyGraph. When a chart has a defined channel connecting from the Emotional Solar Plexus to either the Throat Center, Will Center, Sacral Center, or Root Center, the definition indicates what type(s) of wave(s) a person has. See the Emotional Solar Plexus in Chapter Eight for details on the different types of emotional waves.

Your child can have one, two, or all three types of these waves. The more types of waves they have, the more "emotional" they can appear, varying between wild ups

---

[3] Melanie Zander, "A Milestone Developmental Stage: The Age of Reason," *Scholastic Parents*, (April 12, 2019), https://www.scholastic.com/parents/family-life/social-emotional-learning/development-milestones/age-reason.html

and downs to slow builds of hope and sudden despair to mild ups and downs unless they feel their loved ones or family are threatened.

Understanding what types of waves your child has can be helpful and reveal a pattern to the emotions that they express. Knowing a general outline of their emotional wave can help you both have more understanding when it feels like their emotions come on suddenly. It can also be helpful to understand that this emotional energy is a chemical process of mechanics in action and an aspect of what they came here to experience, but it's not *who* they are. *They* are not their emotional highs and lows. They *experience* emotional highs and lows. Helping them understand this profound yet straightforward aspect can be the difference between them living a life feeling limited by the emotions they experience and a life free to have emotional experiences without attaching their identity to them. Have you been labeled an emotional person? A sensitive person? An angry person? Irritable? Frustrated? Sad? If so, you know how that label can follow you and alter your view of yourself. Now imagine you grew up with a parent who helped you to understand that those emotions do not define you, and they do not have to limit you. How would you see yourself today? Would you have a different perception of yourself?

Emotional Definition at the Different Stages

Early Childhood

At this stage, you can use this chart that shows a scale of mad to excited and ask them to show you what they are feeling right now. After a tantrum or frustration, when they get to the stage where they can talk about it or sit with you, ask them to show you what they feel/felt by pointing to the face they feel/felt like making. Or you can ask them to tell you how they perceive other people they are observing in real life, or how those they're watching on TV might be feeling. Help them to label the feelings so that they can identify them as something separate from their identity. Make sure to use language like "That person looks like they feel sad"

Rather than "That person looks sad" to help them understand how the words make a difference.

FEELINGS

1. MAD	2. AFRAID	3. STRESSED	4. WORRIED	5. SAD
6. MEH	7. CALM	8. RELAXED	9. HAPPY	10. EXCITED

School Age

At this stage, learning to normalize emotions begins with verbalizing feelings. "I feel sad," "I feel happy," etc., rather than "I am sad" or "I am happy." It sounds ideal to identify as happy, but what happens when "happy" disappears and your child hits the low of their wave? Now this emotion that they have identified or been identified with no longer feels true, and they either feel like they must fake it or find a way to live up to it, constantly critiquing why they aren't "happy" and how they arrived here at "not happy." Because happy usually has a positive association and depressed a negative association, we must be careful in how we attach them to our identities, because they are all just expressions of energy in motion, not who we are. Open a dialogue, daily, if possible, about how they are feeling, perhaps asking what they noticed about feeling the emotion they connect with that day. To get them to connect with their body you can use questions such as, "What does happiness feel like in your body?" "Does it feel like little bubbles rising up in your chest?" or "Does it feel heavy like you're carrying a big rock?"

How they respond to a stimulus can provoke emotion, but if they have a base understanding that emotions are just a thing they are here to experience, they can learn to examine what it is trying to communicate rather than judging what it means about themselves. Using the body-based questions above can help them get in touch with emotions that are harder to describe and can be helpful as they learn to navigate their Emotional Authority as well.

Teens

Teenagers whose parents have taught them to separate themselves from their emotional wave early in life can move into this phase of life able to look at their experiences slightly more objectively. I say slightly because the teenage brain is undergoing all sorts of rewiring at this stage, and when you add hormones to that mix, some wild things can happen. If you're finding this book when your child is already a teenager, and you didn't know anything about this emotional wave before now, don't worry, we can all learn to understand emotions better at any age. I have worked with clients in their sixties and seventies who were blown away by this understanding and felt like it gave them more freedom in their lives. The more work you can do on yourself to understand your emotional wave (defined ESP) or emotional empathic abilities (undefined ESP), the more you'll be able to model for and support your child as they learn about their own experiences.

Asking Open and Closed Questions About Emotions

If you have a Generator or Manifesting Generator child/teen, ask them yes/no questions. "Do you feel okay?" "Do you feel happy/sad/angry/etc.?" "Do you want to talk about how it feels?" "Do you want to move your body to help the feelings move through?" or even "I can see that you're feeling some big emotions right now. Do you know what you need to do to help support yourself or to help them move through you right now?"

If you have a Projector, Manifestor, or Reflector, ask them open-ended questions. "How/what are you feeling today?" "I noticed your energy feels a little different today and was wondering if you might be feeling some heavy emotions today."

"Do you think there is a way you could move your body to release the emotions you picked up today?" or maybe "How would it feel if we put on your favorite song and danced it out?" Sometimes simply having them shake their hands out as if they're trying to shake something sticky off can help move emotional energy out of their body.

Use caution to not overdo it with this emotional talk as that can end up reinforcing the feelings by giving them too much attention, moving your child into the mind where they overthink working to figure out why they are feeling what they are feeling. If they decline or say they're fine, leave it be and try again another time.

The Undefined Emotional Solar Plexus/Emotional Empath

When your child does not have a defined ESP, they are constantly being exposed to defined ESP waves out in the world and probably even by someone in your home. They take in and amplify this energy and can appear to be very emotional kids. They are often the kids in the family who seem like they are on the biggest emotional roller coaster. They are simply expressing the emotional energy they are taking in and trying to release it from their systems which are not designed to hold it for long periods. When you have a child with an undefined ESP and they are experiencing big emotional outbursts, it's important to consider where they could have picked up this emotional energy. Even if you think you're hiding your emotions from your children, emotionally empathic children will pick up on them without you even outwardly appearing emotional. Though they may not be conscious of it, you will see it reflected in their behavior. The emotional wave that they feel is chemistry; it cannot be stopped as it's a natural part of life. Rather than try to hide it, take this as an opportunity to teach them how to work with it rather than just run from it, as they will encounter emotional people for the rest of their lives.

These undefined ESP kids are constantly taking the emotional temperature of the room, so it's important if you as a parent have a defined ESP that you understand your emotional wave and how it can be playing a part in the emotions your child is feeling and expressing. Don't be afraid to share how you process the feelings with them. For example, if you wake up in a low part of your wave and your child notices, tell them, "I'm feeling a little sad today. I just need a little bit of time to let it pass. It's nothing you did. It's nothing that I did. It's just how I'm designed and a normal part of my emotions. I know you can probably feel them too, but there's no need to worry about them. I just need some quiet time today."

It's important for you to help your child understand the different emotions and articulate what it feels like for them in their bodies. It's also important to help them understand that they are not the source of the deep sadness or elation or anything in between that they feel. Emotional empathy can be a superpower that allows them to easily read a room, take the emotional temperature and see if it's a place they want to be in. They can become very wise about how others are feeling and know when someone needs a hug without saying anything. They are also aware of who may be unknowingly emotionally charged and should be avoided to not provoke them.

The downside to this ESP Center being undefined is that if these kids are not taught how to navigate this sometimes-overwhelming energy, it can make them want to avoid feeling intense emotions. Confrontation can involve uncomfortable feelings for both parties and for emotional empaths, they anticipate not only their own feelings but also the way the other person's reaction will feel to them. If you're a parent with an undefined ESP, you may recognize avoidance of confrontation in yourself and understand what it feels like. To a child with an undefined ESP, it's not just the low end of the emotional spectrum that feels intense but all the highs and lows. If your undefined ESP child comes home with a great report card, an award, or something you're excited about, as you express that through your defined ESP, that too, can feel overwhelming for your child. Because this feels so intense, they may begin to hide their accomplishments as well as anything that they think may upset you to avoid feeling intense emotions.

Two Emotional Empaths

If both you and your child are emotional empaths and have not been aware of this, you may have found yourself on an emotional roller coaster ride with your child. At times it likely felt puzzling, and the only thing that seemed to resolve it was when one of you stormed off to get a break from the other. After some time, you likely felt the emotional charge of the situation leave and later wondered why you were so upset in the first place. You both pick up emotional energy from the people in your life and can bring it home with you where you may find yourselves nit-picking each other or feel a low level of provocation hanging around. Perhaps it even feels like it needs to be provoked to release it. It's important to check in and be honest with the feelings you're experiencing and ask yourselves and one another, "Where did this come from?" Maybe you can trace it back to someone you were with or somewhere you were earlier that didn't feel great and choose to let it go, but even if you don't know where it came from, you can still choose to release it and let it go. Identifying with its specific source isn't as important as recognizing that it isn't yours to hold and that it's time to let it go. There is no need to attach yourselves to it or to keep ping-ponging it back and forth between you two.

You can also create a temporary definition of an emotional wave with both of your charts together. If one of you has Gate 12 defined, for example, and the other has Gate 22 defined, you create an emotional wave when together. It's not as powerful and sustaining as someone with that definition in their birth chart, however, it can still create some of that ping-ponging emotional energy if you're not aware of it.

Things you can do to release these emotional charges include going for a walk, creating art (channeling emotions from others is a great way to allow a creative process to come through you), writing about it, moving your body, and sometimes just realizing that it's not *your* emotion can be enough to let it go. When all else fails, give each other some room and time to yourselves to let the emotional charge fade.

Parent Emotionally Defined, Child Empath

As an emotionally defined parent raising an emotional empath, everything that you say or do with your child has an emotional charge. This does not have to be negative but being aware of it can help you to understand the interactions you have with your child. Rather than denying your emotions, open a dialogue with your child about your emotional wave (you don't need to explain the mental process you're going through) so that they learn to trust that the feeling they are absorbing is from you and not them and that they don't have to take it on. For example, if you're worried about finances and they feel your worry, it's okay to let them know that you're feeling the emotion of worry, but it's nothing for them to get concerned about. They don't need to know what you're worried about but validating their senses can empower them. Then you can offer to dance it out or go for a walk to release the feelings, which can be helpful for both your child and you.

Empath Parent with Emotionally Defined Child

As a parent with an undefined/open ESP and a child with a defined ESP, you may feel exhausted by the end of the day, especially if you're a stay-at-home parent who is with your child 24/7 riding their emotional roller coaster each day. It's amazing how the emotions of sometimes the smallest person in the family can affect you so much. It can lead to caregiver burnout and a deep need for rest and alone time, especially if you're a non-Sacral energy type or have a 2nd line profile (we'll discuss Profiles in Chapter Nine), who needs time alone if you don't understand the mechanics and dynamics of this relationship.

When your child is young, you may need to work out times with your partner (if available) for you to take daily breaks from your child and their emotional wave. If you're parenting on your own, trade with another parent or hire a babysitter for an hour a day or a couple of times a week. Sometimes at this stage, just having time after they go to bed to be alone and discharge all their emotional energy can be enough. Listen to your needs and make sure you're giving yourself what you need so that you can be the best support for your child and help them navigate the big feelings they experience.

You may also notice that you feel out of control at times. If your defined ESP child is having a meltdown or lashing out at you, you take in (and, if not aware, amplify) and send those emotions back to them unintentionally. You can lash out at them verbally and, depending on the situation, it may even become physical. If you feel yourself taking in these emotions from your child, take a step back, let your child know that you need a moment to gather yourself and step out of their aura. If you have a small child, make sure they are safe and take a break from one another. If there is another person who can step in, let them. Take a break. If you're alone, put them in a playpen or crib or somewhere they are safe and go scream into a pillow. Silent screaming works well too. You can still release all the energy of a scream just without sound. Ironically, it's very effective, and you don't end up feeling hoarse from it so easily. If they're older, let them know that things are feeling intense, and it would be best to take a break to calm down and talk about this later. And do talk about it later. Don't let them feel like you're blowing them off because they are too emotional or think you don't want to communicate. Let them know that you have a high level of respect for each other and yourselves and that you both need time to clear the emotional field to be able to communicate clearly.

CHAPTER EIGHT

THE CENTERS

*To be yourself in a world that is constantly trying to make
you something else is the greatest accomplishment.*
~RALPH WALDO EMERSON

There are nine energy centers in the BodyGraph that correlate with the chakra system. If you understand the chakra system, you already have a sense of what energy each of these centers carries.

HUMAN DESIGN CENTER CHAKRA SYSTEM

Head Center	Crown Chakra
Ajna Center	Third Eye Chakra
Throat Center	Throat Chakra
G Center	Heart Chakra
Will Center	Heart Chakra
Emotional Solar Plexus Center	Solar Plexus Chakra
Spleen Center	Solar Plexus Charka
Sacral Center	Sacral Chakra
Root Center	Root Chakra

The gates (numbers) located in each center have a theme that correlates with the energy theme of the center.

A **defined center** gives it a consistent energy presence in your life and appears colored in on your Human Design Chart. It is consistent energy that you transmit out into the world and what other people sense from you. These defined centers connect to at least one other defined center through a defined channel. Channel definition is created when the gates on either end of the channel are defined (colored in). These are areas where you will learn about yourself throughout your life.

An **undefined center** is an inconsistent energy for you and where you are receiving information from other people. These are areas where you are learning about their energy through your relationships with others all your life. These energies are not for you to try to hold onto but to experience when you're with other people who carry these energies consistently or through the transiting planets. These undefined centers are white or uncolored on your Human Design Chart. The undefined center has at least one gate activation in it. Gate activation will appear as a red or black, or both a red and black line coming out of the gate. The energy of these centers is funneled out through the gate activations within it, which gives you a little more consistency in how you experience the themes of that center.

An **open center is** not colored in on your chart. The way this center is experienced is much more variable. There are no gate activations in it, and it is very open to conditioning and potentially wisdom as you learn more about the center through your relationships.

All centers are susceptible to conditioning, though the undefined and open centers are where most of the conditioning is. One way of looking at the definition in a chart is more of a nature vs. nurture view. The defined areas are nature, and the undefined/open areas are nurture in this example.

We will dive into the centers, what they represent, and how they can show up when either defined (colored in) or undefined/open (white). It is so, so important to **remember that we all have all of the chart. Your child has all of the chart. Nothing is missing.** Look at what is defined in your charts to get to know what is consistent within you, versus what is open to conditioning from the world. When you understand inherently who you or your child is, you can see when you/they are being conditioned to try to be something you/they are not.

Connecting with Other People Through our Charts

Energetically, we are drawn to what we are not, which means we are naturally pulled toward people in our life who have the defined centers, gates, or channels that we do not have defined in our charts. When two people each have a gate definition at opposite ends of the same channel it is referred to as an Electromagnetic Channel, as you are electromagnetically drawn to each other to complete the channel energy. Channels that you share with other people are called Friendship Channels (you both have the same channel definition) and are where you share something in common. There are also places where one person has the whole channel defined and the other person has just one gate in that same channel defined, known as Compromise Channels. The person with the whole channel defined will have the full energy of that channel consistently in their life. The person with one gate in that channel will be the person to compromise with whatever energy that channel represents, which can create a parenting challenge if you have single gates in channels your child has defined, leaving you feeling energetically dominated by your child in that channel. Alternatively, if a parent has the whole channel and a child has one gate in that channel, the child can feel like the energy represented in that channel is dominated by the parent. Dominance Channels are where one person has the entire channel and the other does not have the channel or either gate in that channel defined.

I don't go into detail in this book about all the gates or channels, however, I will touch on a few that come up often in parenting sessions. I would recommend eventually investing in a copy of a body of work that describes these in a way that resonates for you if this level of detail interests you. See the Resources section for some options.

The undefined centers in the chart are where we experience our greatest conditioning. Our mind can become attached to experiencing life through these open centers and try to lead us to making decisions through them, which can lead to living in the not-self. Helping your child see what is consistent and reliable in their chart is helpful for them as they navigate friendships and other interactions where they can become conditioned by family, peers, teachers, or anyone else in their lives. Life is not about avoiding experiences through relationships that can be challenging, but rather understanding self-energy versus not-self energy. Even the people who challenge us most are teaching us something about ourselves.

Head Center

Center for Inspiration | Pressure Center | Yellow in Color When Defined

The Head Center is one of two pressure centers in the chart and is a source of inspiration, doubts, confusion, questions, and mental pressure. This center holds the pressure "to know."

Defined ~ 30 Percent of People

A child with this center defined has consistent inspiration that is designed to ponder life and systems and things that are not yet known whether just to them or to mankind at large. These thoughts and questions can be inspiring to others and can keep them quite busy wondering out of the box things such as "What if people stopped using money and paid each other in potato chips?" and "Why do we build houses out of wood and not hemp?" or "How do you decide which shoes to wear every day?" These children inspire others through their questions and can exhaust their parents with all of their questions at times. Confusion, doubt, and wonder are a normal part of the defined Head Center's process. It's important that children with defined Head Centers understand that not all inspirations are for them to act upon. When the time is right, they will feel called, invited, or inspired to share these ideas or questions and explore them further. Teaching them to follow their Strategy and Authority will help them know when the time is right to share their thoughts. It can be easy for someone with a defined Head Center to get lost in all these questions and not know what to put their energy into, which is why following Strategy and Authority are important here. These kids can feel the pressure to "figure it out" which can create mental anxieties, but they need to understand that they are not meant to figure out every puzzle in life that they wonder about. If the pressure to "figure it out" is turned on themselves rather than letting it come through them in their consistent and natural way, they can become anxious with self-doubt.

The defined channels in the Head Center create consistent ways that information funnels through and can tell you more about how your child processes information. These children can be full of ideas and a great inspiration to those around them. Teaming up for creative work, writing, drawing, and painting at a table with a child with a defined Head Center can help bring more inspiration to everyone at the table. Just being in their aura can inspire the children around them with undefined/open Head Centers.

Because these kids have a direct connection to Source, they receive consistent downloads of information that can feel overstimulating at times, and they can have difficulty shutting their brains off. With so much activity going on up there, it can be difficult for them to sit still without feeling inspired to do or create something. Sitting in a quiet meditation can be difficult or even impossible. As someone who has defined Head and Ajna Centers, I can speak of my own experience as I struggle with traditional meditation methods. To be able to quiet my mind, I must lie down so that those two centers can stop creating so much activity in my mind, as they become inactive when lying down flat. This allows dreaming, possibility, and openness without feeling the need to act.

Undefined/Open ~ 70 Percent of People

The undefined Head Center takes in and amplifies all the defined Head Center energy in the classroom which can feel too stimulating. This can look like a child with what we label as ADD, unable to focus on anything for too long. Remember, this is a pressure center that's trying to sort the information coming in and having twenty-five other students amplifying it can feel very overwhelming. They feel under pressure to have new ideas and to be inspiring.

These children can be inquisitive and interested in learning, especially with Gate 61 defined. They want to know "Why?" about everything and are extremely curious about new things. They may struggle with sticking with one thing at a time (especially if they are a Manifesting Generator as well) so if they can't focus, consider the environment they are in. Do they work better alone in their room? Or perhaps sitting at the dining room table? When in a classroom, are there particular kids that they can focus better with? Hearing all the commotions around them can be stimulating too, so a pair of noise-canceling headphones can help to block out noise when it's time to work.

Their openness in this center amplifies the inspiration they take in from those around them and can lead to incredible insights and wisdom. However, because there is so much coming in when they're around other people, it can lead them to get stuck trying to answer questions or fulfill inspirations that aren't meant for them.

It takes time for them to learn whose questions they are trying to answer and experience. When they can learn to let go of the pressure to answer the questions, they can gain so much wisdom about all the inspirations and questions and realize that they do not have to find the answers to all the questions. They can just observe them, learn from them, and move on to experience the next inspiring person. They need to listen to their Authority for what is theirs to respond to.

A young child is often filled with inspiration; get curious with them. Help them to learn that all the ideas they get inspired by are fun ideas, but not all are for them to act upon. You can even plant the seed of "I wonder who they're meant for?" If you see a manifestation of their idea later on, remind them by saying something like "You told me about an idea that was just like that a week ago!" So that they begin to learn that not all ideas swirling around are for them to act on but are fun to experience and see what's there and how other people can bring them to life too.

The child with a completely open Head Center doesn't have a consistent way of taking in the information they receive and can feel immense pressure to do something with the pressure they feel. They may constantly tell you about all the great ideas they have, and they may appear to be all over the place with their ideas. Help them lean into their Strategy and Authority to know which ones are for them to act on, and which are just fun to watch pass by like clouds in the sky.

Head Gates and Learning Styles

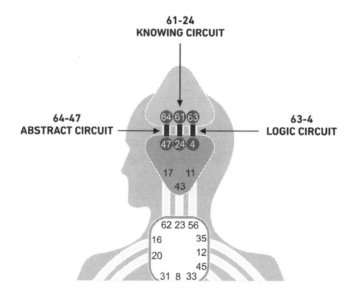

HEAD CENTER CHANNELS

Channel 64-47 - This channel is part of the Abstract Circuit and takes in a considerable amount of information but struggles with order. Kind of like someone is giving you a Lego set without directions. Children with this configuration in their chart tend to be more right-brained and can have a more challenging time with the standard linear, logical school system. A child with this channel might take more effective notes in a Mind Mapping style rather than sequentially.

Channel 61-24 - This channel is part of the Knowing Circuit. Children with this channel will just know things. They will know that they know, but they don't always know *how* they know when you ask them. These kids can be very curious and ask all the *why* questions. These kids are learning in their way, and again the standard school system doesn't always support their learning style best. These kids can probably learn to do complex math equations but not tell you the formula; they just know. They are just taking it all in and might not even take notes or do their homework and can ace the test.

Channel 63-4 - This channel is in the Logic Circuit and is the type of mental processing that the standard school system is built upon. Children who have this and much of the other Logical Circuitry in their chart usually do very well with the way the school system is set up. It's linear, logical, and sequential. These kids may have an easier time with standardized tests. Their note taking is likely more linear and sequential.

*Note - I want to make it very clear here that one of these is not *better* than another. Each is just different and can play a part in how your child learns. If your child has struggled with learning in the standard school system, these channels may help to provide insight into how you can support them best in their learning. These are also just a small part of the chart, so there may be many other factors at play when considering learning style and behavior.

An Invitation

As a parent, if you have a defined Head Center, sitting with your undefined/open Head Center child while they do homework may help them get inspired to write that story that they have been stuck on for the last two days, and you've been reminding them to finish. Rather than hearing an "I know, I will!" or some similar phrase, they may suddenly feel inspired. Or have them bring their writing into the kitchen while you prepare food or some similar tasks that allow them to benefit from being in your defined Head Center presence.

If you have an open Head Center and find yourself struggling to develop ideas or be inspired, take your work to a coffee shop or a communal area where there are other people. There will likely be people who either have a defined Head Center or gate definition that completes a channel in your chart giving you temporary definition. It might occasionally help your child find inspiration working in this type of environment as well.

The Conditioned Self-Talk of the Undefined Head Center

- I have to figure out the answers to everyone's questions.
- Who is inspiring?
- Where can I find the answers?
- I must find a way to be inspiring.

Empower Them by Helping Them Change Their Self-Talk to:

- I receive inspiration from everywhere, but I wait for the right timing to act.
- I don't have to answer all the questions. I can just watch them go by and see who acts on them.
- I don't have to be inspiring. I can be inspired.

Ajna Center

Awareness Center | Process and Store Information | Green in Color when Defined

The Ajna Center is one of three awareness centers and is where we process and store information.

Defined ~ 47 Percent of People

A child with a defined Ajna is confident in their thoughts and understanding of how things are. They have consistency and a familiar way of processing information, they enjoy researching, organizing, and processing information in a reliable way.

However, with a fixed way of thinking about things, they can get locked into a fixed way of thinking how something is and can have a hard time seeing it from another perspective. If you've ever had a conversation with someone with a fixed point of view who *struggles to see* another side of things, you may have been talking with someone with a defined Ajna Center. For example, a child with a defined Ajna who learned math with one method can struggle to learn a new method of processing the same problem. Once they figure out or conclude how something is, they can hold fast to it unless you challenge them in a way that opens their minds to another possibility.

This consistent way of thinking is helpful because once they process how something works, when they encounter that thing again, they don't have to spend a lot of mental energy on processing it; they already know. They can have great systems for getting things done, but if something new is added, it may throw them off for a beat or two while figuring out how they will process and integrate it. Once they've decided how something is, have done the research and work of figuring it out, they can rely on that and not go back to look at it in depth again until it's challenged.

Undefined ~ 53 Percent of People

An undefined Ajna Center is open to new ideas, answers, opinions, possibilities, and concepts. These are the dreamers who see all kinds of possibilities bringing new thoughts and ideas into the world and putting them together with old beliefs or thoughts. They are taking in new information and are not designed to be certain of or rigid about anything. This uncertainty is their gift; they stay open to the possibilities and stay curious about what is possible without falling victim to the societal conditioning of being "certain" about their ideas. The fear that can live in this center is about *not* being certain, so they can double down on ideas they feel like they *need* to be certain of, which can block them from new possibilities.

When these kids are operating correctly for their design, it may sometimes look like they don't know how they think about anything or change their minds a lot. Please use caution to not teach them to pretend to be sure. Let them grow up taking in new information and trying it on, rather than getting stuck in dogmatic ways of thinking because society tells them they must be sure. Let these little dreamers grow up to be open to being wrong. Help keep them humble, honest, and truthful, living in their design. They don't have to try hard to be sure or "smart." They already are! And working with their design will give them confidence that not being dogmatic or certain is a gift.

If your child has a completely open Ajna, they will, by design, have an open Head Center too. They are designed to be open to inspiration and ideas and not get stuck trying to be certain about any way of thinking. They can be great thinkers who find new ways of interpreting information, processing thoughts and concepts leading us to new insights that those with more fixed minds might never reach. We all have a part to play in the game of life. We need the dreamers who show us what's possible and we also need the people who help ground us in what already is known or is reliable.

An Invitation

This center can present difficulty in communicating and understanding one another. Saying it louder doesn't make it any clearer so let's talk about how these defined and undefined/open combinations work in parenting.

Parent and Child with Defined Ajna

If a parent or caregiver has a fixed way of thinking about things and a child also does, you may find that you get frustrated in communicating with one another, or you may think very similarly. If you both have the same defined channel(s) between your Head and Ajna Centers, you will likely communicate more easily; however, different channels for each of you can put you in different Circuitry and present difficulties communicating. A possible learning opportunity for you would be to take a step back when you feel you're both getting frustrated and try to see things from their perspective. As they get older, you can communicate that you need to consider the other's perspective and perhaps even take a break from one another to have some time to consider the other person's position. As the parent, you may have to work harder in those younger years to see things through their perspective. You get the gift of having your mind expanded and opened to new possibilities and your child receives the gift of feeling heard and understood.

Undefined and Defined Ajna Parenting

When a child or parent/caregiver has an open Ajna and the other a defined, the open Ajna can usually adapt to the line of thinking of the defined Ajna. One of you has an openness that allows you to receive what the other shares without getting stuck in your own fixed thinking. There is potential for conditioning here if the child has an open Ajna and the parent a defined Ajna because the parent has a fixed way of thinking, and the child will default to that way of processing information when they are around them. As long as they are around other people and adapting to new ways of thinking, this will just be one more flavor they get to experience.

The Conditioned Self-Talk of the Undefined/Open Ajna Center

- I said I was certain so I must not change my mind.
- I must pretend to be certain.
- I must make order out of this chaos swirling through my brain.
- I don't want to share because people won't understand me.
- I must figure out the answers.

Empower Them by Helping Them Change their Self-Talk to:

- I am open to receiving new information and changing my mind.
- I don't have to be dogmatic in my thinking.
- I can share my thoughts with others when I've been invited to share.
- I don't have to answer all the questions.

Throat Center

Manifestation and Communication Center | Brown in Color when Defined

Manifestation is a Noun, Not a Verb

Before we go any further, let's clear up what manifestation means in Human Design. Manifestation is a big word thrown around in the self-help world at this time. It is implied that if you want something, you can manifest it by visualizing it or making it happen because you *wish* it to happen, which comes from the conditioned mind. Manifestation seems to currently be this idea that if you can think it up, you can dream it into being in the following X number of days, weeks, or months. It's this idea that you can just go make it happen. This sounds great, but if you are first creating something from the mind and then trying to force it to happen, it won't. Not to say that you can't make *something* happen. It just might not be what you'd hoped, and it won't be built on a solid foundation.

To manifest in Human Design is to align with your energy type's Strategy and Authority and wait for the right timing to respond, and what happens next is the manifestation of that. This is true for *all* energy types. Listen to your Strategy and Authority to know how you are designed to manifest.

The Voices of the Throat Center

Each of the eleven gates that come out of the Throat Center has a unique voice, and if you pay attention, you will hear them from your children and maybe even yourself.

Remember that the Ajna is about thoughts, answers, ideas, concepts, opinions, and anxieties. The ESP is about emotions, moods, feelings, desires, food, romance, passion, and nervousness. The G Center is about love, direction, and identity, and the Spleen is related to instinct, the immune system, intuition, survival, and fears.

(AJNA) Gate 62 - I think/I don't think

(AJNA) Gate 23 - I know/I don't know

(AJNA) Gate 56 - I believe/I don't believe

(ESP) Gate 35 - I feel and usually like a change

(ESP) Gate 12 - I know I can try if I'm in the mood

(ESP) Gate 45 - I have, or I don't have

(G Center) Gate 33 - I remember/I don't remember

(G Center) Gate 8 - I know I can make a contribution or not

(G Center) Gate 31 - I lead or not

(SPLEEN) Gate 20 - I am now or not

(SPLEEN) Gate 16 - I experiment or not

Defined ~ 72 Percent of People
Defined Throat Center with a Motor Connection

The connection of a motor center to the Throat Center in Human Design for a Manifestor allows them to act without the support of anyone else once they respond to their inner creative drive. The Manifesting Generator can act on their own with their motor connected to the Throat Center but *only* after they have *responded* to an external cue, such as an offer to join a team, start a project, take a job, begin a friendship, and so forth.

Defined Throat Center Without a Motor Connection

Generators must respond to something with their Sacral (and wait for emotional clarity if that is their Authority) before taking action.

Projectors will never have a motor connected to the Throat Center, so they will need to wait for the right timing to take action, even if they have a defined Throat Center.

A child with a defined Throat Center and without a motor connected to it has more ability to be heard than a child with an undefined Throat; however, they must wait for the right timing or an invitation to be heard. The gates that come out of the Throat Center all have different voices, which is helpful for you to know, as the places where your child has a defined gate in the Throat Center will help you understand more about them when they speak.

It's not fair to expect these kids to speak up for themselves when they really can't be heard. They need you to help facilitate the invitations to speak. Invite them, give them something to respond to so they can share their voice whether they are a Projector or Generator.

A channel connected to the Throat Center will communicate from the center it is connected to. For example, the 57-20 communicates about needs/safety/fears and has the voice of "I Am." Channels 12-22 connecting to the ESP is communicating their emotions and feelings and has the voice of "I know I can try if I'm in the mood."

A Throat Center that is undefined but has hanging gates (a gate definition in a center without the full channel defined) will have common themes that they communicate through, and they may unconsciously seek others who complete those channels to get their voices heard. This unconscious aspect pulls them toward certain people more naturally, as the energy tries to get to the Throat Center where it can communicate the energy it carries. You may notice that your child communicates better with your partner or grandparent than they do with you. Remember that this is not personal. It is a mechanical aspect in action and has nothing to do with them wanting to share more with grandma than they do with you. There is just a natural flow of energy when they connect, and they spontaneously start talking when they're together. Rather than feeling left out and forcing your child to communicate with you more, spend some time debriefing after they come back from grandma's house and find out from grandma what they've been chatting about. This can be helpful if you know something is bothering them, but they don't share it with you. As they get older, you'll need to make sure that you're not pushing the boundaries of trust between the three of you, or they may find someone else to talk to. Follow Strategy and Authority to know when to communicate and manifest.

Non-motorized defined throats have a consistent way of communicating and sharing from any center(s) they are connected to, but they cannot initiate an action like a Manifestor and need to wait for the right timing to communicate so they will be heard.

Manifestor Defined Throat Center

A Manifestor child can speak what they want, and even if they speak it quietly, they have a voice that others listen to. They have the power to get attention and be heard, which can feel a bit disarming if it comes from the youngest family member in the home. Remember, Manifestors don't need anyone to initiate and can take action all on their own.

Undefined ~ 28 Percent of People

The undefined Throat Center in a child is often begging to be heard, especially if they are in a big family. They can be the noisemakers, goofs, or just talk over others. They may say inappropriate things or things at the wrong time trying to draw attention to themselves to be heard. They may also start trying to rehearse what they are going to say beforehand and when they do have the chance to speak come off sounding strange or disjointed. I have also noticed that the more openness the Throat Center has, the more they need for other people to slow down and give them space to get their thoughts and words out or they can easily become frustrated. This can be amplified if they also have a lot of open centers in their chart or are a triple or quadruple split definition. (More on split definitions in Chapter Ten.)

Story of an Undefined Throat Center

When my undefined Throat Center Projector was two years old, I took her to the doctor for a well-child exam. While the doctor was washing her hands upon entering the room, she began asking questions about my child and asked if she was speaking in two to three-word sentences yet, and she looked up, pointed to the doctor, and said "I want to wash my hands too mom!" She was also the child who was very clear about when she didn't want to do something. She would say in response to something like, "Do you want a banana?" "No, I don't want a banana, I do not, I don't."

Open Throat Center

A completely open Throat Center is rare, but if your child has one and they don't know it, or you don't know it, they can have a difficult time feeling seen and heard in a family or with friends and peer groups. Because there is no motor or other center connected to the Throat Center (and there are no hanging gates either), it's harder to make the connection for their voice to be heard. They are often surprised by what comes out of their mouths which can be a source of pain at times as they blurt out the wrong thing at the wrong time in front of the wrong people, but once they learn to follow their Strategy and Authority, they can be the people in the room who say the most profound and interesting things.

I have a child with a completely open Throat Center who is a social butterfly wanting to always be around people and included, and I can't tell you how many times her feelings have been stepped all over because her friends didn't hear her, and she then felt excluded. These open Throat Center children can also have their ideas stolen when they try to speak up in a group and haven't been invited to share ideas. The people around them hear the ideas, and as the ideas filter into their Heads and Ajnas, they say, "I have an idea!" And repeat what the open Throat child just spoke, often receiving credit for the idea, though unintentional.

These kids can be great at mimicking others and picking up a language, or the cadence of others' speech. They can be great singers and actors and adapt to different voices well. They are great at amplifying the voice of others.

Some kids with undefined or open Throat Centers can talk quite early, while others delay talking until later than average.

Taking Time for the Open/Undefined Throat Center to be Heard

Children with an open or undefined Throat Center build up a lot of energy in the Throat Center during the day as they take in all of the defined Throat Center energy around them. At the end of the day, these are the kids who just want to talk and talk and talk, especially right before bedtime. They need a way to discharge the energy they've built up in the Throat Center, and you might find that right before bedtime is not the most convenient or your most patient time to hear all their stories. Try setting aside ten minutes once or twice earlier in the day so that they have a chance to speak and be heard, releasing the energy that's been building up in their Throat Center, especially after they get home from school.

When the Open/Undefined Throat Center Forces Their Voice

When these children try to force their voices louder to be heard, they can create hoarseness and even thyroid issues, especially if this is a pattern they learn when they are young and carry into adulthood. These kids can become class clowns or the most auditorily disturbing because they are trying to get attention. Despite all the advice to avoid giving attention to bad behavior, these kids are looking for a way to be heard, and if you can give them an outlet, the behavior can change.

Whatever the Throat Center is connected to will tell you from where they speak. If the Throat Center is connected to the ESP, then they will speak about their feelings. If connected to the Ajna, then they speak about their thoughts. The G Center will speak about who they are deep within their soul, so be gentle with what they share because it's the heart of them, and these kids wear their hearts on their sleeves. The Spleen will speak about its fears, instincts, and what it senses in itself or others. The Will Center will speak about what it wants or has. The Sacral Center will speak about what it's going to do.

An Invitation

If you are a parent with an undefined/open and non-motorized Throat Center, and you have a child with a defined and motorized Throat Center, your child can talk right over you, overpowering the conversation. You may need to find something to get your child's attention when you talk, like shuffling cards, juggling, dancing, or other high-energy or distracting activities.

As a parent with an undefined Throat Center, you must also make your actions match your words when speaking, parenting, and being listened to. Walk your talk, parents.

The Conditioned Self-Talk of the Undefined/Open Throat Center
- Who can give me the attention that I want?
- Why isn't anyone listening to me? What can I do to get attention?
- Why should I bother saying anything at all, no one is going to listen?
- I feel so much pressure to say something, I'll just talk about the first thing that comes to mind, even if it's not the right time or is inappropriate. (This one might not even be a conscious thought.)

Empower Them by Helping Them Change their Self-Talk to:
- I will wait to share the right information at the right time.
- I don't need to act out to get attention. I will be able to share when the timing is right.
- When I do have an invitation to speak/share people will hear me.
- My thoughts, feelings, and instincts are important, and I will be invited to share when the timing is right; I don't need to force anything.

G Center

Identity | Self-love | Direction | Yellow in Color when Defined

We are not here to be loved but to BE love.

~RA URU HU

Defined ~ 57 Percent of People

These kids have a strong sense of who they are and are here to show others that love is a verb. This love is different from romantic love; it is the embodiment of love. It is a path to acceptance of differences. This kind of love guides them through their life as they travel in a direction that feels set. They may not know how they'll get there, but they know who they are and what they want. When they embrace who they are they will be led to where they need to be for their life to unfold.

The defined G Center, when in alignment, feels secure in their lovability and can love others without having to attach their identity to being connected to another person. They are a source of love and direction for others. A bit of the live-and-let-live mentality when they are aligned, but when they are not, they can have difficulty understanding why everyone doesn't follow their direction. When they follow their own path, others with undefined G Centers get to experience their identity and direction through them. This direction they provide is not through the defined G Center telling others what to do or how to be, but rather influencing them through just living their aligned life.

Their life direction cannot be easily changed or controlled, so when they have people with undefined or open G Centers around them, those people can jump into the defined G's life and align with the journey while together. However, another defined G Center may have a different trajectory and they may experience more conflict in the relationship and need to learn to allow one another the space to follow those paths or part ways. Following Strategy and Authority will help them to know if it is correct for them to travel this path beside one another or not.

In contrast, the undefined/open G Center is influenced by the people they're around. The ability of a person with a defined G Center to lock into a direction and stick with it can be inspiring to those with an undefined/open G who often struggle through conditioning to feel like they should be able to pick a direction or identity and stick with it. They need to remember that they are not designed that way.

Though the defined G Center can easily follow their own direction, they may not always know exactly where it will take them. They anchor into the truth of who they are as they navigate life, and they can help others with an open G Center who feel directionless, through their deep connection to this center.

Their way of giving and receiving love may be more fixed depending on what gates are defined in their G Center. If you look at their defined G Center, look at the themes below and see if you notice the way your child shows and accepts love. Then, consider how this may affect their love language and how you show them love as well as how they receive love from the world and everyone around them.

Kids with a defined G Center connected through a channel to the Throat Center (the 7-31, 1-8 or 13-33) speak from the soul of who they are and worry that they will not be fully accepted. When they share their identity with you, use extra care as words can cut them deeply if it feels like criticism of who they are at their core.

Gate 7 - This is a child that can look to the future and see the direction humanity is taking and see how it can be corrected. This child may be influential, but this gate is not about leading from a place of power, but more of the assistant to the one in charge leading indirectly. Does your child have this gate? Have you noticed them leading the family without telling everyone what to do? Leading by example?

Gate 1 - This is a deeply creative gate and those with this defined have a unique ability to express themselves and their individuality authentically. They march to the beat of their own drum. For example, just because everyone else is wearing skinny jeans doesn't make them want a pair; it probably makes the style less interesting to them, and they'll look for something completely different and start a new trend by just being themselves and wearing something like bell-bottoms instead.

Gate 13 - A child with this gate can be described as an old soul because they are good at listening to the stories of people. People tend to tell them things that they don't readily tell other people. They collect and remember the things that are important to them and learn to share what is relevant to their community when the time is right. They must learn that things told to them in confidence are not to be shared freely as they've been entrusted with someone's thoughts and feelings.

Gate 25 - Universal love. Being loving toward and seeing the world in a way that everything deserves to be cherished. This is a love that can influence and change others and be very innocent despite the circumstances. These kids can be drawn to experiences that lead them to test their faith and deepen their connection to Spirit, becoming an example to the world and empowering them on their journey.

Gate 46 - Love of the body. This is a love of discovering the beauty of every BODY. This child may be the one to appreciate in you what you do not see yourself. They may also struggle with their own body, trying to make it conform to societal pressures rather than embrace the beautiful body that they live in, and allow their physical form in this life to be the vehicle for their soul.

Gate 2 - This gate is about an innate sense of direction that pulls you onto your life path. It's deeper than what can be controlled through willpower. The challenge is to let go of control and allow life to unfold. This child can empower others in finding their direction and resources for their journey. These kids, when aligned, have faith that the support they need will show up when they open themselves to allow the process to unfold.

Gate 15 - This gate is about having a love for humanity and accepting people for who they are. These kids can have their own rhythm and not have a fixed, consistent pattern to their daily life and embrace many changes in routine, which may appear more erratic from the outside. As parents, if you have Gate 5 (the other half of this channel), you are more fixated on routines and rituals, while a child with Gate 15 will feel more erratic. Your challenge is to learn to embrace their rhythm while still honoring your process. Those who have Gate 15 defined are more open to accepting the many different routines and rhythms of others and need you to accept that in them. They may need your support to maintain direction and focus while completing tasks.

Gate 10 - To love being alive as yourself, is the ultimate expression of self-love. When you live authentically as yourself, you empower others to do the same. Kids with this gate defined can express themselves and live authentically; however, it can shut down self-love if this is criticized. If your child has this gate defined, they show you what it means to love yourself and how to embrace who you are. How can you show them you appreciate their unique expression of themselves? This gate is a place where self-love lives and if a child does not have a high sense of self-love, the low expression of this gate, which is self-criticism, can be hard on the person who carries this energy. If this gate is connected to Gate 20 in the Throat Center, it can share either words of high or low self-love with others. In short, they can verbally hurt others when they do not feel a high sense of self-love. This connection can also happen between two people in a family and cause them to say hurtful things to one another that they deeply regret later. If this is the case for your family, focus on improving feelings of self-love rather than putting the focus on the hurtful things that are said out of low expressions of self-love.

Undefined ~ 43 Percent of People

When this center is open, a child will be very influenced by their surroundings, both people and places. If a child does not feel good in their environment, they will not be settled and content. It is very important to them that the place they are in feels right. If you're planning a move and have an open G Center child, it would be wise to take them to the potential home where you are moving to get a sense of it first and ask them how they feel there. If they don't feel good and you have other options, it might make life better for everyone if you keep looking. Sometimes just moving the furniture will be enough or letting them choose their room first. These kids are also the ones who move their furniture around in their rooms and may even want to move the common area furniture to feel settled. Environment is everything to them.

This child can morph into whatever peer group they are hanging around. It's not that they don't know what they like, but instead, they are designed to have the freedom to adapt to their surroundings and try lots of different things on. If you don't like what you see happening with your open G Center child, look around to their friends and get to know them. I would bet you'll find they are the reason your child is changing.

You can help them understand that they don't have to lock onto any one identity: an artist, a writer, a builder, a gymnast, a football player, etc. Those can all be things that they do, but it is not their identity. They can try on many identities in life, what fun!

If you have an open G Center child and they go to a birthday party at a place they've never been before, they may have been bouncing out of their seat excited for the party on the ride there, but once they walk in, if it doesn't feel right, might beg you to stay with them or let them leave. If they stay and are not comfortable, it won't be fun for them so pay attention as this reaction is more than just separation anxiety.

With an open G Center, this is someone who has an unlimited ability to experience what love is like and can shift life directions easily if it feels good to them. Sometimes for the open G, having no direction *is* their direction–moving from thing to thing, place to place, and experiencing lots of people, places, and types of love. If they choose to lock into an identity, it is by choice.

Because they can easily adapt to the people they are around, they can take on lots of different styles, interests, hobbies and make friends with lots of different types of people. Each different group of people with whom they are friends would probably even describe them differently as they all know different versions of this person. This is not manipulation but rather a chameleon-like ability to blend in and get along with many different people. It is important for them to accept this as who they are and not try and lock into an identity that isn't theirs for the sake of "knowing who they are" or being "something." They need to know that they are designed to be flexible, adaptable, lovable, and can navigate the world in a way that feels right to them and that the right people and opportunities will show up when they do.

These are kids who may struggle in school if they do not feel comfortable with where their desk is, who they sit next to, or even the location of their classroom. It may not be an issue with the teacher or a child that is driving the conflict or struggle, but sometimes changing the classroom will shift their relationships with the people or environment which were previously a struggle.

As teenagers, you can tell a lot about who they are spending time with by how they act, how they dress, and what they are into because they will adapt to their circle of friends.

The Conditioned Self-Talk of the Undefined/Open G Center

- I need to figure out where I'm going in life.
- I need to find someone to love me.
- Am I lovable?
- I need a direction.
- What am I even doing with my life?

Empower Them by Helping Them Change Their Self-Talk to:

- – I am open to experiencing lots of different people.
- – I am open to feeling many kinds of love.
- – My life's direction is fluid, and I can embrace not knowing where it will take me.
- – I can trust when I feel like an environment is not right for me.

Spleen Center

Awareness Center | Fears | Intuition | Instinct | Brown in Color When Defined

The Spleen Center is the oldest center in the Human Design Chart and is centered around survival instinct and, therefore, an indicator for immune health, instincts, and safety. Like the immune system, it constantly scans for threats and can become overactive.

When the Spleen Center becomes overactive, the survival instincts of this center can become overzealous, and your child can experience repeating fears that create themes you notice as a parent. Similar to how watching a movie that feels scary to a child can create an inability for them to sleep with the lights off, the Splenic awareness can remain too alert, creating fear patterns and limiting beliefs in all areas of life. The chart below depicts the fears of each gate and how you can help your child reframe them as they come up and shift from fear to awareness.

FEARS of the Spleen Center

Gate 48 - *The fear of inadequacy* can be turned into "I can sense when I need to know more and can take action to learn what I need to know. I also know that I'll know what I need to know when I need to know it."

Gate 57 - *The fear of the future* can be turned into "I can sense that change is coming, and I don't need to fear it. I can use my senses to take any action necessary to prepare when the time is right."

Gate 44 - *The fear of the past* can be turned into "I have had this experience before, have learned from it and will navigate this situation with what I've learned. I can sense what I need to move forward."

Gate 50 - *The fear of responsibility (for others)* can be turned into "I can sense when someone is hurting and needs support, but I am not required to rescue anyone."

Gate 32 - *The fear of failure* can be turned into "I don't need to fear failure because when I trust in the right timing, I will know when the time is right for me to take action. Whatever happens, when I try, I learn."

Gate 28 - *The fear of death* can be turned into "Life is an adventure, and some adventures teach me to know what's worth standing up for. I know when to take action and when it's worth struggling for, and when to quit."

Gate 18 - *The fear of authority* can be turned into "I can see where patterns need correcting, but I will wait to be invited to share what I know so that it can be helpful to others."

Defined ~ 53 Percent of People

People with a defined Spleen Center, may be more likely to have a strong immune system and get sick infrequently, however when they do get sick it can be significant. With their strong immune system, they do not as easily pick up on the nuances that tell them something is off until they can't ignore it anymore.

If you have a child with a defined Spleen Center, they have an innate sense of timing and are more likely to arrive places, such as school, on time.

People with a defined Spleen Center have consistent ways of connecting with their intuition in one or more specific ways. Their intuition may be sensed through an innate knowing, a sense, smell, sound, vision, etc., that gives them clues into what is off, harmful, or not working. If your child has a defined Spleen Center, listen to the phrases they use to describe when something is bothering them that they can't specify. For example, they may say things like, "I just know they don't like me"(knowing). Without a specific reason, it may be tempting to say something in response that overrides their knowing because we don't want our child(ren) to feel like someone doesn't like them. But are we doing them any favors by telling them not to listen to the intuition that tells them this person is not for them or doesn't feel safe around them? This is an opportunity to help them trust their intuition and for you to understand more about what is happening. Ask your Sacral energy types yes/no questions and ask the non-Sacral energy types open-ended questions when navigating this.

Undefined ~ 47 Percent of People

Children with undefined Spleen Centers take in the immune energy around them and amplify it. If not aware of this difference, your child may sense the illnesses of people around them and begin to think they themselves are unwell or that they have the same condition. These children have more sensitive (but not weak) immune systems and can be much more sensitive to medications and even supplements. Due to their sensitivity, you may learn to request the lowest possible effective dose of medication, should they need it, or ask to titrate up to the optimal dose depending on the medication, which is a conversation for you to have with their medical provider. Don't alter prescribed meditations on your own but communicate with your child's medical provider if you have concerns about potential reactions. Sometimes as parents, you may keep quiet when you think someone else is more educated than you, but you are the one who is with your child every day and knows them best. If your intuition says something doesn't sound right, don't be afraid to ask questions.

As they get older, if they decide to experiment with drugs or alcohol, they are likely to be more sensitive to it.

Easily sensing that something is off, the child with an open Spleen Center can become wise about others' health and safety as well as their own, which can grow to be one of their superpowers and lead them to have a healthier life. They can grow up to become gifted contributors in the healing arts, easily reading the other person, and getting a sense of what is going on with them. You may find them to be the children who instinctively know when you're not feeling well and curl up with you to snuggle, or just know that you need a slower-paced day.

These children may seem much more sensitive than other kids in general and may feel unwell more frequently and be clingier than other kids to a parent or other child with the defined Spleen Center. They can be the kids who don't want to go to school and leave their parents all day, especially if they've been home with a parent or grandparent until they start school. They can also have a more challenging time letting go of things or people, even if it's not good for them to keep hanging on.

The undefined Spleen Center can have more consistent themes of how they receive their intuition based on the gate activations in that center.

In contrast to the kids with defined Spleen Centers who can more easily keep track of time, these kids can lose track of or misgauge time causing you to panic when they aren't where you told them to be. Of course, the flip side to this is that they could be the child with forty-seven alarms on their phone, so they don't forget things, causing them to become hyper-aware of the time due to being reprimanded for being late.

Open Spleen Center (No Gate Activations)

The child with the open Spleen Center is more open to conditioning through this center. However, without any gate activations, all energy they experience in this center is inconsistent and variable depending on who they are with and the planetary transits.

The open (no gate activations) Spleen child can be highly intuitive. Their way of intuiting can change depending on who they are with, so the way they receive information is not as consistent as a child with a defined Spleen Center.

Intuition in the Spleen Center

The Spleen Center is scanning for threats constantly as a cat in the wild would. And because the perception is constantly shifting depending on what it senses, it does not repeat information. Their knowing, gleaned from listening to the Splenic awareness, is in the moment and not repeated, so it's important to listen carefully. Even if this is not the Authority in the chart, it is still an awareness center that can be an additional source of information. If they have an Emotional or Sacral Authority, then you must also get clarity in those centers before taking action. If the Spleen Center were a news station, it would be the reporter pitching ideas, and the Authority is the editor telling them when to run with the story. If you miss the story, it's too late to circle back and try to find it because time has moved on, and that story is no longer relevant.

I have heard many stories from parents who said that their child told them something felt wrong about a place or a person, and because of their age and what the parent thought they knew of the situation or person, they sent them back into the situation. When information later came to light, they wished they had listened to their child's instincts. Children are never too young to have intuitive awareness, but people and time condition it out of them. The more you can allow your child the gift of listening to their fears and their senses, the more you can help them to trust their knowing.

An Invitation

Children (and adults) with undefined/open Spleen Centers are drawn to people with defined Spleen Centers because they feel like safety and security to them. If you have a defined Spleen Center and your child has it undefined/open, they may want to be near you all the time, which can be a little frustrating when you need a break, and your child only wants to be with you. And if your child has a defined Spleen Center and yours is undefined/open, you may find yourself going to them, wanting a hug, or being near them when you don't feel well or need a feeling of safety. Additionally, if you have one child with an undefined/open Spleen Center and another with a defined Spleen Center, you may see this relationship dynamic play out between them too.

If you're a parent with an undefined or open Spleen Center, consider this: What are you holding onto that is no longer serving you? Do you have a child with a defined Spleen Center and struggle to let them become more independent? Are you holding them back through your conditioning or fears?

Parents with open Spleen Centers can sometimes find themselves in relationships that are not healthy: Their partner does not treat them well or abuses them. If this is you, and you know that this partner is no good for you, but you keep going back to them, I would invite you to run charts for you both and see if this defined/undefined Spleen dynamic exists within your relationship. The feeling of safety that a defined Spleen Center gives to an undefined/open Spleen Center can be so strong that leaving feels impossible. I want you to know that you are worthy of being treated well. Your children are worthy of being treated well, and your partner needs to do their own work in therapy to understand the wounding that has led them to this behavior.

A child with an undefined Spleen Center raised by an abusive parent with a defined center can easily grow up to unconsciously seek a partner who treats them the way the parent did. But, when you have the courage and ability to break that cycle, you can stop it from affecting future generations as well as heal the relationship with your parents, by doing personal growth work. Can you imagine the legacy you leave for your family?

When you can see the energetics at work, you can begin forgiving yourself for accepting behavior that you know is unhealthy or wrong. You are worthy of and deserve healthy relationships.

The Conditioned Self-Talk of the Undefined/Open Spleen Center

- I need that person/thing.
- I am scared that...
- I think I have (medical condition).
- I am not good enough to...
- I can't trust my inner knowing.

Empower Them by Helping Them Change Their Self-Talk to:

- I know things and I don't have to explain how I know them. Knowing I know, is enough for me.
- In every fear there is potential for wisdom and insight.
- I can trust my instincts.
- I can sense when others might need support.

Sacral Center

Motor Center | Vitality | Lifeforce Energy | Workforce Energy

Defined ~ 70 Percent of People

The defined Sacral Center is a powerhouse of a motor and an Authority for a lot of people. This center, when defined, gives them access to seemingly limitless energy. These kids are your Energizer Bunnies going all day long, climbing everything, building, moving, and on the go! Because this energy is so renewable and powerful, you'll need to drain your little Energizer Bunny's battery every day so they can power down for sleep. If they don't get enough exercise, they can have a hard time getting to sleep, staying asleep, and may then wake up feeling tired and cranky the next day. If they're in school, it can show up as an inability to pay attention in class or acting out. Plenty of physical exercise is a basic need for these kids (and adults too).

These kids can grow to be people who do all the grunt work if we do not teach them to learn to commit to the work their Sacral responds to and say no to the things it does not. Remember back in the Authorities Chapter, I mentioned the Sacral Center responds to yes/no uh-huh/unh-uh sounds? If not, no worries, just take a quick trip back to Chapter Six to review, or to the Appendix for details on how to ask Sacral response questions. It's important. What these kids are saying yes to with their Sacral sounds is an agreement for how they are going to use their energy. If they put their energy into work that they don't love, it dims their light and can lower their energy in an unhealthy way. They will still have the energy to keep going, but you'll watch the magic, sparkle, wonder, and awe dim within them. This can go on all their lives. You probably know plenty of these people who have been taught to do the work that needs to be done, even if they despise it. They'll do the work, but there isn't much joy left because they must force their energy into it. If you teach these kids to follow what their Sacral response tells them to do, they can grow up having a strong sense of where to find work they would enjoy. It doesn't mean that their work will always be their life's purpose (sometimes that happens, but that's not necessarily what we're aiming for). We want them to find work that they feel good about putting their energy into. If their life's work is not in the job they do to pay the bills, they have the energy left over at the end of the day for their passion project, creating, volunteering, or whatever makes them feel whole and alive in the world.

When these Sacral defined kids say yes with their Sacral response, they are saying, "YES! I want to put my energy into this job/project/art" or whatever they're responding to.

Undefined ~ 30 Percent of People

The undefined Sacral Center kids are the Manifestors, Projectors, and Reflectors. They need to approach things differently than the Generators and Manifesting Generators because their energy fluctuates. They do not have a consistent source of workforce and lifeforce energy and need to listen to their Authority on what they choose to respond to. These kids do not have the sustainable energy to keep doing a job that they do not like. Their energy is not well-suited for a typical 9-5, Monday to Friday job (at least not without some flexibility), so we need to help them from a very young age to understand what work/play/projects are correct for them. However, I want to make clear that any child can be anything, no matter their design energy type. How they approach what they do, determines how long they can do it, however. Former President Obama is a Projector and did a very high-stress job for eight straight years, and I'm sure he had systems in place to make sure he got the help and support he needed in his life to do so.

Non-Sacral energy kids take in and amplify the Sacral energy from the defined Sacral people around them and can temporarily look like super Generators. Even though they appear to have limitless energy when amplifying Sacral energy, they will hit a time in life where they can't continue in this way. It's important to teach them when they're young to find healthy sustainable work patterns to show them that they don't have to keep up with everyone else.

An Invitation

If your child is a Manifestor, Projector, or Reflector, they may be nappers, which is normal for their energy pattern. Please also make sure you check out Chapter Eleven on sleep as well because proper rest is super important to these kids.

Undefined Sacral children need to learn to use their Authority to understand what to respond to and invest their energy in and not to say yes because they think they have to. There is pressure on these kids who do not know when enough is enough to keep working. They may need you to step in when you recognize that they are pushing with their energy or over-committing and help them see that it's time to stop.

The Conditioned Self-Talk of the Undefined/Open Sacral Center

- I can't quit.
- I just need to push harder to get it all done.
- Why can't I keep up with everyone else?
- I feel like I should do more.

Empower Them by Helping Them Change their Self-Talk to:
- I don't have to keep up with other people.
- I honor when my body needs rest.
- I know when I can use the borrowed Sacral energy of others for the short term, but I don't rely on it.
- What I can do is enough. I trust my body to tell me when enough is enough.

Will Center

Willpower | Ego | Integrity | Self-Worth | Resources | Motor Center | Red in Color when Defined

If you have a child with a defined Will Center, you'll want to see who else in the house has this center defined. When there is a fight, the defined Will Center can always outlast and get in the last dig. If parent and child have defined Will Centers, the battle is a bit more even, but the parent must consider which battles are worth fighting.

Defined ~35 Percent of People

If a child has a defined Will Center and the parent does not, the child will be able to assert their willpower over the parent more easily and influence them. If the parent has a defined Will Center and the child is undefined/open, be conscious of when you use that willpower, so that you don't accidentally crush their spirit. Whoever has the defined Will Center will outlast the undefined/open Will Center because they have consistent willpower. If both parent and child have a defined Will Center, there can be considerable power struggles, but it won't break the other's spirit as easily as it can with a defined parent vs. undefined child.

These children care for their things and can seem possessive of them or not want to share. The desire to control and care for their resources is not for the sake of being materialistic or greedy. This center has Tribal Circuitry running through it and is about having access to resources to help the community more than it is to simply possess things. If you have a child with this center defined, consider how they behave with their resources and how the need to support their community with those resources may be expressing itself.

Parents need to help their children with defined Will Centers find an appropriate use of their power and empower them without allowing them to become bossy. The issues that arise can often be around things or people, like attention from parents. Appropriate use of power and feeling empowered is essential as these kids get older, so they don't feel disempowered and then try to assert their power with their parents or others as they become teens and beyond.

The Will Center has a pulsing rhythm and is not constantly on, so it works best if it powers through a period of commitment and then rests, and then powers through and rests. If a child with a defined Will Center continues to push with their willpower even when they're worn out, they will push themselves into burnout. It's a situation of just because you can, doesn't mean you should. As parents, we need to help them understand when their body needs a rest. If your child also has a defined Sacral Center, they can force their Sacral energy to keep working even after it's ready to quit. This is a great opportunity to ask them Sacral questions to see if it's time to stop and not push through with willpower. If they do not have a defined Sacral Center, then you really need to make sure they learn to *not* push through on their willpower when they need to rest.

Kids with a defined Will Center help others to feel empowered by just being in their presence. They may draw other people to them with this empowerment. However, they may find that their friends commit to things that they can't or don't want to commit to through their borrowed Will Center definition and later have difficulty keeping the commitment.

When people have a defined Will Center, others will expect them to follow through with what they commit to. If they commit to a task and do not follow through this may become damaging to their reputation as others expect them to do what they say they will do. If they can't follow through with a commitment, they need to quit correctly for their energy type and communicate that they cannot meet the expectation this time.

It can be difficult for children with a defined Will Center to realize that other people don't have this ability to commit to something and see it through. This can lead them to become disappointed with others with undefined Will Centers who are not designed to have consistent willpower and don't follow through in the same way they do.

Undefined/Open ~ 65 Percent of People

If your child has an undefined Will Center and you have a defined Will Center, then you need to understand that your words, threats, punishments, and promises all carry a lot more weight. If you say you're going to take them to the park tomorrow, you'd better mean it. If you put your foot down over a matter, it has more finality than a parent who has an undefined/open Will Center. It also means that when your child is with you, they will feel more easily able to commit to things like taking the dog for a walk daily, doing their laundry, mowing the lawn, etc., but once you leave and take your aura somewhere else, their willpower wanes, and they can't stick with that commitment so easily. This is not because they are lazy; they just don't have consistent access to willpower like you do and if they don't have a defined Sacral Center, they can slow down when on their own.

Someone with an undefined/open Will Center learns to be wise about who can keep their promises and follow through. Because self-worth is found in this center, they can struggle to know what is valuable and often question their worth and try to prove their worth by doing for others or over-committing. When they fail to deliver (because they are not designed to have consistent willpower), they beat themselves up over not being worthy because they can't follow through. Your child can become conditioned here to try and prove their worth to you, their teacher, their coach, etc. Help them understand their worth is not connected to what they do or achieve. They are worthy just because they exist and do not have to prove it by how much they commit to or accomplish. How many adults do you know that are trying to prove their worth through all of the doing? Social media only exacerbates this issue as we compare ourselves to each other's curated profiles that only show what we want others to see.

An Invitation

Sixty-five percent of the population does not have a defined Will Center. Are you surprised? I was when I first learned of this. How many times a day do you hear statements like "If you want it badly enough, you'll find a way," "Just do it," or "Make it happen." Can you imagine if even half of the world understood that only 35 percent of us have the ability to exert willpower consistently? How would we work differently? Would we hold each other to different expectations? How would we have grace for the times when people couldn't follow through with their overarching commitments? How many times as a parent have you committed to something and then found you just lost steam? How many diets have you started and quit? It is not because you are not good enough. You're not designed to ride on willpower and never falter. How can you give yourself more grace around being a parent? What have you promised and then had fall through? Are you ready to let go of that self-punishment and find grace for yourself? I invite you to consider trying to say a phrase such as "I don't know. Let's see how I feel when it gets closer. When do you need to know by?" or "I'll try" rather than "Yes, I promise" when asked for a commitment from your child or anyone else.

The Conditioned Self-Talk of the Undefined Will Center

- I said I was going to do it, so I have to keep trying.
- I can't follow through with anything.
- I'm worthless.
- I have no willpower.

Empower Them by Helping Them Change their Self-Talk to:

- I am worthy just because I exist.
- I do not have to prove my worth to anyone.

- I can say I'll try rather than I promise, and it will be okay.
- I know my power.
- If I make a promise and then realize I can't do it, I will tell the person I cannot finish the commitment.

Emotional Solar Plexus Center (ESP)

Awareness Center | Feelings | Moods | Creativity | Passion | Desire | Brown in Color when Defined

If your child has a defined ESP, they will have one, two, or three types of emotional waves and experience emotional ups and downs that are a normal part of their lived experience. There are three types of waves that come from the ESP: Tribal, Individual, or Collective, which relate to the circuitry in the chart that they are a part of.

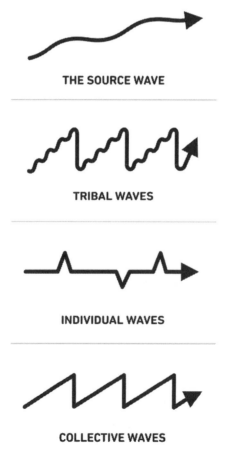

THE SOURCE WAVE

TRIBAL WAVES

INDIVIDUAL WAVES

COLLECTIVE WAVES

The Tribal Wave - Channels 37-40, 59-6, and 19-49

This emotional wave operates in a ratchet-type mechanism. It ratchets up one annoying or frustrating thing at a time until it explodes or reaches clarity and is reset before it begins building again. How long that ratchet action takes to explode is individual to the person. If you keep a journal or note it somewhere when the blow ups occur, you may see a pattern to better understand when that might happen, but you likely will notice your child has a shorter and shorter tolerance for things right before the explosion. This emotional wave responds to touch, so a gentle hand on the shoulder or offer of a hug may be able to diffuse the emotional ratcheting before it explodes if you notice it reaching its peak. Generally speaking, these children have a fairly balanced emotional appearance, unless something or someone affects their loved ones/tribe, then they can have a big emotional response. This ratcheting is also often related to a need that is not being met, whether it was communicated or not. These needs could include the need to feel loved, to feel heard, to be useful, to be left alone, to rest, etc. As a parent you can likely sense when your child is tired for example, though they often try to keep pushing and going until they crash or have an emotional outburst. If you can see that a meltdown is coming, try shifting them to an activity that allows them to recharge, especially if you have a non-Sacral emotionally defined child. Remember: because they take in and amplify all the Sacral energy around them (roughly 70 percent of people), they can have a hard time knowing when to quit and take a break.

Once the pressure builds to the point of eruption, the person with this wave just needs a little space to cool back down. Sometimes it's immediate, but there is often a bit of embarrassment or resentment that is felt after losing their cool. Give them a bit of time to sort out what just happened and then offer to talk about the situation. You can help them identify what their unmet needs are and help them learn how to ask for them to be met or to set a boundary so next time they don't have to explode to get their needs met. As an example, this wave is like the pressure building (ratcheting emotions) in the Instant Pot and then someone comes along and pops the pressure relief valve once the pot is fully pressurized. The pressure is released (emotional explosion), and eventually, you'll be able to open the lid, but you've just released steam all over the kitchen cabinets and probably even the ceiling. To make matters worse, you realize it was over-filled with tomato sauce, and you'll probably have some stuff to clean up after that (the emotional fallout of those around you).

I can speak from experience about this ratcheting, as I have the Channel 37-40. I can remember even as a child how I would tolerate things until suddenly, I wouldn't, and I'd explode. I'm a Leo, so I always thought it was the lion in me roaring. But now I also see through the lens of Human Design that this is the ratchet wave in action and that on the other side of the explosion, there is relief. The explosion can be followed by guilt, shame, or vulnerability, and immense relief from the pressure that had been building. Unfortunately for the undefined/open ESPs around me, when I exploded and felt relief, there was emotional fallout. Even though I would feel relief and reset, the effects would be felt by others for a while after, or they'd need to have space from me. As a child it was confusing because I felt relief and clear to start again, while those around me needed time or space before playing with me again.

As an adult I have noticed that if I am ratcheted high in my wave, and I snap at someone, if I have not waited for my wave to come back down to where I am ready to apologize or fix things between us, everything I say is still emotionally charged to the undefined ESP person. I've learned that some sort of emotional release, whether yelling into a pillow or putting on sad music and crying, can help. I've also found that for me, time alone, going for a walk, exercising, or just putting on music and staring at the wall can help as well to physically move the emotions. These things all allow me time to come back down from the height of that wave and to see clearly again.

I've had to learn through trial and error that the height of this wave is not a time to reply to emails, texts, or other requests unless absolutely necessary. Not only because what I say feels emotionally charged to the person receiving it, especially the undefined ESP, but because these things usually require a decision, and deciding in the moment while feeling emotionally charged does not lead to aligned decisions.

The Tribal Wave - The Source Wave – Channel 59-6

This wave is emotional energy related to caring and providing for the people you love and are bonded with the most. People with this wave generally do not appear emotional unless someone or something threatens the people they care most about.

If your child has this wave, you may see it show up, for example, when someone threatens or says something mean to their sibling, and they react aggressively to the threatening person. Another example of this wave is a parent who is very mellow and even tempered until someone or something threatens their child's safety and then they roar like a lion at the threatening person or thing.

The Collective Wave - Channels 36-35, and 41-30

This wave is a slow build where it begins at the low part of the wave, gradually climbs higher and higher based on desire or expectations, and then crashes when those expectations are not met. When the wave crashes, these people can spend time in the low of the wave before it begins building again. The length of this wave is individual, meaning that each person who carries this wave has a different amount of time they spend in the different parts.

I cannot stress enough how important it is that you don't get stuck in identifying your child with the emotion they experience. This is simply an emotional wave they ride, and they do not need to judge themselves or overly identify with it. If you can learn to avoid identifying them by the highs or lows, they will learn also that those highs or lows do not identify them. The more they identify with the emotion, the longer they may spend time in that part of their wave, so consider helping them when they wake up feeling low with the reframe from "I'm so sad and low today, what's wrong with me?" to "I feel sad today, what do I need today?"

For the younger kids, maybe snuggle time, hug, watch a show with you, read books quietly, or draw to go more inward and allow space to process the feelings they experience.

For older kids, talk to them about not identifying with the feeling by saying "I am sad" but rather "I feel sad today." The more they identify themselves with that part of their wave, the more time they will spend there. To be clear, this is not about bypassing the feelings but acknowledging them, creating space to feel them, and making it okay to feel the lower vibrational feelings. Of course, there are many factors to this and if you have a child who has very low lows (or stays in them), seek professional help to guide you and give them the support they need. The earlier we can teach our children these lessons about their emotions, the more resilient they can become, thereby seeing them as just a thing they experience rather than who they are.

The kids who have this wave in their chart need to be reminded to enter into something just for its experience, and release expectations. I've watched this channel play out time and time again in a child who gets their hopes up, invests all their energy into something happening, and when it doesn't work out, they crash and say things like "I never should have gotten my hopes up!" or "Why did you make me think that was going to happen?!" or "I shouldn't even try. Nothing ever works out for me!" There can be elements of fantasy in these channels so the expectations they have may not be something that was actually agreed upon by both people. You'll benefit as a parent from being clear when tossing out ideas of things that *could* happen, ensuring they are not promises but ideas. Saying "We should go to Disneyland" casually in conversation because you'd like to make that happen one day can easily be heard by children with this channel as "We're going to Disneyland!" You can imagine the disappointment they will feel when they realize you weren't promising anything and are not actually going anytime soon.

It is, however, important to understand that some days will be down days which doesn't mean there is anything wrong with them or they need fixing, but that it's one part of the emotional wave.

Because this wave is defined in a person with an Emotional Authority, you as a parent or caregiver, can help them by checking in with them on bigger decisions. Rather than spending all their savings on a toy they just saw, help them learn to wait a couple of days and make sure it's what they truly want to spend all their money on. Practice asking them when they are feeling happy and excited, versus pouty and sad, frustrated, etc. When they've come back to a neutral place without a lot of emotional charges, ask if they still want to spend ALL of their savings on just one toy.

The Individual Wave - Channels 12-22, and 39-55

This wave is more even keel with sudden ups and downs occasionally, but they generally don't spend a lot of time in the highs or the lows. These kids can go along feeling emotionally neutral until they experience sudden hope and excitement over something. This usually doesn't last long and then they're back to neutral. The same goes for the lows, where they have a sudden low feeling of deep despair and then return from it. There can be a feeling of melancholy in this type of wave that they will never feel anything again when they are in the middle of their wave. Because the wave is more random and their highs are so high and the lows so low, being neutral feels "meh" or like "What's the point?" They don't know when they will *feel* deeply again. It is through these deep emotional feelings, both high and low, that they can create incredible, passionate art whether through traditional methods, music, cooking, designing, or more.

However, as with the Individual wave, it is important to understand that some days are down days and that it doesn't mean there is anything wrong with them, it's just one part of the emotional wave. These low days provide a time when they may need to retreat and have more alone time to feel all their feels and then come out of it. If you push them to know why they feel so blue or down, it only reinforces that low, and they may stay there longer. Find ways to give them some space when they are in the low and know it's part of their emotional process.

Parents of Children with any of the Emotional Waves

Human Design gives you information about the mechanics of how emotions work. If your child is experiencing lots of extremes or long periods of lows, it does not mean that you should not seek help with your child's emotional health and assume it's just Human Design at work. We are complex human beings, and Human Design only tells part of our story. Listen to your inner guidance as a parent and know when to seek additional help.

Defined ~ 51 Percent of People

If your child has a defined ESP, when they walk into a room, they will affect the emotional temperature of that room. Wherever they are in their wave is what the undefined/open ESPs will emotionally feel from them, even if they don't understand where it's coming from. If you know your child is in a charged part of their wave, or feeling low, it probably isn't the best time to take them to meet new friends or for pictures. (I think we've all seen those family photos.) Not that we can always choose these things but knowing where they are emotionally can help you understand why they respond to things the way they do. What would help them to feel grounded? What would help them blow off some of that steam? Skipping rocks on the water? Hitting a baseball? Kicking a soccer ball? Dancing? Blasting some music and headbanging? Yelling into a pillow? Time alone? Emotions are the lifeforce of creativity so encouraging them to create art or music could help them to process what they're feeling by allowing emotions to move through them.

Most kids probably don't even realize that they are sending out these waves or that anyone can feel them because it is always happening within them, and they think everyone feels this way. It is our job as their parents and guides to help them understand how the expression of their emotions affects others and that there is nothing wrong with having emotions; it's a natural part of their life. The more they try to resist them, the more erratic they may feel.

Emotional kids can be thrilled about something one day and then totally uninterested the next. If it doesn't feel good to them and you force them to continue with it, it likely won't be as great as you thought or hoped it would be, so be prepared and know that this isn't personal, it's mechanics. If your emotionally defined child says, "I don't feel like going to Sally's house to play," and you force them to go anyway, be prepared. They're telling you where they are in their wave and forcing them to try and be in another part of their wave won't work.

When we ask our children over and over, "What's wrong?" "What happened?" or "What made you feel that way?" It tells them that there must be a reason, a cause for the emotion they are having, rather than letting it just be *a part* of who they are and what they experience. It tells them that it's wrong to feel anything but joy and that if they're feeling unhappy, they must find a reason for it and try at all costs to eradicate it. What if we just let our children know that it's part of this emotional wave they experience and it's not who they are? *They* are not sad, but they do *feel* sadness.

Undefined/Open ~ 49 Percent of People

Similar to how a person with an open G Center can feel who someone is, an open ESP can feel how they feel. The undefined/open ESP is a child who is very emotionally empathic. They take in all the emotional energy in the room and amplify it. Ironically, this can make them appear as the most emotional person in the room. The defined ESP can walk through a room without saying a word and change the room's entire mood for anyone with an undefined/open ESP. With roughly 50 percent of the population emotionally defined and 50 percent undefined/open you'll likely have a mix in your home. Knowing who is more emotionally sensitive to others can help you understand their behavior and reactions as some are more affected by argument, conflict, and even celebration.

People with an open ESP do not like conflict or confrontation. The kids hide in their rooms if you are arguing with someone or even if you're very excited about something. All intense emotions feel big and overwhelming to them. These kids can become bullied because they don't want to confront the bully. They can avoid telling you when they've done something they think you'll be mad about (even if that's unfounded) because they don't want to deal with (feel) your response. As teens, they may go along with what other kids are doing or cave to peer pressure to avoid dealing with their friend's emotions or having to respond to aggressive or pushy energy. These undefined ESP kids can also avoid answering your call when they're late to come home because they know you'll be mad, and they want to avoid feeling the intensity of your reactions expressed through your defined ESP. In that case, it may be helpful to have another person such as a parent/grandparent or friend with an undefined ESP call to make sure they're okay.

These children need to be taught that all the intense emotions they feel do not belong to them. When they can understand the origin of the emotions, they can disentangle themselves from taking responsibility for other people's emotions and learn to deflect the emotional energy from other people or learn to let it move through them rather than get stuck.

EXERCISE: You can help your young child by asking them about other people (people on TV or in movies, cartoon characters), and how they perceive what the characters feel. Help them understand that what they feel when they watch them is not coming from themselves, but from the emotion being expressed from the character or other person whose emotions they feel. Then turn off the TV and ask them what they feel.

Have them shake it off by getting up and moving their body to discharge some of the energy and then ask them again how they feel. You can then ask them if they feel a difference between what they felt watching the show or person versus what they are feeling now. Sometimes it takes longer to shake it off depending on the emotional intensity but helping them to understand firstly that it's not their emotion to attach to and, secondly, that they can find ways to discharge it, will be immensely helpful in their lives.

Kids who don't understand this and feel everything from everyone can grow up to be people-pleasers. They become non-confrontational so they don't provoke anyone's emotional response, and can avoid conflict altogether, often at their own expense.

Teach them to be a screen and let the emotions go through them rather than a sponge that holds on to all the feelings and tries to understand why they feel the way they do.

Two Undefined/Open ESPs

Two undefined/open ESPs can come together and create a temporary definition of a channel. This allows them to amplify emotional energy back and forth until it reaches a point of real conflict. If this happens, remember that neither one of them created this energy, having picked it up elsewhere and brought it into the relationship. If they can recognize it and agree to have a bit of time apart to discharge this energy, when they come back together, the emotional field should feel neutral again. The time apart needs to be truly alone, so they don't pick up more emotional energy elsewhere and bring it in when they come back together. As an emotional empath, time alone is best for discharging other people's emotions.

The Conditioned Self-Talk of the Undefined/Open ESP Center
- – I can't tell the truth because it will hurt their feelings.
- – I am a pushover because I don't want to stand up for myself.
- – I am too emotional.

Empower Them by Helping Them Change Their Self-Talk to:
- – I am not "too emotional," but I can deeply feel others' feelings.
- – I am empathetic to others' feelings, but I don't have to take them on as my own.
- – Emotional sensing is my superpower!

Root Center

Pressure Center | Motor Center | Brown in Color when Defined

The Root Center is where we find both pressure and adrenaline in the chart. The pressure from the Root Center funnels into the Spleen Center, Sacral Center, or ESP. If the Root Center is defined, you will have a consistent theme of pressure and operate under your own timing. If this center is undefined/open, you will have varying energy pushing into the chart based on the people or planetary transits affecting you.

Defined ~ 60 Percent of People

A defined Root Center operates in an on/off pulse, which means there will be times that you feel fueled by adrenaline to act, and there will be times that you won't feel so driven. It is crucial to listen to this on/off pulse because if you force action when you don't feel like it, it's kind of like pushing a boulder up a hill–you work hard and make little progress. If you work with the pulse of the Root Center and use those "on" times to get in the flow and do what you want or need to do, you'll be more efficient and get it done in less time; it just may not be on the schedule you'd planned with your mind.

If your child has a defined Root Center and they are in an "off" pulse, and you ask them to clean their room, prepare for a battle of prodding, coaxing, or coercing. You might even find yourself bribing them to get them to do what you ask. You can't pressure a child with a defined Root Center to do anything; it must be on their timing. Consider how badly you need them to complete the task on your terms. When we consistently push our children to work against their design, we condition them to do what other people say rather than what their body says, disconnecting them from their truth, Strategy, and inner Authority. Instead of forcing them to work on your schedule, try giving them a window of time to get a task done.

Sacral Energy Types

If you have a Generator or Manifesting Generator child, you can ask them through yes/no questions to do what you want as the Sacral is more consistently powerful than the Root Center. But before you do, I would ask you if you might be teaching them to ignore their body's signal for rest. The Sacral is a more powerful motor, and if you make it turn on, it can overpower other centers like the Root Center. There will be times when you need your kids to do things, and life needs to carry on, but when it's not critical, could you wait until tomorrow to have them clean their room? Remember, we're trying to raise children who know their bodies as their inner Authority rather than their minds or other people.

Non-Sacral Energy Types

If you have a Projector or Reflector, you can invite them to engage their energy. That could sound like "I'm noticing that it's hard to find things in your room lately. How do you think we could improve it?" or "What could you do to make it feel more peaceful/calm/organized in here?" or "Can you tell me about your system for organizing your room?" And, after they clean up or complete the task you ask of them, make sure to give them recognition for the effort they put into it. Notice them. Let them know you see their actions and efforts. They might also need you to stay and be there with them to borrow energy if you're a Sacral energy type.

If you have a Manifestor and they don't feel like doing what you ask of them, it can be a real challenge unless they have some ability to choose. You could inform them, "I would like you to clean your room; when do you think you'd like to take care of that before Friday?" for example, which gives them a window of time, so they have some say in when they do the task you ask.

This one screams to parents that they're giving away their power, but when you can honor who your child is and how their energy works, things don't have to be a power struggle. Power struggles are created when one person is trying to dominate the other. There are many outdated ways of parenting that are about dominating your child(ren) to get them to do what you want them to do, no matter what they want or feel like they can do. We have many generations of ancestors who bought into this way of being, but there is a better way. Again, this is not to say you should let your child(ren) have excessive power, but appropriate power for their age. Giving them ways to lean into the trust of themselves and their bodies allows them to grow to be independent people who are successful in life and confident in their abilities.

Undefined/Open ~ 40 Percent of People

The undefined/open Root Center is under tremendous pressure to be free of the pressure. Because this is where we find adrenaline in the chart, when this center is open, it leads to a tremendous amplification of the adrenaline from the defined Root Centers around them. Energy that comes from a person with a defined Root Center feels like it holds so much charge that the open Root Center person needs to respond or react immediately, even if the person with the defined Root has said, "Whenever you can get to it."

When you don't know how you take in and amplify this energy, you feel like you have adrenaline running through you all the time. You rush through life and burnout early because the consistent presence of high stress hormones in your body is not sustainable. You end up overdoing, over-committing, and generally taking on or being given more than you can handle long-term. Short term, you can be the fastest at tasks because you are running on amplified adrenalized energy. You may also be more likely to become an *adrenaline junkie* if you have this center open, getting hooked on the feeling of adrenalized energy and the thrill it provides.

As a Projector with a completely open Root Center, I'm personally familiar with burnout. I found myself burned out at thirty-two, complete with panic attacks and anxiety. My cortisol levels had been elevated so long that upon testing, my body was no longer producing appropriate levels of cortisol to regulate my circadian rhythm, affecting sleep, wake, and stress response. I was running on fumes and had no idea what I was doing wrong. I could barely care for my kids throughout the day and spent most of the day on the couch resting. I felt worthless. I'd lost myself and was doing everything for everyone else and didn't even know what I liked to do for myself anymore. I can now look back on that time as a great wake up for me, and while I'm grateful that it put me on the path that I'm currently on, I don't wish anyone to have to live through that level of burnout.

If you have a child with an open Root Center, they may experience overwhelm easily from pressure. As a result, they may struggle with anxiety to perform in school or other activities. You can help by talking with them about the pressures and breaking the tasks down into smaller parts to avoid feeling overwhelmed. Conversely, children with an open/undefined Root Center sometimes rush through things and don't spend enough time on the details because they want to get it done to be free of the pressure.

My children have open or undefined Root Centers, and I've seen how the pressure affects them in school and with peers. Being at home full-time during 2020 highlighted for me how much less pressure they feel at home, even though many other areas were challenging.

Open Root Centers can feel pressurized energy the way open ESPs feel emotions. They take the energy on themselves, thinking it is their own, but it is really borrowed. If you or your child has an open Root Center, learn to discern what it feels like to be around someone with a defined Root Center. The adrenalized energy you feel is not your own, so if you feel pressure to do, check in and see if you are the one who needs to be doing everything. Also, if your child has an Emotional Authority with an open Root Center, they may have a harder time waiting to respond to invitations or opportunities because of the pressure they feel through this center.

Undefined/Open with a Defined Root Center

If you have an undefined/open Root Center and have a child with a defined Root Center, you may always feel like they are pressuring you for things, answers, playdates, toys, etc. The open Root Center perceives pressure from the defined Root Center and wants to be rid of the pressure. Ask yourself, "What would happen if I said no?" before responding, buying, or committing if you have an open Root Center.

If you are co-parenting with someone with a defined Root Center and you have an undefined/open Root Center, you may feel that they are always pressuring you for things, time, pushing boundaries, wanting more than you agreed upon. Creating clear boundaries can help everyone know what is expected from each of them from the beginning. Even with clear boundaries, life happens, and circumstances change so when unexpected things come up, ask yourself, are they demanding, or are they just asking?

The Pressures on an Open Root Child

Children with an open Root, especially combined with other open centers, can take in so much energy from other people that they appear to become numb to the pressure when asked about what they feel. They may appear to mentally be unaware of the stress they are experiencing, but their body tells. This can show up as children who don't eat enough due to stress, or who over-exercise. It can also show up as overeating to self-medicate the pressure they feel. I've also witnessed a child who became so overwhelmed by this unrecognized stress that their physical body stopped functioning as normal, losing the ability to walk unassisted, mentally shutting down, going somewhere else when confronted with a stressful situation. There was nothing physically wrong with this child, but the pressure and stress overwhelmed their body. In a joyful situation, this child could appear normal, leading people to think they were faking, but when it got too stressful, they shut down again mentally and physically. Eventually, after taking a break from regular activities in their life for most of a school year, things improved, and they got back to a normal way of life. The parents learned to watch for less obvious signs of "too much" rather than taking the child's word at face value that things were "fine."

If you are a parent with an open Root Center, how much of your time are you spending on tasks that can wait until later? For example, does every dish in the sink need to be washed the moment it lands there? Can the mopping wait until tomorrow while you get down on the floor and play Legos with your kids instead?

If you have an open Root Center, consider what is most precious to you. What do you hold most dear? Will you look back on your life and say, "I sure wish I'd mopped the floors more when my kids were young?" Or will you say, "I wish I'd let the little things go more often and engaged with my kids at every stage?" It's a balance—this dance we do in life and parenting. We won't always get it right, and if you have a 3rd line in your profile (more on Profiles in the next chapter), you'll have to get in there and try some stuff to figure out what works for you and what doesn't. Keep an open mind and know that it's all a learning process for both parent and child. You are doing the best you can with what you know and remember to be gentle with yourself too.

An Invitation

This is an invitation for you to look at the stories you play in your mind of how parenting must be. Were you raised to do what your parents told you to do and not given any compassion for where you were in life? Were you forced to push beyond if you were having a low emotional day or a low energy day? What conditioning can you identify in your own experience that is leading you to want to make your children do things in your way, on your time?

The Conditioned Self-Talk of the Undefined Root Center

- I can't figure out how to do all the stuff I need to do, so I just won't do anything.
- I feel so much pressure, so I just act without waiting for the right timing.
- I just want to be free from the pressure.

- Why is everyone always pressuring me?

Empower Them by Helping Them Change Their Self-Talk to:
- I can learn to ground into my own sense of timing and not have to be on anyone else's schedule.
- Just because I feel pressure doesn't mean I have to act right now.
- I honor myself enough to slow down and run on my own time.
- Just because someone asks me for something, doesn't mean I have to act right away.

CHAPTER NINE

PROFILE

It takes courage to grow up and turn out to be who you really are.
~E.E. CUMMINGS

The Profiles in Human Design help you to understand the role that you play in this life. Profiles can tell you more about how you learn and how you interact with other people. Understanding your child's profile can give you a lot of insight into their personality.

5/2 PROFILE

How To Find Your Profile Numbers
Profile lines come from the conscious and unconscious sun. They are listed as the conscious line first, followed by the unconscious. This chart is a 5/2 profile.

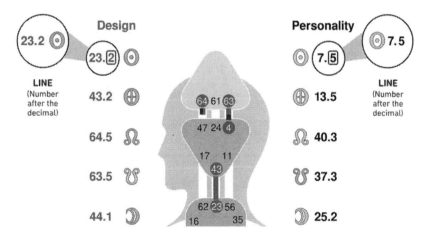

The Profile lines are found in the Conscious and Unconscious Sun. When you look at the chart, you'll see these represented in the black and red sides of the chart where the planet symbols are listed. In the Sun signs, you'll see a gate number followed by a decimal point and a number (1-6), or on some charts, it is written as an exponent or raised number. In the example above, you see the Conscious Sun in Gate 7 followed by a decimal and then the profile line of 5. Your Profile is read as the Conscious Sun line first, followed by the Unconscious Sun line. This example shows a 5/2 Profile.

THE HEXAGRAM LINES

The numbers in the Profile originate from the hexagram of the I Ching. Divided into lower trigram lines one, two, three, and upper trigram lines four, five, six, your child's profile is a combination of two of these lines.

There are only twelve combinations that become known as the Profile.

Now that you understand where to find the Profile numbers, let's learn about what they represent and mean.

Role Model / Martyr	6/3	
Role Model / Hermit	6/2	Left Angle Transpersonal Life Path
Heretic / Hermit	5/2	
Heretic / Investigator	5/1	
Opportunist / Investigator	4/1	Juxtaposition Fixed Life Path
Opportunist / Role Model	4/6	
Martyr / Role Model	3/6	
Martyr / Heretic	3/5	
Hermit / Heretic	2/5	Right Angle Personal Life Path
Hermit / Opportunist	2/4	
Investigator / Opportunist	1/4	
Investigator / Martyr	1/3	

Left Angle Profiles

The Profiles 5/1, 5/2, 6/2, and 6/3 are considered left angle or transpersonal karma Profiles. These Profiles carry transpersonal karma, which is about the relationships in a person's life that influence the trajectory of their life story.

Right Angle Profiles

The Profiles 1/3, 1/4, 2/4, 2/5, 3/5, 3/6, and 4/6 are considered right angle or personal karma Profiles. A personal karma Profile's life story unfolds based on the personal experiences that they have, rather than through relationships with other people.

Juxtaposition Profile

There is one Profile, the 4/1 that doesn't fit into either right or left angle Profiles, and that is a juxtaposition or fixed karma Profile. This Profile travels along on a predetermined or fixed trajectory. In many ways, they are observers experiencing life and are often found to be people interested in studying other people's patterns, like psychology, Human Design, personality typing, etc.

Breaking Down the Profiles into Separate Parts

Line 1 - The Investigator

This foundational line supports the hexagram structure, so kids with a 1st line in their Profile want to investigate and get to the bottom of things. They want to learn, understand, and feel competent in anything new before sharing it with the world. If you push them to share what they are working on before they are ready, it can create insecurity in their knowledge and drive them to feel the need to know even more before they share the next thing. They can hide away until they feel competent in that area before sharing. Encouraging them to realize they know more than they think they do may be helpful at times, so they don't get lost in "not knowing enough." Use care not to push too hard and allow them their pace sharing what they know.

Whether through formal education, studying independently, or finding a mentor that they feel is competent in what they want to learn, 1st line profiles are lifelong learners. They are constantly digging into things to get to the bottom of them—to the truth. When they feel they know enough, they feel secure. The underlying fear they can experience is that they don't know enough, which can stop them from moving forward or sharing what they know.

Surround these children with plenty of books and resources. Get them a library card and teach them what is available in books. Help them understand reliable sources of information and how to locate them. They need a solid base of information to make their decisions. Ask them questions about the things they're interested in and help them learn to share what they know to bring out their wisdom.

And lastly, they need time alone to integrate what they are learning. You might have a 1st line child who likes to read a lot and retreats to their room or one who gets lost in learning from YouTube tutorials and then goes for a walk by themselves to process the info they just took in.

Line 1 Parents

If you are a parent with a 1st line in your Profile, you will likely be the researcher. If something is challenging as a parent or you are dealing with a medical issue for example, you will investigate and learn more about that subject than anyone you know. You gather information to make decisions for your child based on the knowledge you have acquired.

When making a big decision around parenting, you need to retreat for some time alone to process your knowledge and formulate your thoughts on what to do next before acting.

Line 2 - The Hermit

This 2nd line in the trigram has a bit of aloofness about it. Contrasting to the first line, which is driven to investigate and figure things out, the 2nd line inherently knows things. They are often the children described as old souls who seem wise about life. You don't know how they could know some of the things that come out of them, and if you asked them, they probably wouldn't know how they know, but they know. They are quietly observing life and the world around them, taking it all in, and they need time alone to process and integrate what they're learning through observation.

Theirs is a knowing that is certain until questioned too much. In a logical world where we want proof that things are a certain way or why things work in a particular fashion, this kind of knowing can come under scrutiny of friends, teachers, and adults in their lives. This questioning can cause them to want to hide, because if they are not out and exposed in the world, people will question them less. The 2nd line child can be found in the corner of the room watching everyone, learning by seeing the interactions in front of them while pretending to be buried in a book. They are noticing and taking it all in, processing in their unique way where it becomes the wisdom that others will seek them out for later in life.

As they get older, they will notice that the more they try to hide away, the more they are called out to be social and share their insights. They need to be allowed space to be quiet and still, and alone to integrate what they learn. To a parent with a large family, it may seem strange that a young child wants to be alone in their room, but they will need quiet time. This need is especially important when they are in school, after a long day of being social. If they're being tested on what they know and how they know it, they will need downtime to recharge. Being alone allows them to regenerate their energy and integrate their learnings into wisdom.

Other people can see things in the 2nd line Profile they themselves cannot and call them out for it. These are the kids that don't need other people to help them, and they are content to do their own thing in their hermit-like way, and it can seem self-absorbed. Imagine a child who dances appearing to be in their own little world, and then you notice they have natural talent in their movement. When you call them out for it and tell them how great they are at it, they may run to their room as they've just realized you recognized something in their inherent abilities, and they may believe that you now have expectations of them and what they can do or know. They'd prefer to keep dancing on their own, BEing in their own aura, doing what they feel called to do, in their way, with no one watching.

Line 2 Parents

If you are a parent with a 2nd line Profile, you may parent in a way that causes other parents to believe that you know something they don't, and they want to know how you do it. You may also find that your children realize you know things and ask you about them. And, if your child has a Profile with a 1st line, they may want to know how you know and where you got your information, which can leave you feeling called out and put on the spot and wanting to avoid the questioning. A child with Gate 61 defined can ask a lot of why questions which can leave you feeling tested if you can't give a source for your information. You'll also need more downtime/alone time than the other Profiles as there is a lot of internal processing after interacting with people all day.

Line 3 - The Martyr

The 3rd line child is curious and will not accept "Because I said so" or "Because that's how we do it" or "Because that's how it works" as an answer. They need to get their hands in there and try it out for themselves to see if it is true for them. As a parent, when they challenge these types of answers, consider if this is the best way to do things *for them*. It's not that they are saying "You're wrong" but that they need to see if it's true for them too. The 3rd line is very much the "Let me try" child who needs to get their hands dirty and immersed in the process to see how it works. Experiential learning for this Profile is critical. When they're small, hands-on children's museums are wonderful, as are science experiments, testing theories, and questioning the process of everything. A great approach to take with a 3rd line Profile child is to take their hand (whenever possible) when they ask why and say "I don't know why we do things this way. How do you think we should do it?" Get down to their level and get curious with them. Help them explore their world and know that it's okay to question all the things because they are learning immensely through their process to become wise and share with others.

This Profile could lend itself well to a great scientist, or chef or any profession with great possibilities in varied outcomes, as they think outside of the box and are willing to get messy to see what works. The same can be said of their relationships which is why there is a theme of bonds made and broken through this Profile as they see what works and what doesn't. Teaching children with this Profile to embrace this ability to learn from and move on can help them avoid getting stuck in a limiting belief or fear that they are going to fail if they try something new.

If you have a 3rd line Profile teenager, these can be the kids who want to experiment with things like drugs or alcohol to see what it's like *for themselves*. Not to scare you, but just telling them that it's a bad idea is not enough (remember they are highly experiential). Having this Profile does not predict that your child will experiment with drugs or alcohol or have a problem with them, but it's important to consider that through the experimental qualities of this Profile, this is a possibility. The same could apply to speeding or other reckless behaviors. Add to this an undefined/open Root Center, and the peer pressure of being a teenager can lead to some riskier experimentation.

No matter what your child is working through, allowing them to try and see for themselves is a big part of their process. You can help them make connections between how they do things and what they learn, rather than focusing on what didn't work out. Consider how you felt as a child, and whether harsh criticism or punishment ever led you to open up more to your parents? With this learning style, try to stay curious rather than critical. You may learn differently from them, and simply watching others make mistakes may be enough for you, while this child will need the room to learn through their own process. These children are not making mistakes, they're just learning through a very experiential process. When things don't go as they'd hoped, help them reflect and consider why it didn't work out like they thought it would, what they would do differently next time, and what they learned through the process.

Again, of course, please do not knowingly allow your child to make harmful decisions just for the sake of learning. But also know that some of what they do is never going to be in your control. Hopefully, they have been allowed to experiment early on with more minor consequences so that when they get to the teens and beyond, they understand their process a bit more and can use that wisdom to make good decisions for themselves.

Line 3 Parents

If you are a 3rd line Profile parent, you too, will learn by doing. It's not that you're doing it "wrong," but it might feel that way when you see other parents who seem to have it "all figured out." But just like everything else in your life, you learn by doing, so lean into your Strategy and Authority and find *your* way to parent your child. It won't always work out as you thought, and that's okay. You do your best, learn from it, and keep going. Handle your parenting expectations with a healthy dose of grace for your process.

Line 4 - The Opportunist

The 4th line is the foundation of the upper trigram (lines 4, 5, 6), and building relationships with others is important to them. It's not about *how many* people they know but the *quality* of their connections. Their quality of life is related to the network of people in their life. They tend to have a group of friends that last, and family is essential to them. The opportunities they receive will come through the people they know. Perhaps not directly but for instance, when they go to get a job, someone they know may say, "I know someone who is looking for help. I'll connect you two."

Like how the 1st line Profile needs to know enough to be prepared to share, the 4th line needs to know what to expect to feel prepared. Kids with the 4th line in their Profile will ask many questions about what things will be like, who will be there, what they will do, etc. when going somewhere new. They need to know ahead of time what to expect so they can prepare to leave the foundation they are currently in and move into the next thing. Whether it's a new house, school, friend's house, sports competition, or anything else where they haven't experienced that place or the people they might encounter, they anchor into security by knowing what is coming next. All the questions can sometimes leave parents feeling a bit exasperated, but once they learn about this energy, parents can understand what their child needs to move forward in an easier way to new opportunities.

Ask them what they need to know to feel comfortable taking action to move to the next task. For example, if you're moving to a new location or town, if possible, let your child go to the area or place to see what it's like, and they will understand better how they will fit into it and what to expect allowing for a less stressful move.

Spontaneity can be harder for these kids because they need to know what's next. Adults too, just because you grow up doesn't mean you outgrow this Profile, though you can mature and become more comfortable with change. You will always feel more secure if you have another job lined up before quitting the one you have. And you'll want to go check out the new city before moving there because it helps you feel secure in your foundation; however, when you learn to embrace it, you can become a great example for others of how to adapt to change.

The 4th line child will have a close network of friends they connect with, though they may have many acquaintances. This Profile may be a child who goes through school with the same group of friends. It's important that their network of friends feels supportive and leaves them feeling connected and nourished. After a day of networking, these 4th line children will also need some time to themselves.

Parents with a 4th Line Profile

Parents with the 4th line in their Profile are always scanning for what's next before leaping and asking things such as "How will this impact my family and me?" "What will I need to feel comfortable with this transition?" Finding a group of parent friends can support you as you raise your children if you don't already have that in your friend group or family. When taking your child somewhere new to go to school, childcare, or even a friend's house, you want to know what it will be like, so don't be shy to ask to come over and meet the parents or see where the friend lives. You need to know for your own sense of safety and security before you let them go.

Line 5 - The Heretic

These children are here to show us what's possible with their out-of-the-box thinking, but they can be heavily projected on to be the saviors or fixers. They can be the kids who seem to always want to help, but if you aren't careful, they may overly identify with this role and feel like they must always try to save everyone around them. Because they feel best when helping, they can look for more opportunities to help rather than waiting for the correct opportunities. They may end up feeling used by people who just want them to help and who then disappear when help is no longer needed.

A 5th line child needs to understand that because of this projection field; if they say yes to something and can't follow through with it, their reputation can suffer. They can become known as the kid who makes promises and can't keep them. A poor reputation can be garnered because of the projection field even if the child never actually made a promise in the first place. If the other child perceived a promise and your child doesn't deliver, they could be alienated by their friends. Help them understand that they don't need to help everyone or fix anyone's problems. They need to learn to be clear when making plans or agreements with others, to be very specific with what they say they will do, and only commit to something if they know they can follow through. If they enter into an agreement and find they can't follow through, they need to be honest and let the other person know. It's important that they learn to use their Strategy and Authority to know which things they should get involved in/with.

People with a 5th line Profile also have an ability to see the best in others and what they can become. If they are not careful, they can end up saying yes to helping someone who is not operating from their highest self and wind up hurt and confused in the end. They can't imagine someone wouldn't want to be the best version of themselves. It's important to note that while it can be hurtful to the 5th line child to have this experience, it can be unfair to expect someone to live up to the standards that someone else set for them through what they see is possible. This is why teaching them Strategy and Authority to navigate friendships, relationships, work agreements, and projects is critical for children with a 5th line Profile.

Karmic Mirror

The projection of the 5th line holds up a karmic mirror to the people in their life, showing them what needs to improve in their lives, which can feel painful at times when the other person projects onto them their wounds that need tending. Unfortunately, these children can feel like others take things out on them for no reason or are bullied or blamed for something they didn't do. If you have a 5th line child and you're commonly coming up against a repeating feeling that you think they aren't doing things right or they just need to do things like everyone else, it would be wise to do some self-reflection and ask yourself what this child might be trying to show you. This is an opportunity to learn about yourself and where you might have some wounds that need tending.

The 5th line Profile may start to believe that they need to be the savior, particularly if that is the role they've played in their family home growing up. These kids can take on responsibility very early for other family members' physical, mental, and emotional well-being if the parent for example, cannot care of themself or if they are unaware of the projection they are placing on their children through this energetic field.

If the child remains in a relationship with a projection field that has them always saving someone (a friend, parent, and later a partner), they will not get to live out the highest expression of this energy because they are in the wrong place with the wrong people. They need to get out of that projection field to soar. Their time in a relationship with a projection field like this can cause them to lose their sense of value and continue hiding out and not fulfilling their true purpose as a 5th line Profile, which is to see the potential in others as a visionary leader and trust their Strategy and Authority to know when to respond, guide, or initiate.

When they are with the right people in the right place, they lead others to fulfill their potential to help them see what else is possible. They look for people to align with that, live up to their word, and take accountability for their actions.

Like the 2nd line Profile, they need time alone to reflect and be able to consciously enter a relationship before offering their leadership to avoid a "saving other people" role.

Line 5 Parents

If you have a 5th line Profile, you get an extra dose of, "But you promised we'd go to the mall!" Or, "But you said ..." thrown your way from your child as they project their expectations onto you. If you are not very clear in your promises, any implied promises or hinted-at promises could become fuel for argument and hurt feelings.

If you have a child who likes to wait until the last minute to get their schoolwork done, and you are the one to push them to finish it, are you empowering them or disempowering them by teaching them to rely on you to pressure them to do it? If they don't get the project done or are cramming at the last minute, freaking out that it won't be ready to turn in on time, and they're going to fail the class, are you always rescuing them? Knowing that you have a projection field that can give off the feeling of "I'm going to help/save/rescue you" will help you understand how you get into situations like this and why it's important that you not reinforce this role. Recognize the projection field and become very clear about what you will and won't do and your role in agreements.

If you co-parent, and you have the 5th line Profile while your partner does not, be careful not to get into the habit of being the one who always saves the day, as you can easily become expected to save the day, every day.

Line 6 - The Role Model

The 6th line is different from the other lines in that it goes through three distinct phases in life. These kids can feel like they have a life purpose that they must find and live out. They can become fixated later in life with what they should be DOing with their life, but really, it's about who they are BEing.

The first phase lasts until about age thirty when they reach their first Saturn Return, living life as a 3rd line Profile. If you have a 3/6 or 6/3 Profile child, you will experience all your childrearing years parenting a 3/3 through their first phase. Remember the third line child is all about experimentation and figuring out what works for them and seeing if it's true for themselves to learn and gather their own wisdom. They *need* to experiment with life in this phase. They know they are here for something meaningful and can sometimes be hard on themselves because they aren't getting it "right." They need your encouragement that, like the 3rd line

Profile, life is not about perfection. These kids need to know it's okay to try things and not have them be the way you wanted them the first time around but to try again and help them see what they are learning with each attempt.

The second phase of the 6th line life lasts roughly from ages thirty to fifty, from the first Saturn Return to their Chiron Return and is a time described in Human Design as being "on the roof." It is a time to go more inward, slow down, and contemplate all the things they learned living their 3rd line lives up to their Saturn Return. They are also watching others, healing, and restoring energy for the next phase and can appear more like a 2nd or 5th line Profile during this phase with their need for alone time. This shift may be more challenging for a Generator or **Manifesting Generator, who is used to having plenty** of **energy to go and** experiment. They still have energy but leaning deeper into Strategy and Authority will help them navigate what to use it for. If they do not take the time to reflect and integrate their learnings during this time, they can have a bumpy landing coming off the roof. From the outside, it may look like their life is falling apart, but in reality, it's the Universe helping them align to where they need to be and helping them become the role model that they're destined to be by walking their talk. The second phase is about alignment and clearing out the stuff that hasn't been working to allow for their life purpose to continue to unfold.

When the 6th line is in the 3rd phase of their 6th line life, they share it with the world as the wise role models they become. This phase of their life is about who they are BEing and showing others what it means to live an authentic life by being themselves.

Those first thirty years, though: Hang on parents, because it can be a wild ride! If you're a parent who likes a lot of control and order, welcoming a child with one of these Profiles can be quite a challenging and learning experience for you. I invite you to lean into the learning and become curious with your child rather than resist this curiosity and try to shut it down. During the 6th line's 3rd line phase, these kids will find ways to experiment with or without you, so you'll likely sleep a lot better if you are involved in their processes. You might earn some gray hairs over it, but at least you'll know what they're up to!

The term *role model* is a heavy one for a child, so keep in mind that this doesn't happen for decades. The work you're doing as a parent is to help them stay curious, adventurous, and experimental. They will likely want to try different foods, go to new places, meet new people, and have all the adventures. So, buckle up parents, this one is a wild and fun ride! Think of all the stories you'll have to tell!

Line 6 Parents

Consider what phase you are in when you become a parent and when you will go onto and come off the roof experiencing these key changes in your life. For example, if you become a new parent at twenty-seven and hit your Saturn Return at thirty-one and are a Generator, you can move from feeling like you have a ton of energy and are rocking this parenting gig to feeling like your four-year-old just wore you out. It's not just because your child turned four, and four is a hard age or that you're "getting older." It's also because you just went "on the roof," and now you've entered a more inward process and need more time to retreat and reflect. Your energy quiets during this time, and it can feel like you lost your groove. Knowing this ahead of time can help you prepare for how this shift may affect you (and how you parent) while also allowing you space for this period of deep integration.

If you're "on the roof" when your kids are young and come "off the roof" while you have teenagers, for example, as a Generator you may find that you suddenly have more energy again and connect with your kids in a new way.

No matter where you are in your timeline as a 6th line Profile, keep these phases in mind as you navigate your parenting and your feelings. It's not only their different developmental stages you navigate but your own as well.

CHAPTER TEN

SPLITS AND RELATIONSHIPS

I can do things you cannot, you can do things I cannot;
together we can do great things.
~MOTHER TERESA

Splits in Human Design refer to the number of groups of centers in the Human Design Chart. If you were to print your design and put your pencil on one of the **defined** energy centers, could you draw **one continuous line** through all the **defined centers** in your chart without picking up your pencil through the **defined channels**? If not, then you have at least one split in your design. Also, if you get an advanced chart from www.geneticmatrix.com, it will tell you if you or your child has a split definition.

When a child or adult has a split definition, they unconsciously seek out people who bridge those gaps in their chart. The gaps can be small or large, depending on where the definition is. It may take only a single gate to bridge the gap, or they might need a whole channel or a channel and gates to unite the areas of center definition. There can also be multiple gates or channels that bridge a split, however not all gates need to be bridged, just enough to connect the centers by drawing a single continuous line from center to center without picking up the pen from the paper.

Remember, conditioning comes mostly through openness in your chart, which leaves the areas where you have a gap between defined center groupings open to more conditioning as you are always looking for what you don't have. Creating a single definition and getting energy to the Throat Center to communicate and manifest are higher priority, so gates and channels that bridge splits or connect the Throat Center to a motor are areas where there is likely more conditioning. A single definition or a triple (three groups) split definition will experience the most conditioning around their open centers in their chart, while a single split or quad (four groups) split definition will have most conditioning around the gates or channels that bridge their splits.

Because we are always unconsciously seeking others who help us bridge these groupings of centers, a child with a split, triple split, or quad split in their chart is energetically looking for someone to be in a relationship that helps them have a single definition, or at least fewer splits when together. You can think of it as people with splits need other people, while people who have a single definition in their chart don't need other people to feel whole and easily express their definition. Single definition people are content being on their own in a way that split definition people are not.

Please note that we should not specifically go looking for people to be friends with or in a relationship with or work with who have these gates. There is nothing you need to do but follow your Strategy and Authority to guide you to the people who are destined to play a part in your life. Allow your child to find the people they need to experience in their life by helping them learn to enter friendships and later relationships through Strategy and Authority. We are not trying to design the perfect relationships but rather gain understanding and insight into how we are all different and energetically supported. A perfect combination on paper can be terrible in real life because of conditioning, trauma, and other influences like living out a lower expression of your design and/or having low self-worth. Remember, each part of the chart is an archetype, and there are a variety of ways it can be expressed. You need not ever feel limited by your design.

Single Definition

A single definition means that there is no split, and all the defined centers can be connected through one continuous line if you draw through the chart without lifting your pencil from the paper. This means that all your defined energy centers can talk to one another and send information back and forth easily. Single definitions receive most of their conditioning through their undefined centers in their chart.

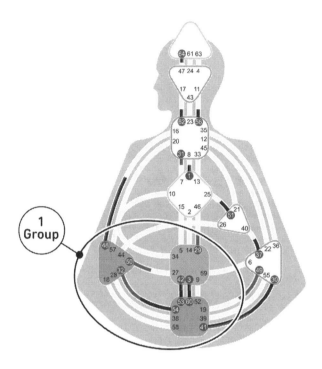

If your child has a single definition, look at your chart to see if your defined centers are conditioning your child's open centers. Because this is the energy you transmit out and will be experienced by your child, it's important to focus on how healthy your relationship with the energy of that center is.

Split Definition

A split definition is when there are two distinct groupings of defined centers in the chart. A split definition can take a beat longer for the two groups of defined centers to communicate unless someone is helping to bridge that gap. Depending on where this shows up in the chart can determine how that is experienced. Look to see if the split is small (needing one gate to bridge the gap) or wide (needing a whole channel or more to bridge the gap). Split definitions receive most of their conditioning through their bridging gates (the gates that connect one area of definition to another).

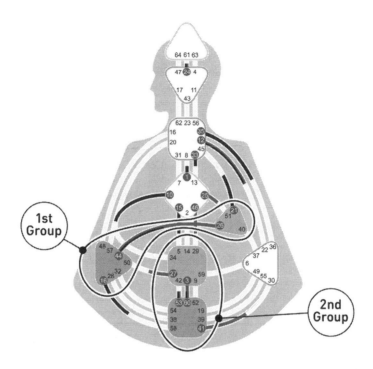

If your child has a split definition, look at your chart to see if your defined gates or channels bridge the gap in your child's chart. Then, get to know the energy in that gate or channel and your relationship with it, as your child receives conditioning around that gate or channel through you and anyone else they are close to, who has it defined. These are areas to focus on how healthy your relationship with the energy of that gate or channel is because that energy is what you transmit out into the world and will be experienced by your child.

Triple Split Definition

A triple split definition is when there are three distinct groupings of defined centers in the chart. The triple split configuration can take a bit longer for all defined centers to communicate as groups and send info back and forth unless someone helps bridge that gap. Triple split definition receives most of their conditioning through their undefined/open centers in their chart.

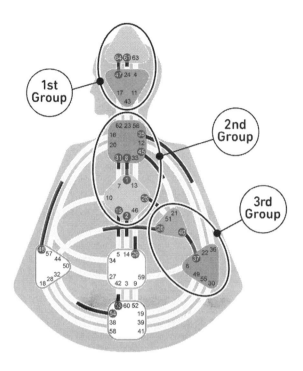

If your child has a triple split definition, look at your chart to see if your defined centers are conditioning your child's undefined/open centers. These are areas to focus on how healthy your relationship with the energy of that center is as that energy is what you transmit out into the world and will be experienced by your child.

Quadruple Split Definition

The last and rarest split type is a quad split, which is four distinct groupings of defined centers in the chart. With this type of split, the communication between centers can be slower, as there are now four separate groupings trying to send information back and forth. Particularly when communicating, it can take longer to filter the information to get it to the Throat Center unless someone helps to bridge the gaps. If someone in their life has a motor center connected to the Throat Center and your child does not, they may have an easier time communicating with them than with other people. You may also need to slow down to give them space to process their thoughts and get them out with their voice. The quad split is rare; however, the adults I've worked with who have a quad split definition have told me that it feels like there are four different parts of them. They have shared with me that they must wait for these groups to sync up when communicating, which can slow them down or cause them to speak before they've fully processed their thoughts, emotions, or senses depending on who they are with.

These quad split definitions receive most of their conditioning through their bridging gates (the gates that connect one area of definition to another). These gates are areas to focus on how healthy your relationship with the energy of them are in your chart as that energy is what you transmit out into the world and will be experienced by your child. Because this is the energy you transmit out and will be experienced by your child, it's important to focus on how healthy your relationship with the energy of that center is.

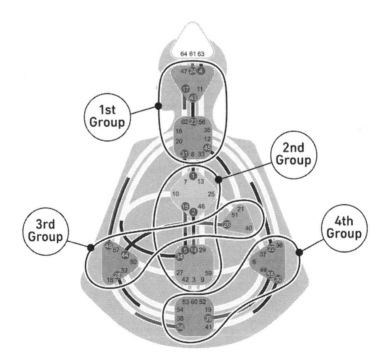

If you have a child with a triple or quad split, it may take them longer to process their thoughts and emotions and be able to communicate them to you. Learning in a typical school environment *may* be more difficult for them, and adjusting to how they take in the information, how much time they have, and if they feel under pressure can change the experience of learning for them. These kids need to not be rushed in order to be able to check in with themselves fully. However, in a classroom, they are likely to have their gaps bridged and can also thrive in this setting sometimes even more than in a homeschool environment, depending on the charts of the people they are with and how they bridge the gaps in the child's chart. These kids need people around to collaborate and explore different aspects of themselves. Notice what works for your child and experiment with ways to support them in processing information and being heard.

CHAPTER ELEVEN

THE BODY AND ITS NEEDS

A bird does not sing because it has an answer.
It sings because it has a song.
~CHINESE PROVERB

Feeding Your Child

There are elements in the deeper layers of the chart that are entire classes on their own, including information about digestion type. The very high-level portion of digestion here is not meant to be read as an absolute but as a starting place for experimenting with your child to find what works for them. Digestion is considered the primary focus up to the first Saturn Return (around age thirty) in Human Design. Digestion is an important aspect of helping parents narrow down ways to support their children. Experiment with this and see if it works for you and your family but don't take it as an absolute.

Having worked with clients as a Nutritional Therapy Practitioner for the last eight years, I have seen how much food affects us all. The food system has been altered and adulterated, and our once nourishing foods are now void of nutrients or filled with pesticides and hormones. It's not one food or food group causing all the issues. Each person has a unique combination of foods that work and foods that don't work for them. It used to be that food sensitivities and allergies were rare and digestive issues were deemed a rare or adult problem, but I see younger and younger children suffering. I've worked with kids as young as a few months old who had food sensitivities, including my three-week-old child who began having issues with her food through what I was eating as a breastfeeding mama. *What* we eat is important, there's no doubt in my mind about that, but *how* we eat often gets overlooked, which is why I love this element of Human Design for parenting.

Something to consider is that food is never just about food. There are so many things wrapped up in food including traditions, cultures, bonding, connection, memories, food chemicals, and more that we must consider when we look at foods and decide whether they work or don't for us and our unique bodies. It takes connecting into our bodies at a deeper level and paying attention to figure out what is truly working for our children and ourselves.

In my own experience as a child, I had a quirky way of eating. I hated for my food to touch on my plate, and I liked to eat all of one food on the plate before moving on to the next. For example, if I had steak, corn on the cob, and salad, I would eat all the steak, all the corn, and then all the salad, not necessarily in that order, but all of one food before moving onto the next. To not eat this way was incredibly frustrating and stressful for me. I couldn't exactly explain why I had to eat this way, but I just knew that it was what felt best to me. Only in my late thirties did I find out that my Digestion type is Consecutive, which means that I am designed to eat this way just as I take in information one thing at a time. Does it mean that I only eat single foods, one at a time now? Nope, that doesn't always work for me, though I do notice I digest much better when I eat simple foods, and if they have fewer ingredients, all the better. For example, I often eat an apple, then an hour or two later some nuts, then a couple of hours later, maybe I'll have some cucumbers, and I might follow that up with some carrots. This way of eating digests so much better in my body than if I ate three larger meals in a day with several foods combined. We are all unique individuals and need to find what works optimally for each of us.

Take a moment and think back to when you were a child. How did you like to eat your food? Did you have a preferred way of eating that was conditioned out of you? How about your kids? Do they have particular ways of eating foods that you've noticed or even tried to "correct"?

In Human Design, there are twelve different ways of feeding your child so that they can digest optimally. Keep in mind that this is not telling you what to feed your child but is more about the way you feed them and, in some cases, what the environment is like when they're eating. You can find your child's eating Strategy in the Advanced Pro chart in Genetic Matrix under Design -> Determination. It is critical to have an exact moment of birth for this information. If you do not have an exact minute listed on the birth certificate or are not confident its correct for any reason, you can still explore all these options and observe your child and what they naturally gravitate to. Considering these as possibilities that can help you embrace your child and the way that they eat, as natural for them.

What's interesting about this aspect of the chart is that it doesn't only apply to eating, but also other activities like learning and taking in information. Anywhere your child is taking in information, you can play with these concepts based on your child's digestion type. For example, if your child has a digestion theme of Calm and is trying to do homework or learn in a chaotic environment and struggling, try moving their study area to a quiet area in the house and seeing if their concentration improves.

All of these digestion types are just one aspect of the chart. It's important to remember that your child is an entire human being and not one part of their chart only. Please take this information in and play with it. Observe how they naturally want to eat and learn, rather than insisting on how you want them to eat or what and how you want them to learn. It's all just a big experiment that continues to grow and evolve. See what works for your child and let this be a starting place. Don't let it be the only way. As we evolve and grow, we have different needs. The best dietary approach takes that into account and asks you to stay curious and open to what your body needs, not fixed in a dogmatic way of eating or learning. Simply following what someone told you to do, or because it worked at one time, or even because your Human Design Chart said so still doesn't allow you to connect to your innate wisdom of what's best for you. We must stay open to the possibilities that it can all change because we are complex human beings, and our bodies are constantly reaching for homeostatic balance and doing the best they can with what we have given them. Your children's bodies are the same, but the younger they are, the less dietary conditioning they've experienced. Try sitting back, getting curious about what is working for them and decide how you can work with it rather than against it.

Twelve Types of Digestion

The first six digestion types are centered more around the way your child eats their food and what they gravitate toward eating, while the rest are more about the environmental conditions than the foods themselves.

Figuring out what foods or subjects they like and how or where they prefer to eat their foods or do their homework can be supported by asking them the right kind of questions for their energy type.

1. **Consecutive Appetite:** Consecutive Digestion is considered the oldest digestion type, going back to the eating patterns of the hunter-gatherer era. As you can imagine, without supermarkets and foodstuffs aplenty as they are today, if you found a bush of berries, you ate them—all of them. Then perhaps you wandered on and found a stream where you caught a fish, and you ate the fish all by itself. People who have this digestion type do best eating one thing - literally one food at a time.

If your child has this digestion type, you may already know this. They are likely the kid that does not like all their food smushed together on their plate. They eat all the peas, then all the rice, then all of the meat, etc., consuming all of one food on the plate until it's gone and then moving to the next. This type may also be the most innate digestion type, meaning that the body has a natural ability to know what is good and right for it that is based on how things taste and feel in their bodies versus what is not. As humans, we used to know what this felt like, but as more and more foodstuffs have become the norm with food chemicals designed to light up our brains and make us want more, it's hard to know what a genuine need for our body is and what is our brain on foodstuffs. If you've ever had the opportunity to watch a wild animal such as a deer eat, they take a bite of a leaf and chew it, and if it's what their body wants, they can eat an entire bush, but if it's not, they simply move on and eat the next thing. The deer have not been given food chemicals and social conditioning and remain eating in a pattern very similar to how this digestion works. Your child may be obsessed with a single food such as blueberries, and that's all they want to eat for a day, or they might need separation on their plate and eat one food at a time. Also, this can mean one thing like potato, or for your child it could mean mashed potatoes that have milk and butter in them, combining a couple of foods but generally not many. You'll have to experiment to see what works for your child, but it doesn't always have to mean one single food only at a time. It could also mean eating a muffin alone rather than a muffin and eggs at the same meal.

If this is your child, do you let them eat this way already? If not, what would it take to allow yourself to experiment with your child eating this way?

Learning

The Consecutive Appetite Digestion type may do best focusing on one thing at a time. Limiting distractions around them and helping them learn to open only one browser tab on a computer may help them limit their overwhelm, stay focused, and learn efficiently.

2. **Alternating Appetite:** This digestion type is based on the previous Consecutive Appetite but allows a bit more variation. Their food is separated but rather than eating all of one food before moving on to the next, they eat one bite of kale and finish it, then one bite of blueberry and finish it, and then one bite of applesauce and finish it, and so on. So, it's still separating the foods but allowing more variation between bites rather than only eating one thing at a time until it's finished.

Learning

The Alternating Appetite Digestion type may do best by having a couple of browser tabs or subjects open at one time and do a little bit of one thing and then a little of the next, jumping back and forth between them. Learning in this manner is not how we've been taught in our standardized linear, logical learning system, and it can feel difficult for parents to try. If your child has this digestion type and is sitting down to do homework while struggling to keep their attention on one thing or feeling overwhelmed by having to be so focused, experiment with them. Try giving them two to three options at one time and let them do the work in the order they wish and see if things change. Again, help them follow their Strategy and Authority on the right choice for them in approaching getting the work done.

3. Taste - Open: With this digestion type, they are open to trying new foods and learning new things. If you have a child with this type of digestion, they may be a more adventurous eater than many kids. Offer them lots of different foods, and make sure to remain open to the idea that they may like foods that you don't. As parents, we can assume that our children will like similar foods to us, especially when they are young but if your child has this type of digestion, let them experiment. Take them to the grocery store with you and see what they are interested in or let them look through cookbooks to see what sparks their interest.

Learning

The Open Taste Digestion type may be open to learning lots of things, possibly even multiple languages or different variations of one thing. For instance, if they have an interest in dance, they may want to try several types of dance classes to figure out what they want to dive into more. Offer them different opportunities to learn, so they don't get bored with the limited options given in school. Follow their curiosity. This type correlates with the 3rd line Profile: your child needs to experiment and try lots of things to know what they like.

4. Taste – Closed: This digestion type represents a child who has a list of things they like and stick with them. You may get them to try new foods sometimes, but they will have the tried-and-true foods that they prefer. There is a certain safety in knowing what their food is going to be like, how they will feel eating it, and in this security, they gravitate toward the foods that make them feel good. This does not mean that they need to live off of chicken nuggets and sugary treats, but maybe they only like three kinds of fruit, and don't want to try the others you give them. As they develop and change, keep offering them new foods because something new may appeal to them later that didn't initially. Kids' taste buds change dramatically as they grow. They may start with very simplistic palates and develop the taste for more complex flavors.

If your child has this digestion type when you go to restaurants, do they order the same foods? Do you let them, or do you pressure them into trying something new? How has that worked for your child?

Learning

The Closed Taste Digestion type is likely to be the child who has figured out which subjects they really enjoy and want to dive deeply into those subjects. Obviously, there are more areas they need to learn about but may not enjoy as much as others, so you'll need to get creative to encourage them to learn new things. Can you negotiate with them to complete the work they don't love doing so they have more time to learn more about the things they do want to learn about? Rewards such as trips to museums, camps, classes, the library, or other opportunities to dive more into their favorite subjects can power them through the things they don't love so much.

5. Thirst - Hot: This type does not have as much digestive fire and needs some support to properly digest. They tend to gravitate toward warm foods (as it takes less effort and energy to digest) like soup, oatmeal, and cooked veggies rather than salads, smoothies, or cold foods (more effort to digest).

Learning

The Hot Thirst Digestion type may need to adjust where they are learning to be in a warm temperature space. Depending on the time of year and where you live, you may be inside more or outside, and learning may become more challenging if your child does not feel the temperature is comfortable. Likely to be interested in being cozied up on the couch under a blanket or their bed to do their homework, ask them if something would make them more comfortable to study.

6. Thirst - Cold: This digestion type belongs to a fierier system that needs cooling down and gravitates toward room temp or colder foods. These kids enjoy snacks like finger foods, charcuterie plates, appetizers, or colder foods like cold cereals, smoothies, salads, sandwiches, frozen fruits, and similar items.

Learning

The Cold Thirst Digestion type may need to adjust where they are learning to be literally in a cool temperature space. Depending on the time of year and where you live, you may be inside more or outside more, and learning may become more challenging if your child does not feel the temperature is comfortable. Likely to be interested in being on the floor where it's cooler, or by an open window, ask them if a temperature change would make them more comfortable to study.

7. Touch - Calm: This is a digestive type that does best in calm, quiet environments. What works best for these kids is a nice quiet family dinner, dinner one on one, or in a quiet restaurant. Keeping the commotion down around them helps them relax into a state where they can digest their foods better. If you have a large family or chaotic mealtimes, consider other options to allow everyone to get what they need, such as having them eat at a different time in a quiet space or eating in another room. You can still connect as a family at other times but allowing each of your children to eat in the way that feels best to them means they will feel good while eating and digest their food better. If your child with Calm Digestion asks to eat alone, it doesn't mean that they are depressed or don't like you. Nothing about this is personal to you but is optimal for their digestion.

Learning

The Calm Touch Digestion type needs a calm environment for optimal learning. For example, if your child normally sits at the kitchen counter to study and do homework and many other family members are coming in and out of the kitchen, this can be very distracting to them. They need a calm and peaceful space to learn best. Take inventory of your home and where the calm areas are at different times of the day. This does not have to mean silence, but a place where there is not a lot of movement or commotion.

8. Touch - Nervous: Opposite of Calm Touch Digestion, the Nervous Touch type needs to move around for optimal digestion. These kids have a hard time sitting still at the table and want to be up and moving about. They can also be the child who takes a bite of food and runs around the dining room or living room while they chew it before coming back for another bite.

I grew up with a cousin who did this every meal. She just couldn't sit still while she ate. I remember her mom getting an old seat belt from a car and buckling her into her seat at the table until she was done with dinner when she was about three. Later, when I found out about Human Design and looked up her chart, lo and behold, her digestive type is nervous. Turns out she was just digesting the way her body felt best and moving during dinner.

Learning

The Nervous Touch Digestion type needs an environment where they are allowed to move around while they study. Taking frequent breaks may be necessary for them to get up and move around, dance even, and be able to sit back down and focus again. You may even find them tapping the desk while reading to move energy while they work.

9. Sound - High: This digestive system is about being in a space where there is a higher sound level. Noisy restaurants, a TV on in the background, or music playing is preferred for this type. They may also be the child that makes a lot of noise or clinks their spoon on their glass or taps it on their dish, which may or may not drive you bonkers, but it's part of their process. The more commotion and chaos, the more at home and relaxed they feel. Big chaotic family dinners with extended family? That's right up their alley. They digest well when dining out or with friends or family.

Learning

The High Sound Digestion type may very well be the child who blasts their music in their room while doing homework, leading you to want to walk in and tell them to turn it down and focus, but it's important to be open to the possibilities of what works for them, even if it wouldn't work for you. They may want to take their homework to a coffee shop where there is noise and busyness around them while they work.

10. **Sound - Low:** This digestion type is also about the environment, but prefers mellow music, quiet conversation with their meals, or even silence. This type could show up as the child who enjoys classical music with meals or a modern variety of music with a mellow vibe to it while eating or one who wants to eat alone for the quiet.

Learning

The Low Sound Digestion type may learn best with some classical music or other mellow music playing in the background. Experiment with different mellow music preferences and see how your child's focus responds. They may also prefer to learn in a more intimate setting with one other person who has a similar learning style, or they may prefer going somewhere like the library where it's quiet.

11. **Light - Direct:** This digestion type has more to do with the environment they eat in. Direct light relates to times of day when natural light is available, which changes throughout the year. If you can sit outside to eat in the sunshine (when the weather permits), this brings happiness to this digestive system. If not, sitting in or near a window with good natural light can be sufficient. Does your dining

area have natural light? If not, can you let your child eat in another room where access to natural light is better? If natural light is unavailable, try having them eat in a more well-lit area, or earlier in the evening.

Learning

The Direct Light Digestion type child may prefer to get their work done earlier in the day when there is still light from the sun. They may prefer to sit outside in the natural light or in the window to do their work. They may also have difficulty getting their work done or staying focused later in the evening. If you're a working parent and don't have time until later in the evening to help with homework, it may take some creativity as to how you can navigate this design. Is there an older sibling or neighbor who could sit with them while they do their homework earlier in the day? Is there a space at their after-school program to allow them to work on their homework with access to natural light?

12. **Light - Indirect:** This digestion type also has more to do with the time of day and lighting when eating. This type prefers to eat in indirect light, which can mean eating or being hungrier after the sun goes down. Still, it can also be supported by altering the dining area to be dimly lit or drawing the curtains to create a more intimate space like when the sun goes down. Dinner by candlelight might be preferred as this is a less harsh light than LED light or incandescent light which can feel too stimulating.

Learning

The Indirect Light Digestion type child may prefer to put off doing their work until it gets closer to bedtime, and it gets darker out. A lot of parents want their child(ren) to get their homework done earlier in the day so that they can relax the rest of the evening; however, this may be a battle with a child with indirect light as their digestion type. Waiting until the conditions feel best for them can allow the child to get their work done more efficiently once they dive into it if they're not forced to do the work earlier, which means less struggle for you, the parent, and less stress for the child. You could also stage a low light vibe in their room with curtains if this helps them study better. Ask them what works for them and experiment.

With all these designs and suggestions, remember that following Strategy and Authority for your child's energy type is most important. You might recognize all twelve elements of digestion in your child, and that's okay¾in fact, it's normal. We are complex beings, and we all have all elements of the chart. Even those of us with definition in particular centers or channels and gates can experience variations of that energy, especially due to the conditioning of the people we spend the most time with. Conditioning does not have to be experienced as a negative. Our conditioning shapes us to be who we are and helps us learn the lessons we need in this life to become wise about ourselves. No one escapes without conditioning, nor should they. We are all just traveling through life interacting with each other, affecting one another, and learning from one another.

Get Curious About Learning

Consider how you learn and where your preferences may influence how your child learns. What could shift with mealtimes or learning if you experiment with their digestion type? What do they need to feel supported and successful in their learning?

How do You Work with Multiple Different Digestion Types?

I know how overwhelming it can feel when everyone in the house has different digestive needs or requirements due to food sensitivities, allergies, or preferences. Add in these different eating styles, and it can feel overwhelming, but most of these type combinations can be navigated together when eating.

If you have a child with Nervous Digestion and one with Calm Digestion, you may have to feed them in separate rooms or at different times, which can feel disappointing when you prioritize eating as a family. It's not to say that you can never eat together. But if you notice at the family table that one child can't sit still and the other child can't handle the movement of the first one, perhaps small shifts can help. It might make for a much less stressful mealtime if you divide the table or create two dining areas if possible or try eating at different times with the kids as another option.

High and Low Digestion can be navigated by having a child wear headphones for music to create the high sounds optimal for them, while the child with Calm Digestion may need noise-canceling headphones or earplugs and both can still be present at the same table.

Children with Consecutive Digestion can be served meals with different foods on different plates or plates with dividers if that feels good to them. Children with Open Taste Digestion may benefit from your bringing home a new ingredient every week, or at least once in a while, so they can try something new or try a restaurant that serves something they've never had before. Open Digestion types can make excellent cooks if they choose because they are willing to try new things and be open to combining things that others would not.

If a parent has Calm Digestion and the kids have Nervous or High Digestion, sit with them and have a beverage while they eat and engage in conversation and then eat your meal after their dinner, allowing yourself the space to eat in a calm environment.

I assure you, you can work with these different digestion types; it just takes an open mind and some creativity. We must break open the boundaries that we have set or perpetuated from our ancestors and what they expected from us. The way forward is the way that works for you and your family. The times we live in are different from forty or fifty years ago, and indeed different from 100 years ago. Tradition can mean everything to people who hold it in high regard. Tradition can still be a part of your life; you just may need to get a bit creative with how you approach it and how you define it. What new traditions can you create?

If creating connection at the dinner table feels too tricky with many different digestion types, consider another way you can connect with your child(ren) and family that doesn't involve mealtimes. Family game night? Evening dance party? Family walks or nature hikes? I'm sure you can get creative with whatever your family is interested in and develop something that allows you time to connect, even if it's not around the dinner table.

Sleep

Sleep can be a big challenge for parents, both for themselves and for their children. According to WebMD, the current research on sleep shows that children need the following amount of sleep based on their age.[4]

RECOMMENDED SLEEP FOR CHILDREN

Age	Amount of Sleep Needed
1-4 Weeks	15-16 hours/day
1-4 Months	14-15 hours/day
4-12 Months	14-15 hours/day
1-3 Years	12-14 hours/day
3-6 Years	10-12 hours/day
7-12 Years	10-11 hours/day
12-18 Years	8-9 hours/day

This research is an average of what kids need, but your child may not fit right into the middle average which is why looking at your children as individuals can help free you to live a less stressful life around bedtime and sleep. Just as with dietary advice, exercise advice, business advice, and anything else in life, parenting advice

---

[4] "Grow" by WebMD, "How Much Sleep Do Children Need?" accessed on 12/17/2021, https://www.webmd.com/parenting/guide/sleep-children#1

is given based on what works for the person who wrote it or based on a study of a specified number of kids, but your child may be different. This book is about reminding you that you and your child are individuals. What you need, your child needs, and your family needs will be unique to you and them, and I want you to feel free to embrace that. There is enough judgment in parenting, especially around this topic, so let's consider some key ingredients to getting optimal sleep.

Here Are Seven Things That You Can Try to Help Improve Your Child's Sleep

1. Reduce screen time in the day.

Replace some screen time with other things such as games, dancing, sports, nature walks, trips to the library, puzzles, imagination games, bike riding, and more. Ask them questions for their energy type to find out what they would like to do more of.

2. Get them outside and move their bodies.

For children with a defined Sacral Center, if they are not sleeping well, make sure they have physically moved their bodies enough during the day. If they do not move enough to discharge all of the energy their little Sacral energy factories are churning out each day, they won't sleep easily. This energy buzzing within them needs to be used up so they can sleep well. Without adequate sleep this can lead to poor attention the next day, hyperactivity with fatigue, and poor ability to take in information at school. Often, the kids who get labeled with hyperactive disorders or attention disorders benefit hugely from just moving their bodies more. We've become a society that sits too much, and is fed information at lightning speed, without taking time or space to digest the information by getting up, moving our bodies, or doing something creative. Instead, we just keep pushing more information into our brains. Don't underestimate the transformation more movement can make in a Sacral energy type's well-being.

Of course, all these recommendations must begin with the parents first. If you're on your devices all day and night, while you're watching TV, or while you're at the park with them, that is what they will think is normal and imitate you. You set the example for the behavior your child exhibits, which is a lesson I've had to work hard to remind myself of regularly. It's easy to check out by scrolling social media for a break or work when you're self-employed or work from home. Set timers, turn your phone off, lock them up if you have to, and ask your children to hold you accountable too. We all could use better boundaries when it comes to screen time and social media.

3. Have them get their bare feet on the earth.

If you live near the beach, even better, but any natural ground will do. Earthing is a process that can help neutralize free radicals, reduce inflammation, and lower cortisol as you absorb electrons from the earth.[5] The book *Earthing* by Ober, Sinatra, and Zucker explains the benefits of earthing in great detail. It can also just feel good to connect with the earth in this way, particularly for kids who may not have conformed to wearing shoes all day. If your child has sensitivities to different sensations, try various textures such as sand, water, grass, mud, dirt, etc. Making mud pies isn't just fun; it also has health benefits!

4. Teach them mindfulness practices like yoga or meditation.

Download an app to teach yourself some yoga sequences that you can do with your kids. Have the video lead you, or learn on your own, and then put on some music and move your bodies together.

---

[5] James L. Oschman, "Can electronics act as antioxidants? A review and commentary," *Journal of Alternative and Complimentary Medicine*, 2007 Nov;13(9):955-67, https://pubmed.ncbi.nlm.nih.gov/18047442/

5. Get creative.

Encourage creative expression like drawing, writing, building, exploring, dancing, acting, or cooking. They get to move energy *and* emotions, whether self-made or absorbed from others- double win!

6. Reduce exposure to Electromagnetic Frequencies (EMFs).

Check out the section a little further on in this chapter on Devices and EMFs.

7. Create a safe place with loving attention and physical contact.

Try going a whole day without touching anyone and see how your feeling of safety and connection change. Although for some parents who are in the thick of the young childrearing years, a day of not being touched sounds heavenly as your body often does not feel like your own when it's in service to kids all day. I see you, parents. It won't always be like this. Your body will be yours once again one day.

Some Other Considerations for Optimal Sleep

Pineal Gland

The pineal gland produces melatonin, the sleep hormone. Without enough of it, we can have trouble sleeping. Though there are supplements, I do not recommend them for kids unless your doctor recommends them in a rare instance. Taking supplemental melatonin can tell your body it doesn't need to make its own any longer and it will begin to down-regulate making this hormone. The pineal gland is deeply involved with sleep and regulates the circadian rhythm—the pattern of when your body is awake and asleep through rising and falling cortisol levels.

The endocrine system involves the thyroid, sex hormones, pancreas, (which makes digestive enzymes, insulin, and glucagon for regulating blood sugar), the adrenals (cortisol and adrenaline production), as well as the pituitary and the hypothalamus which is the master gland of the endocrine system and controls all of the others. If there is a dysfunction in one of these areas, it can affect many other areas of the body. Sleep affects not just mood and concentration, but the entire endocrine system and is critical to health.

Things That Can Affect Pineal Gland Functioning

1. Fluoride, bromide, and other halogens calcify the pineal gland over time, compete for thyroid receptor sites, and contribute to thyroid issues.

2. Artificial lighting, including LED lighting which flickers, may overstimulate the brain and stress the body.

3. Pesticides and other environmental chemicals contribute to the calcification of the pineal gland over time.

4. The pineal gland is said to be the "seat of the soul" or the "third-eye." It is deeply related to your connection with Spirit and feeling disconnected from Source/Spirit/God/Goddess/Divine/Universe can affect your ability to sleep as well.

Napping

Some kids give up napping at two, while others continue to need naps all through grade school (especially non-Sacral energy types). How we perceive the world and how much energy we take in from others can play a big part in how well we rest. If your child has a lot of openness in their chart and is not designed to hold specific types of energy for long periods, they may be a child who needs more downtime, more naps, earlier bedtimes, or later wake-up times.

Downtime

Non-Sacral energy type children need more downtime, and this may or may not include more sleep. Remember that these kids take in and amplify the Sacral energy they are around all day. If they share a bedroom with a sibling or family member with a defined Sacral Center, they are likely not resting as deeply as they would if they were sleeping alone. These kids (and adults) do best if they get into bed at least thirty minutes before lights out and unwind with a book or guided meditation, have story time, or can listen to an audiobook. They must be lying down while they are unwinding as the BodyGraph changes when they lie down and some of the centers essentially go to sleep until you get back up and are vertical again, so it's not all about just having quiet alone time, but also about lying down. I have found for myself as a Projector that even if I am watching a show on my iPad with Night Shift or blue light blocking glasses on (which still exposes me to some blue light) before bed, if I'm lying in bed while doing so, it can still help me relax. I notice with my defined Head and Ajna that when I lie down, I can quiet my mind in a way that I can't in the daytime when I'm upright, and they're so active.

Blue Light

Blue light is one of the more significant concerns we have for sleep currently as we are exposed to it all day long, and children's brains are particularly lit up (excited) by exposure to it. Ideally, we wouldn't expose children to it later in the evening, but we live in a modern world, and we're all just doing the best we can. You can download apps like f.lux for your computers or use Night Shift on iOS devices which changes the color of the light to a more amber tone that is not so harsh on the eyes or brain.

Blue light blocking glasses is another option, and if your child wears glasses already you can get a blue light blocking coating added to their lenses, so the time they spend on their computers is not quite so harsh to them. Some retailers include this coating on all children's glasses at no extra cost.

Sleep Hygiene

The environment where your child sleeps can make a big difference. For example, consider a child with touch sensitivity and a blanket that's too scratchy or too soft. Are their blankets too heavy or too light? Weighted blankets can help calm anxious children and have become more prevalent in the last few years, as they act like a big body hug that calms the nervous system. Are the blankets the right thickness for the temperature, time of year, or location? Is the air temperature too hot or too cold? Do they prefer to sleep with a nightlight on? It is optimal for melatonin production to sleep in darkness, but not all kids can tolerate that. Try to use the lowest light setting to make them feel comfortable and get restful sleep.

Food

Have they eaten a bunch of sweets in the day or before bed? Do they drink caffeine? Even if it's much earlier in the day, these things can impact their sleep quality and ability to fall asleep quickly. Do they eat foods with lots of food dyes? Food dyes have been found to correlate with hyperactivity.[6] If your child is sensitive to any of these, they don't have to ingest a lot to have an impact. Do they have any food intolerances like gluten or dairy? Tummy aches often make for a difficult time sleeping or can cause constipation, affecting sleep quality.

Body

Have they moved their body enough today? Do they need to release the energy they built up from other people throughout the day? Don't forget the non-Sacral kids can dance or do other movement to shake out the energy they absorb all day.

Creativity and Imagination

Reading to your child before bed can help them grasp language, inspire their creativity and imagination and depending on the stories, help them understand morals and values. This can also be a special bonding time where kids feel important and have your full attention in a busy world which allows them to fall off into sleep feeling nurtured, important, and loved.

---

[6] Prabasheela Bakthavachalu , S Meenakshi Kannan , M Walid Qoronfleh, "Food Color and Autism; A Meta-Analysis," *Advances in Neurobiology*, 2020; 24:481-504, https://pubmed.ncbi.nlm.nih.gov/32006369/.

Additional Human Design Aspects

Does your child have a non-motorized Throat Center? If so, they build up a lot of energy from being around defined Throat Centers all day. They need to have time to release all of that stored Throat Center energy, usually by telling you all about their day and what Sammy did on the playground and what Mrs. Turner did when Erika wouldn't listen in class, and, and, and... Try giving them time to talk about their day before bedtime, or plan for that at bedtime so you don't end up frustrated that you just want to get some downtime at the end of the day and bedtime is taking forever! If you have a Reflector, they may want to stay up late talking, processing, and discharging all the energy they took in that day, or they might just want to be left alone at bedtime, needing most to get time alone and in their own aura. Try not to take it personally.

Downtime for Sacral vs. Non-Sacral Energy Types

Defined Sacral Energy Type Kids - Generators and Manifesting Generators

These Sacral defined energy types are the source of the go, go, go energy. To properly slow down enough that they can rest and sleep at night, they need to use up the energy that their Sacral Center generates each day with enough physical activity to be able to drop down into rest and relax mode. The more cranky, frustrated, and unfocused the Sacral energy type child is, the more likely it is that they need more physical activity in their day-to-day life.

I've heard many parents tell me that if they don't force their children to wind down before bed, they fear they won't sleep (these are usually non-Sacral energy type parents). However, if you have a Sacral energy type child, you may still need to let them run out their Sacral energy batteries, even if it's right before bedtime with a run in the yard, jumping-jacks, dance party, or another way your child likes to use up energy.

Non-Sacral Kids - Manifestors, Projectors, Reflectors

The non-Sacral kids need ways to release the energy they take in and absorb all day long, especially if they live with defined Sacral energy types. These kids don't need more physical exertion the way the Sacral energy types do, but more time for relaxation and unwinding. Non-Sacral kids need to get into bed at least thirty minutes before lights out so that they can discharge the energy they absorbed throughout the day and allow the body to slow down, ideally alone in their own aura.

Another thing to note is that if you have a Projector or Reflector who has an undefined Throat, they may need some time to release the pressure that has built up in their Throat Center by talking about their day. You may need to set some time aside for letting them talk and be heard while releasing this built-up pressure so they can wind down for sleep, especially if your bedtime routine is taking longer and longer each night.

Non-Sacral energy types can be amped up from all the Sacral energy around them. If they are around this energy a lot, they may need to dance or jump it out on a trampoline for a few minutes to move the energy through their bodies physically, but it's not the same level of intensity of needing to physically move as a defined Sacral energy type child. The difference between them is that the defined Sacral Center is the creator of the energy, and the energy buzzes around in them until it's released through physical work or play. On the other hand, the non-Sacral child is in energy overload in a system that isn't meant to hold this type of energy for very long, and they just need to move enough to let it flow through them.

Devices and EMFs and Health

Electronics are a huge part of our daily life. Do you even remember a time before everyone had a cell phone? I do. It was amazing! We had the freedom to play and create and do without worrying that someone would film us, put us on social media, and bully us with it. It also meant we were forced to find other things to do with our time, like playing games, going outside, reading, learning, exploring, or even simply looking out the window on a road trip and playing silly games in the car. We had the time to be bored, which allowed the space to imagine and create.

We've likely all heard by now that we should limit children's TV time and electronic time. I'm a firm believer that you know what's best for your child *when you're paying attention*. If you're regularly handing your child a phone at eighteen months old so you can shop in the store uninterrupted while they zone out, that's probably not considered paying a lot of attention. Instead, consider the opportunity to connect with your child, teaching them about shopping, budgeting, selecting good fruits and vegetables, sales, quality items vs. stuff that is going to break and end up in a landfill sooner rather than later, and so much more.

Jordan Shapiro, author of *The New Childhood*, says that if we deny our children electronics until they are a certain age—thirteen or whatever you choose—that when you do turn them loose, they don't know how to manage it. They go overboard because it's new and addictive and has so much access. But if we teach them how to be responsible with it from a young age and they see it as a tool, rather than a toy, they can grow up understanding that it's a tool and it has its place, but it does not have to be all-consuming. Technology does not appear to be going anywhere, so we need to learn how to embrace it in the healthiest way possible to navigate this world we've created.

Screen Time

How much screen time is too much? How much avoidance is living in an ancient world? This topic has been studied and researched for years. Results from such studies change as different factors or variables are introduced, but what we do know is that children's brains are highly affected in just a short amount of time by holding a cell phone up to their head. Here's an article[7] in *Clinical and Experimental Pediatrics* from as recent as November 2020, that says "The developing nervous system is more conductive and absorbs more electromagnetic energies than those of adults." I think most people know it has the potential to affect them, but to what extent? New technology is always developing, especially with the widespread rollout of 5G nationwide in the U.S. and we have yet to see the effects of this new technology. There is also Wi-Fi on every corner, usually multiple signals. If you live in an apartment building, you're exposed to smart electric meters, your neighbor's Wi-Fi, cell phones, and any other devices they use, such as smart thermostats, stoves, washing machines, Alexas, and on and on.

We can't always control what is happening around us, but we can control how much we expose ourselves to EMFs and electronics directly, which is especially important at night. When we sleep, our bodies go into a regenerative state, our defenses are lowest, and we are more vulnerable to the effects of radiation. There are ways to protect your sleep area and create a sleep sanctuary free of EMFs, but it's expensive. Short of investing hundreds to thousands of dollars on creating this space, you can do some simple things to limit exposure for you and your family.

1. Set your Wi-Fi router on a timer so that it goes off at night; you can even set it to come back on in the morning, so it's not a bother to anyone. This not only limits EMF exposure to everyone in the house at night, but it also keeps your kids from getting on the internet in the middle of the night and disrupting their sleep.

2. Turn your cell phone on Airplane mode, silent, Do Not Disturb, or vibrate mode when you go to bed at night. Again, fewer distractions equal better

---

[7] Jin-Wha Moon, "Health Effects of Electronic Fields on Children," *Clinical and Experimental Pediatrics*, 2020 Nov; 63(11): 422–428, http://www.ncbi.nlm.nih.gov/pmc/articles/PMC7642138/#:~:text=In%20today's%20world,%20most%20children,effects%20of%20EMFs%20are%20increasing.

sleep. Airplane mode also stops the phone from trying to connect to the towers nearby. Did you also know that if you live in an area with poor cell reception, the lower the bars of service, the higher the radiation emitted from your phone as it tries harder to connect to service? Additionally, if you're driving around town or on a long trip, your phone is ramping up and down how much radiation it sends out as it connects and disconnects and reconnects from tower to tower. In the more remote areas, you're better off downloading some music or maps and then turning it on Airplane mode until you're back to full bars of service to lower radiation exposure, especially if you're sensitive.

3. Keep your and your kid's phone charging in another room so that any pings or alerts do not wake you. I hear of so many kids sleeping with cell phones under their pillows, putting this EMF emitting device right under their heads all night when their defenses are down, and their bodies are most vulnerable.

4. Even if your child does not connect to cell service and you turn off the Wi-Fi router at night, many kids are still up past their bedtimes on their devices playing games. Consider keeping all devices in a locked drawer until morning if you find this is a problem in your family.

If your child has many open centers in their chart, they may be more sensitive to EMFs. EMF sensitivity can show up as agitation, anxiety, irritability, ringing in the ears, dizziness, tingling, and fatigue, to name a few symptoms.

In my coaching practice and talking with parents of children with an undefined or open Spleen Center, I have noticed that they tend to be more sensitive to EMFs. I've also noticed children with undefined or open Root Centers have a more challenging time letting go of the electronics and knowing when to put them away.

CHAPTER TWELVE

WHY CHILDREN MISBEHAVE

Do the best you can until you know better.
Then when you know better, do better.
~MAYA ANGELOU

Children act out, they react, and they can test every ounce of patience you have, but they don't do it initially to frazzle your sanity. They act out because they want to know they are loved, they belong and are worthy, that you value them, and that there is a place for them in your family and in the world. They also need to be allowed to explore, experiment, and learn through doing, rather than having things done for them or being told how things should be done. This autonomy allows them to feel capable and self-sufficient for their age. I've always felt that if I've done my job right as a parent, my kids will grow up and not need me, but they'll come back and share their lives with me because I've provided a space in their lives where they feel seen, heard, valued, and free to be themselves.

We get so caught up in the moment with all the multi-tasking and problem-solving that what we don't often see on the surface of our kids' behavior is the uncertainty and hurt that they are feeling inside. Kids will cover up their insecurities through acting out, engaging in a power struggle with you, trying to get even by hurting you back, or just giving up on things that are difficult for them. They're challenging you to make sure that you care, and they're often not even consciously aware that this is what they're doing.

These four basic ways that children misbehave are described in detail in Rudolf Dreikurs' book, *Children: The Challenge*, which was introduced to me through my mentor Karen Curry Parker. I use these four elements when looking at the behavior a child is experiencing when working with parents so we can see how parents can best support them. When we understand these four basic behaviors, we can then look at our children's Human Design charts and see where their needs are not being met and what we can do about it.

The way we can understand more about what their needs are that aren't being met is by how their behavior makes *us* feel. The response they elicit in us gives us clues as to why they are behaving the way that they are.

The four basic behaviors that children use are:

1. **Attention** - With this behavior, children try to get your attention to make sure that they still belong, that you love them, and that they can push your buttons and you'll still be there. They want to know that you still care about them. What they can't seem to come right out and say is "I don't know where or how I fit in, please make me feel loved and secure." This can show up when they feel they aren't getting enough attention, such as when you're working late or working from home, or when you bring a new baby or sibling or partner into the home. *When a child is trying to get your attention, you, the parent, will feel frustrated or irritated/annoyed.*

2. **Power** - With this behavior children try to assert some sort of control over themselves, which can look like they're trying to overpower others. They simply want a say in what's happening in their lives. They want you to help them know that they can be *appropriately* powerful for their age. What can they do themselves that you are not allowing or encouraging? If what they want power over is not appropriate, where can you help them see that they *can* have power in their life? We're not trying to create power monsters here, just making sure that they know that their voice is heard and that they can

have some control over what happens to them. *When a child is not feeling powerful in their life, they will engage in a battle for power with you and you will feel challenged and provoked.* You can probably think of an instance where you asked your child to do something like pick up their toys, and they replied, "No." You then replied more forcefully that they need to pick up their toys, and they replied with "You can't make me, you're not the boss of me!" This is an example of a power struggle where who wins? Nobody wins when it ends in tears for either of you. Consider how you can give them opportunities to help them feel appropriately powerful in their lives. Give them some power to choose, for example, ask, "Do you want to pick up your toys now or after your snack?"

3. **Inadequacy** - This behavior is the "I can't do it all by myself, I need help" or "I don't know how" when asked to clean up their room or start their homework. The child who says "I'm too stupid. I just can't do this" and gives up, is often overwhelmed by the task, and they need your help to understand how to break the task down into manageable pieces. If they have an open Root Center, the pressure of getting the task done might just feel like too much for them. Help them break it down into steps that they can take to get it done. If they have an open Sacral Center, they might need some borrowed energy to complete the task. *When a child is feeling inadequate, the emotion you will feel is confusion or exasperation.* With this behavior you feel confused because you know that they are capable, and you end up frustrated because you don't immediately understand what the issue is. Step back and consider if they are overwhelmed. Do they need some support? How can you make them feel adequate and successful? Don't forget to ask Sacral or open-ended questions depending on their energy type to get them going again.

4. **Revenge** - This is usually reserved for the teenagers or the children whose needs have gone unmet for a length of time, and they've become mad and hurt so they want you to feel those things too. These kids often do not feel lovable. What has shifted in the family? Have you brought someone new into the

home? A new baby? Are you caring for a family member that takes up the time that you used to spend on them? Are they *feeling* left out, disempowered, or not good enough for you to love? Are they getting enough attention? Are they feeling appropriately powerful in their lives? Are they feeling inadequate somewhere in their lives and need your support? *When a child is feeling the need for revenge, the parent will feel like they want to hurt the child in response, often with a gross overreaction like saying something horrible and hurtful to them or kicking them out of the house.*

When our children act out, if we can take a moment to pause and consider how we are feeling before reacting, we have an opportunity to see what we miss when we simply react without thinking. However, before we can use our own emotions to gauge how we are feeling in response to our children, we must look at ourselves and consider if our needs are being met. Are we feeling grounded? Are we getting enough time to ourselves to rest, reset, and rejuvenate? Are we feeding ourselves regularly and well so that we feel steady energy throughout the day and are not getting hangry? Are we being realistic about how long things take, or are we trying to cram too many things into a single day and then feel irritated with our kids when they want our attention? Not only does the way we take care of ourselves affect how we respond to our child(ren), but our children are learning their habits from us and watching how we take care of ourselves. We must consider what we're teaching our children or how we are conditioning them to live as they watch us race around stressed out, not prioritizing ourselves, and not nourishing our bodies. If we want more peace, success, satisfaction, or surprise (their signature emotions that show alignment for their energy type) for them, we must make sure we want more of those things for ourselves as well.

CHAPTER THIRTEEN

GENDER ROLES

You wander from room to room hunting for the diamond necklace
that is already around your neck.

~RUMI

Gender roles are being challenged now more than ever, and we are finally societally beginning to redefine what it looks like to be a family. While society has long held specific ideas of how men, women, and children should be, behave, do, and what roles they should play, we are finally seeing that not everything in life or everyone in life fits into a neat and tidy box that we can wrap a bow around and put on the "correct" societal shelf.

The time has come where society is breaking down social constructs and redefining where all of us fit and what a family looks like on a larger scale. Families often feel like they don't fit the "norm" and struggle to explain their lives, parenting, and relationships to others. I wish they all knew just how much everyone feels like they don't fit into those boxes.

Boxes are meant to hold things, not people.

It is time for change on so many levels, and our traditional gender roles are no exception. Gone are the days of moms staying home to raise the children, volunteering for the PTA, and having dinner waiting with a cocktail-ready at 5:00 for their husbands to arrive home from a busy day of work where he sits and is catered to while mom takes care of it all.

I spent a lot of time with my grandparents growing up. My grandfather was a long-haul truck driver and was gone for days at a time. When he'd come home, dinner was served at 5:00 daily to him on a tray in his recliner in front of the TV. I remember being in high school, and thinking *Oh my god, I'm never going to do that*! And when I got married, I remembered that and told my husband, "Don't expect me to cook for you every night," and he didn't. He's always grateful when I cook, he's never picky about what I fix, and when it was just the two of us, we were much freer about what we ate, when we ate, and where we ate. I remember one time at midnight, my husband wanted tortillas, and we didn't have any, so he found a recipe online and made his own, and we ate those delicious tortillas after about two hours of hard work.

But then kids came along, and they relied on us to feed them, clothe them, nurture them, make sure they're safe and happy, and our world revolved around them and their needs. I wanted to be a "good mom" and do it "right," and I fell into patterns that became unsustainable when later I started a business that I was passionate about and wanted time for too. One day I woke up and found myself feeling like a maid fixing everyone's meals, making sure they ate and showered, did their homework, and all the other things that we as moms take on and feel expected to do. I realized that I'd just stepped into the role I promised myself I'd never get stuck in. I began to resent that it continued to be my role in keeping up those things while building a business. The most frustrating part is that my husband would help, but I had a hard time allowing him to help in his way. I still felt responsible. I felt like I wasn't doing "my job" as a mom.

Who was I really mad at? First, I was angry at society for telling me I can have it all, but only if I'm willing to fulfill my traditional roles first before fulfilling myself and my contribution as a person to the world. Second, I realized I was mad at myself for perpetuating these outdated ideas. I was keeping this pattern alive!

The time is now to shift these expectations and change the story. I talk to women every day who are in the same position and feel guilt for wanting to be something in addition to their role as mom. If you genuinely enjoy cooking and caring for people, great! The world needs you to do what you're designed to do! But if not, the family dynamic can shift to allow everyone to have their needs met and share the workload at home too.

Even the moms who love to do for their family get burned out on all the selfless doing. At some point, we all need to feel appreciated. And for us non-energy types, we can't keep going on without some recognition, appreciation, or support. The more we must do, the less we want to do. We become bitter, frustrated, angry, or disappointed. Nearly every mom I work with in my coaching practice initially comes in feeling some level of burnout because they are expected to keep fulfilling the role of traditional mom and wife in addition to any work or professional life they have to or choose to have. And they are tired, so, so tired.

Human Design shows us that we are all designed differently and that it doesn't matter your gender, race, religion, or anything else. The Human Design Chart has the same possibilities for every human and is determined by your birth date, time, and place. When we look at this chart that has seemingly endless possibilities how could we ever categorize traits through gender alone? This is not just about women's roles either. How are we supporting the men in our lives, if we aren't allowing them the space to do the nurturing and caring roles they crave, to feel like they're living an authentic life? How are we allowing the folks who are not defined by gender to fit into the story if it is only operating through a binary with outdated ideas? When I look at a chart with a client, I look at energy and what is consistent (defined) versus what is variable (undefined), and from there we look at how this is showing up in their lives. For example, sometimes, when I look at a family's charts, I can see and am told that the man has more nursing and nurturing capacity than the woman, who would rather be out working a job that makes her feel fulfilled. Yet they struggle with allowing each other to fill the roles they're designed for because family and society have conditioned them to believe that they can't. It's getting better, but the judgment is still there.

Human Design shows us there is no right or wrong way to be a family or to divide up the chores and responsibilities. What works for you and your family is right for you, as long as everyone feels good about their roles, no matter how it looks to anyone—family or otherwise—on the outside.

Let's all break each other out of these boxes, by embracing who we truly are and allowing each other to do the same!

CHAPTER FOURTEEN

PARENTING AND CHILDREN WITH DIFFERENT ENERGY TYPES

Each child is an artist. The problem is
how to remain one after growing up.
~PICASSO

A common question I get is "How do you manage when you have children with different energy types?" The most foundational piece of advice I can give you is to honor who they are as individuals. Find their unique gifts and strengths, focus on those, and know that their contributions to the family will be different as they are designed to be different.

Your Manifesting Generator, for example, has the energy to work and do and can be helpful with household chores, and can act on their own once they respond to something in their external reality (you've asked or invited them to do something for example). On the other hand, Projectors have a different approach, so it's not fair to expect them to do the same things. Now, to be clear, this does not mean that the Projector shouldn't have to do household chores, and, when these energy types are together, your Projector child can take in all that Sacral energy, amplify it, and for short bursts, outdo the Manifesting Generator. But remember, just because they can doesn't mean they should make a habit of it. Expecting them to sustain the same level of physical work as a Manifesting Generator, conditions them to grow up trying to behave like a Manifesting Generator, and this is not sustainable. When a Projector doesn't understand how to use their energy correctly, they burn out early and can end up bitter that things aren't working out for them like they are for everyone else.

You can team them up to work on tasks together, but it's also good to recognize that your Projector child is naturally inclined to learn systems and make them more efficient, and also to guide after being recognized and invited. Are there tasks they can help with that they would be more naturally talented and inclined to do?

Movement

Non-Sacral energy types need to move their bodies as much as anyone else for optimal health; however, what movement looks like for a Projector, Manifestor, or Reflector can be different from a Manifesting Generator or Generator. While a Manifesting Generator child needs to physically move every day until they have physically exhausted their Sacral energy, a non-Sacral energy child needs to move, but not to the point of exhaustion. Yes, they can play together and do the same things, they can even participate in team sports, but the intensity and duration will be different. Your non-Sacral kids may be perfectly content to sit in the park and read a book rather than run around. Notice how your children are naturally inclined to exercise (and how much) and ask them questions for their energy type to know if they need more or less exercise. Ask your Sacral energy types yes/no questions and ask your non-Sacral energy types open-ended questions.

For example, at the end of the day, ask your young non-Sacral energy type child if they'd like to pick a song to dance it out to before dinner. Then ask your Sacral energy type child after dancing "Do you need to move your body more before dinner?" and if they reply "No," ask "Do you need to move your body more after dinner?" and if they say yes, check in with them again after dinner. On the other hand, if you have a non-Sacral energy child you can ask "How would it feel to dance for a few minutes before we sit down to dinner?" This type of movement for them will help to move any energy they picked up in the day in their open centers out of their bodies, which are not designed to hold this energy for long periods.

Sleeping Arrangements

If you have multiple children and have the space, it's ideal to have each child have their own room for sleeping. Most people who have multiple children have at least one room with two or more kids in it. If this is the case for you, try to pair them up by energy type, particularly if you have Sacral and non-Sacral energy type children. Consider that Sacral energy types need to wear out their Sacral before sliding into bed. In contrast, non-Sacral energy types need to have at least thirty minutes lying down in bed reading or having quiet time before sleeping to discharge the energy they picked up in the day. If a non-Sacral energy type is sleeping in a room with a Sacral energy type all night, they don't get the same level of rest that they would alone or with another non-Sacral energy type. Even with two non-Sacral energy types, it can be too stimulating. For instance, if you have a Mental Projector and a Manifestor with two or three centers defined, it can still be too stimulating for them. While it doesn't always make sense age-wise, or if you've had them separated into same-gender rooms, everyone might get better rest if you try experimenting with how your energy types are roomed together for sleep.

How Do Our Designs as Parents Affect Our Children's Conditioning?

How we define work begins when we are children. Seeing how our parents and other adults use their energy and when they push through even though everything in their body says stop, teaches our children to ignore their body's signs and signals. When we as adults ignore our bodies' signals, we.teach our children to let their minds decide to overpower what their bodies need.

Now, I don't think most parents intentionally want to teach their children to ignore their bodies; however, conditioning has been passed down for generations about work ethic and working hard. The way our parents worked was hard. They were taught that with hard work comes reward, which is the conditioning many parents grew up with. It is up to us to change how we teach our children to view work and teach them to work with integrity. Working with integrity means honoring yourself, your body, your resources, your expectations of others, your needs, and your energy.

When we raise our children expecting them to work or behave like us, we ignore who they truly are, and we teach them to ignore who they truly are. Consider if you're parenting them as they are designed to work or as you think they should learn work.

I'm so glad that Human Design found you because right now is the perfect time to begin seeing your child for the unique person they are. Honoring your child(ren)'s gifts, accepting their limitations, and showing them grace and support as they navigate their challenges in life is one of the most valuable things you can give them.

A Projector child that grows up in a household of Generators learns to work hard. Depending on how aligned the Generators are, they may learn to people-please or become martyrs about all the work they do for everyone else. They learn to act without waiting for the invitation and try to make life happen. Even within the most aligned Generator families, children still receive conditioning through the family. You can make a conscious effort to help them see how they are different and help them learn to honor how they work and how their approach to life needs to be different for them to feel successful.

Even a Projector child in a house of all Projectors can be conditioned to live out of alignment if the family is operating out of alignment, pushing to make life happen. So, it's important that the parent and the whole family learn how they are all unique and how they can support one another in their uniqueness for the greater good of the family and humanity. The more we allow ourselves to be uniquely ourselves, the more we allow and support everyone to become uniquely themselves.

Reflector children are being conditioned by everyone they live with which can determine who they seek out in life to partner with or avoid. Help them see and honor their uniqueness and needs. The Manifestor child is often conditioned to be a Generator and not wait for the right timing to take action, again, trying to make life happen, rather than letting it happen and then taking action when their timing is correct. There are many ways that we condition each other, but remember the goal is not to avoid conditioning. The goal is to see each other for who we are, recognize our stories as parents that we need to work through, and course-correct when we see how we're trying to make our children work or behave like us that goes against their design. Our job as parents through the lens of Human Design is to see who our children uniquely are and help them navigate what it means just to be themselves.

CHAPTER FIFTEEN

RECOGNITION IS NOT JUST FOR PROJECTORS. EVERYONE LIKES TO BE ENCOURAGED.

Fill your life with tiny and large adventurous moments.
~SARK

As you have read through this book and looked at the chart(s) of yourself and your child(ren), I hope that you've found ways that you can take action and create a stronger connection with your child. I hope you see a way forward that isn't necessarily always easy but feels healthy and aligned and a way for you to grow together.

Human Design is the closest system to a user manual I've ever seen for a human being. What is found within the chart allows the potential for profound freedom to be uniquely you, which is the greatest gift you could ever give yourself, your family, and the world.

In Human Design we talk a lot about recognizing the Projectors, and as one myself, I appreciate that as it can often feel like no one sees us. But the truth is we all need to be seen, recognized, valued, and appreciated for who we are. There has never been anyone like you before, and there never will be again, because this moment never existed before, and it never will again.

My great-grandmother (also a Projector) used to watch me as a young child during the days my parents were at work, and I remember her always sitting on the couch and doing crossword puzzles. She always had a great big red hardback dictionary next to her as she puzzled. She died when I was twelve, and I remember asking for that dictionary which I still have. Inside the cover, she had written, "Use the dictionary and learn all you can, as it will never come out in movie form," which to me, speaks to the significance of language and how we connect with one another, how we describe things, people, and our relationships. Our words matter. Choose them wisely. For me, it also speaks to the point that the world is not given to us in a tidy little package with a pretty bow. It's available for us all, but we must put the pieces together and do the work to understand who we are, and through our greatest struggles often comes our greatest and most profound growth. We must take the pieces we know and find ways to understand them better, work with them, and see how they fit into the big picture of our lives. When it seems hard, know that you're on the edge of something great: great wisdom, great insight, or just one great day. Once we have the dictionary, we can find the right words, we learn how to spell the words we do not already know, and with this book in your hands, you have the resources to begin learning about that which you do not know so your language as a parent can expand.

My great-grandmother also used to say some wise things, which didn't always make complete sense to me as a five-year-old. However, it clearly left an impact because I remember them today. I remember her looking at the clock one day and saying that "It will never be this time again," and I replied, "But it will be this time again tomorrow" not understanding the impact of what she was saying. Kids can be quite literal. Indeed, the clock will make its rounds, and it will show this same time again, but it truly never will be this precise moment in time again. This is your moment. Every moment you have as a parent is fleeting. It exists, and in a heartbeat, it's gone. There is a saying that the days are long, but the years are short. I was told this when my children were babies, and I've held tightly to that saying many days when life was rough. Those words held me when it felt like I didn't know what to do next or how to help my child through what was happening. We are parents. We find a way. I wish that I had known about Human Design when my children were babies, but I am so thankful that it found me when it did. It gave me a map, a guide to help me navigate these uncharted waters, and I hope it helps you too. Of course, other parents have come before us, but no one has ever parented your child before, and I trust that you will find *your* way.

APPENDIX

Sacral-Response Questions

If you have a Sacral energy type child (Generator or Manifesting Generator), you'll need to get familiar with Sacral-response questions. Learning how to ask your child questions that they can respond to will change your life. If you're a Sacral energy type parent, have someone do this exercise with you as well, so that you can get to know how your Sacral responds, and you can teach your Sacral energy type children to respond with theirs.

If you're a Sacral energy type parent with a non-Sacral (Projector, Manifestor, Reflector) energy type child(ren), **do not** do this exercise for them or ask them Sacral questions, as it conditions them to try and live as a Generator energy type. Non-Sacral energy types need open-ended questions.

If you have a young child that has a Sacral energy type, practice always asking them yes/no or this/that questions. This will help them remain connected to their Sacral response to help them navigate life, staying connected to this powerful inner knowing.

As your child gets older, you can play a game with them. Make up a name for it or call it "The Yes/No Game," or the "I Decide" game. Get creative but make sure to keep it fun. You can use this to help them stay connected to their Sacral sounds when they are young, but you can also use it to get to their truth about something in particular.

You'll start by asking them simple questions about their surroundings, or what they're wearing. And once you start asking questions and they respond, you pick up the speed and ask them questions faster and faster until you know that they couldn't possibly be thinking them through, and this is when you'll know that they are answering from their truth. I'm listing some sample questions below but do use caution in asking them anything that you're not prepared to hear their truth on, such as "Do you like me?" or "Did you like dinner?" You might not like the answer you get. They may be mad at you that day and not like you at that moment–which is probably not the best time to ask these questions. Their Sacral is responding to what the question is in the present moment.

One caveat: You must warm up the Sacral before dropping in the question you need to ask; you can't just jump into the desired question right away.

If your child has an Emotional Authority, you'll want to do this several times throughout their emotional wave so that you can see their truth *over time*, which is what the Emotional Authority needs. You can read more about the emotional waves in Chapter Six, under Emotional Authority. It is generally understood that if the Sacral says no during the questioning throughout the wave that it's a no to the question. Keep a list of the questions you ask, so you can repeat them in the next few sessions.

Sample List of Sacral Response Questions

- Is your name (enter their name here)?
- Are you sitting down?
- Is it daytime?
- Is it nighttime?
- Do you like to play soccer?
- Do you want to paint your room?
- Are you wearing shoes?
- Am I your (mom/dad/etc.)?
- Do you like your teacher?
- Do you like swimming?
- Do you like to get presents?

- Do you like to give presents?
- Are you excited about summer break?
- Do you have a best friend?
- Is the sky blue?
- Do you like swimming?
- Are you excited to see (friend's name)?

Start with simple things about what is around them in the room, or what is obvious. Then you move to things that are not so obvious, as you notice them answering quickly and you know that they've stopped filtering the information through their minds, then you can drop in the real question you need to ask them. If you need more questions to get to that point, keep adding them until you can tell that they aren't answering from their mind anymore.

If your child is older, you can still ask yes/no Sacral questions this way; just make them age appropriate. If your child is not connected to this Sacral response due to conditioning away from using it and relying on the mind to make their decisions, i.e., the pro/con list, you may have to do this several times to engage it. Explain to them that rather than stress themselves out over whether they are making the "correct" decision, which usually considers other people's expectations and feelings, they can first understand their truth without the influence of other people, yourself included. Let them know that this is their truth and connecting to it can help them navigate the world and the opportunities that come to them in a way that preserves their energy. This way, they learn to only commit to the things they genuinely want to do and feel aligned with in life, and not say yes out of obligation.

Open-Ended Questions

If you have a non-Sacral energy type child, you'll need to be familiar with asking open-ended questions, as that is what they respond best to. This applies to Projectors, Manifestors, and Reflectors.

Open-ended questions allow the space for possibility, room for exploration, and the freedom to speak enough to find the way to their answer. If you are a Sacral energy type, this may be frustrating for you initially as you would like a quick yes or no and to move on to the next thing. It's important for you to get what you need as well, which is to be able to respond to yes or no questions so you can also teach your non-Sacral family members to ask you those yes/no, this/that type questions.

Examples of Open-ended Questions

- What would it look like if you said yes to _____?
- How do you think you could make that happen?
- Where do you think you'd have to go to learn more about that?
- Who do you know that would be a good resource to learn more about that?
- What sounds good to eat?
- Why do you feel that this is the correct choice for you?
- If you go to ___, what do you think you'll need to bring?
- What is your plan for___?
- Who do you think would be good at _____?
- Why do you think that?
- How do you know?
- How do you understand _____ to be?
- What do you think you need to know before moving forward with this project?
- I'm curious, how did you come to that conclusion?
- I wonder what would happen if you _____?
- What was your favorite part about____?
- Tell me more about_____.

As you're learning, you'll find you still ask yes/no questions. When you get those blank stares back at you, just try rephrasing the question and make it more open-ended and see if it shifts their ability to answer you more easily.

If they've been used to hearing yes or no questions from you, they may be quickly answering but from a conditioned response. The more open-ended questions you can ask them, the more you help them connect with their truth. Just keep practicing and reframing when needed. You've got this!

RESOURCES

Books

I Ching: The Ancient Chinese Book of Changes

Quantum Activation Cards Companion Book by Karen Curry Parker

The Definitive Book of Human Design, The Science of Differentiation by Lynda Bunnell and Ra Uru Hu

The Gene Keys by Richard Rudd

The Wisdom Keepers Oracle Deck and Inner Guidebook by Rosy Aronson, Ph.D.

Understanding Human Design by Karen Curry Parker

Where To Get Your Chart

Genetic Matrix - www.geneticmatrix.com. You can get a free copy of your basic chart, or for a small fee, you can create charts for your family and get the advanced features including information on digestion.

To find your Digestion type, choose the Advanced Membership plan. Under the Quantum chart in Genetic Matrix on the left side of the chart listed under Body, you'll find the Determination, which will tell you your Digestion type.

For bonuses and to access more resources directly from Aypril Porter that accompany the book and enrich your learning experience:

- – Images from *Parenting the Child You Have* in color and enlargeable

- – *Parenting the Child You Have Workbook*

- – Parenting by Human Design Classes

Just open up the camera app, and your phone will automatically open a web browser and take you to the embedded link.

BIBLIOGRAPHY

Bakthavachalu, Prabasheela, Kannan, S Meenaksh, Qoronfleh, M Walid. "Food Color and Autism; A Meta-Analysis." *Advances in Neurobiology*. 2020; 24:481-504. https://pubmed.ncbi.nlm.nih.gov/32006369/.

"Grow" by WebMD, "How Much Sleep Do Children Need?" accessed on 12/17/2021, https://www.webmd.com/parenting/guide/sleep-children#1

"Just Now Chart," Jovian Archive, Discover Your Design, Live Your Life, accessed on 12/17/2021, https://www.jovianarchive.com/Just_Now.

Moon, Jin-Wha. "Health Effects of Electronic Fields on Children." *Clinical and Experimental Pediatrics*. 2020 Nov; 63(11): 422–428, http://www.ncbi.nlm.nih.gov/pmc/articles/PMC7642138/#:~:text=In%20toda y's%20world,%20most%20children,effects%20of%20EMFs%20are%20increasing

Oschman, James L. "Can electrons act as antioxidants? A review and commentary." *Journal of Alternative and Complimentary Medicine*,.2007 Nov;13(9):955-67, https://pubmed.ncbi.nlm.nih.gov/18047442/

Zander, Megan. "A Milestone Developmental Stage: The Age of Reason." *Scholastic Parents*. (April 12, 2019). https://www.scholastic.com/parents/family-life/social-emotional-learning/development-milestones/age-reason.html

GLOSSARY/INDEX

Anger - The not-self emotional theme of the Manifestor and a secondary not-self signature emotion of the Manifesting Generator. Usually results from being interrupted in taking action and having to explain to others what they are doing. In the Manifestor it can also result from not getting enough rest between initiating.

Authority - Refers to the inner Authority in your chart. Inner Authority is how you are designed to make aligned decisions for yourself.

Bitterness - The not-self emotional theme of the Projector. This emotion usually appears when the Projector is trying to force their way in the world by not waiting for invitations and is met with resistance, or when the Projector is fatigued and tries to keep going. The emotion that they project is bitterness, which can be felt by themselves and others.

BodyGraph - Your unique chart based on your birth time, date, location and shows your centers, gates, channels, planets, and lines.

Center - These are the energy centers in the chart and include the Head, Ajna, Throat, G, Spleen, Sacral, Will, Emotional Solar Plexus, and Root Centers.

Channel - A channel is a connection between two centers, with gates on either end. When the gates are both defined, the channel is defined. When the gates are both undefined, or if only one is defined, the channel is undefined.

Electromagnetic Channel – When two people each have one of the gates in the same channel, they are drawn together through the electromagnetics between them like two magnets coming together.

Friendship Channel – When two people have the same channel defined in their charts, they share a commonality through this channel.

Compromise Channel – When one person has one gate in a channel and the other person has the entire channel. The person with one gate will always be compromising the energy to the person with the entire channel.

Dominance Channel – When one person has a channel, and the other person has no channel or gate definition in the same channel.

Circuitry - Refers to groups of energy in the chart that have common themes, such as the Tribal, Individual, or Collective Circuits.

Conditioned Self/Conditioning - When a person is not living in a way that works *with* the energy of their chart but is doing what they have been taught or think is expected of them. Not living true to their energetic self. Conditioning mostly comes from the family of origin or who raised them.

Defined - An element of the chart that is colored in. The centers will be colored in either brown, green, yellow, or red. The gates and channels will be colored in red or black, or red *and* black, if defined.

Disappointment - The not-self emotional theme of the Reflector. Usually results from the Reflector seeing the unmet potential in other people.

Emotional Theme - An emotion associated with a particular energy type when they are living their design or living in the not-self/conditioned self.

Energy type - Refers to the energy type of an individual i.e., Manifestor, Generator, Manifesting Generator, Projector, Reflector.

Frustration - Not-self emotional theme of the Generator and the primary not-self emotional theme of the Manifesting Generator. Frustration can tell them when they are pushing against right timing, not waiting for something to respond to before taking action, or when they are about to move into the next stage of skill in their process of work. It can also show up when they are saying yes to people, jobs, projects that they want to say no to.

Gate - An energy archetype associated with the center it is located within, for example, the G Center is about love, direction, and identity, and Gate 10 within that center is about self-love more specifically. Gates can be located by looking at your BodyGraph. The gates are represented by the numbers located in the centers. They can be defined (colored in) or undefined (white/no color).

Generator - A Human Design energy type defined by having a defined (colored in) Sacral Center.

Hanging Gate - A single gate on a center that does not have the whole channel defined. A hanging gate can be located on a defined or undefined center and is attracted to someone with the other half of that particular channel. For example, Channel 43-23 contains Gates 43 and 23. If you have only Gate 43 Defined, you have a hanging Gate 43.

Initiating - The energetic action that the Manifestor puts out into the world is initiating energy. They are here to bring new things/ideas to life.

Magnetic Monopole - Located in the G Center, this invisible one-way magnet draws life and experiences to us.

Manifesting Generator - A Human Design energy type defined by having a defined Sacral Center *and* a motor center connected to the Throat Center. They are here to wait to respond to what life brings them and then can act quickly after responding through their Sacral Center.

Manifestor - A Human Design Energy type defined by having a motor center connected to the Throat Center, *without* Sacral Center definition. They are here to bring new things/ideas to life and can act on their own.

Motor Centers - Centers that create energy: Emotional Solar Plexus, Sacral, Will, Root Center.

Not-Self - Also known as the conditioned self, referring to a person operating out of their life/environmental conditioning and not living true to their energetic self in their Human Design Chart.

Open Center - An energy center that has no definition or gate activations within it.

Projector - A Human Design energy type defined by having at least two centers defined and no Sacral Center defined. They also do not have a motor connected to the Throat Center. They are here to guide after they've been recognized for their abilities and invited to share.

Reflector - A Human Design energy type defined by having no centers defined in their BodyGraph. They are here to reflect the health of the community through their ability to adapt to any environment and reflect to them what is happening in their environment.

Right Timing - To wait for the time, place, and/or people to be correct before taking action. For Manifestors they must feel their inner drive to create. Generators and Manifesting Generators must wait for something to show up in their external reality to respond to. Projectors must wait to be recognized and invited. Reflectors must wait a lunar cycle for clarity on whether to act.

Sacral Response - Unique to Generators and Manifesting Generators this refers to the communication with the Sacral Center on whether to say yes or take action in response to what life brings. Can be a yes or no response, or a push/pull sensation, or even more guttural sounds of uh-huh, unh-uh.

Satisfaction - The signature emotional response of the Generator or Manifesting Generator when living in alignment with their energetic design.

Saturn Return - Refers to the time it takes Saturn to return to the exact place in your chart at the time of your birth. Occurs roughly every 28-30 years from your birth date.

Signature Emotion - An emotional response unique to each energy type that tells you when you are living in your energetic alignment, or through the conditioned self.

Stairstep Learning - This refers to the learning process of the Generator and Manifesting Generator. They ascend in their understanding or proficiency of a subject and then hit a plateau where they gather the energy/resources to take the next step up in ascension.

Story - A long or deeply held belief that a situation or relationship must be a certain way, usually developed as a protection mechanism for what was happening at the time but may no longer be true as time goes on. For example, if you were told you were a shy child, you may grow up believing that you are a shy person. You've been carrying that story around with you because that's what you were told or believed about yourself, but as you grew you became more confident and were no longer shy but unconsciously or consciously still hold onto the story that you are a shy person.

Success - The signature emotional response of the Projector living in their energetic alignment. Not necessarily about financial success, but a general feeling of recognition and alignment in life.

Surprise - The signature emotional response of the Reflector living in their energetic alignment. They are surprised or delighted in other people and life in general.

Undefined - Refers to the centers in the chart that are not colored in but have at least one defined gate or hanging gate.

Uranus Opposition - The point in life where Uranus is halfway back to the original position it was in at the moment of birth. Also known as the mid-life crisis, this energy brings about a change signaling the end of the young life and the beginning of mature life. It is often a time where we take notice of what is working and what is not in our lives and make significant changes.

GRATITUDE

Without my children, there is no way this book would exist. Imogen and Athalia, you filled a hole in my heart that I never knew existed before you appeared in my life. I never expected that you would teach me so much about who I am through watching you grow and you just being your unapologetically authentic selves. Never forget that just being you is all the world needs from you. You both care so deeply about others it humbles me. Keep being the change you want to see in the world. I love you with all that I am.

Thank you, Imogen, for drawing the children illustrations for the cover. Your natural talent and commitment to refining your art are infectious, please don't ever stop drawing, dancing, or being uniquely you. You show others what is possible every time you put pen to paper, and your resilience through all the challenges life has thrown your way, inspires me every day.

Athalia, you have taught me more than I ever expected from day one. Your journey has brought me to my own path of self-discovery, healing, and expansion. Thank you for showing me the way and for showing me how much I love hugs! Your empathy for everyone and every animal reminds me to stop, be present, and appreciate what is right in front of me.

And of course, without my parents, I wouldn't exist. A special thank you to my mom, Tami. You always saw *me* and let me be me, even when you didn't understand me or the choices I made. You knew how to guide without even knowing you were a Projector, and I am forever grateful to you. You are my compass, my touchstone, and my Google all in human form. Thank you for calling me to Earth.

I've said from the beginning that this book came fast and quick, through the right timing and a state of wonder. It might have been another project I threw myself into and then set aside somewhere were it not for my husband who believed wholeheartedly in me and my ability to share what I know with the world. Jeff, thank you for being my number one supporter and encourager through all my entrepreneurial journeys over the years. The last seventeen years together have been a wild ride for you, I'm sure. Sometimes I bring the sunshine, other times I'm the hurricane, but I know you wouldn't have me any other way. No matter what I dream up, you always get on board for the ride with me—except for painting the house purple. I see your boundary and I honor it. Thank you for letting me be me and growing with me. Thank you for always being there and always seeing my potential. I hope I do the same for you. Thank you for your long hours of designing the graphics for this book as well as the cover art.

Human Design came into my world in the same way this book did. Fast and intense. When Human Design found me, I was all in. I consumed everything I could find produced by Ra Uru Hu, the founder of Human Design. I took classes and then felt lost. Like Ra said, "You have to live it, experiment with it." I could not just learn it through reading about it, which initially was incredibly frustrating. However, the more I let go, the more I saw that the process worked, and the more trust I had, the more understanding I had. I am so thankful to Ra Uru Hu for bringing this system forth for all of us. Ra always said that this system is for the children, and now as the world reshapes and the potential of what we may become is limitless, this feels like the most important time to share my interpretation of his transmission with our children and the people that are raising them.

My deepest gratitude and appreciation for the work of Karen Curry Parker who has taken the original teachings from Ra and brought a new language to it with Quantum Human Design™. My life has exponentially changed since becoming a student of Karen's. She teaches with the most compassion and biggest heart while honoring each of her students. She allows them to grow as unique individuals, or as she says "the once in a lifetime cosmic event" that they are. Thank you for being my mentor.

To my editor Shauna, thank you for seeing my vision and sharing my enthusiasm on the subject of parenting by Human Design. Thank you for holding space for me while it felt like at times the world was falling apart. From one Projector to another, I see you and appreciate you.

To my editor Laurie, thank you for helping me shape this book into what it was meant to be, for bearing with me navigating the language rules of HD, while still upholding the rules of English. I am eternally grateful that you nerd out on words, like I nerd out on HD.

To all my nutrition, life coaching, and Human Design clients over the years, you have taught me so much by sharing yourselves with me and allowing me into your lives. Thank you for being you and trusting me with your stories.

A special thank you to Genetic Matrix, who allowed me to use their beautiful BodyGraph images for the graphics for this book.

And lastly, thank you GracePoint Publishing for leading the way in telling the stories the world needs to hear, and for giving people like me a way to share their voice.

ABOUT THE AUTHOR

Aypril Porter is a Human Design 5/2 Projector. Born raised in the Pacific Northwest to Projector and Manifesting Generator parents, she lives with her Projector daughters, Manifestor husband, and Projector mom. She has spent her entire adult life working in service to others as a Medical Assistant, Nutritional Therapy Practitioner, stay-at-home mom, and even a scuba instructor, among other jobs. She currently serves others through her Life and Human Design Coaching practice, where she helps people live the life their soul desires and bounce back from burnout. She also helps parents to raise their children in a way that allows them to remain true to themselves, so they don't have to grow up and have a crisis to remember the truth of who they are.

Aypril believes that we can create a world where people feel seen, heard, loved, and valued for being themselves—one where we can embrace who we authentically are and allow others to do the same. She believes that when we feel seen for who we are, we have more compassion for each other and understanding for the people who challenge us most. She is passionate about giving people the tools to develop a new life story that empowers them to live their truth and raise their children to do the same. Having personally shifted relationships with family members who always felt difficult to her by seeing them through the lens of Human Design, she is a huge advocate of the freedom found within this system. She believes that anyone can change ancestral patterns by utilizing Human Design to see beyond the emotional responses to the truth of who they and their loved ones are. She also believes people can stop the wounds of childhood from being passed on to future generations by showing up and doing the work of staying curious about what is possible.

Aypril enjoys working with clients of all ages. She is available for Human Design Sessions, Human Design Parent Coaching, Human Design Life Coaching, and classes. You can find her at www.ayprilporter.com.

For more great books, visit Human Design Press online at

books.gracepointpublishing.com

If you enjoyed reading *Parenting the Child You Have* and purchased it through an online retailer, please return to the site and write a review to help others find this book.

86661300R00164